THE END OF EXISTENCE

The End of Existence:
Membership and Metaphysics

together with

Mental Fight:
A Memoir

GARVIN RAMPERSAD

sunday hill
PRESS

Sunday Hill Press
Sunday Hill Farm
Brinkworth
Wiltshire
SN15 5AS

Cover design: MBM Europe Ltd

First published by Ashgate 1998.

Reissued in expanded form by Sunday Hill Press 2011.

Printed by Short Run Press, Exeter.

British Library Cataloguing in Publication Data
A catalogue record for this book is available from the British Library.

ISBN 978-0-9568722-0-3

Contents

Foreword

Garvin Rampersad is one of a small number of people who have been genuinely troubled by philosophical problems, and who have tried to solve them according to their own lights and without retreating behind walls of academic jargon. I first knew him when he was a student at Birkbeck College in the University of London, where I was teaching, and was immediately struck by the original nature of his personality and his mind. In republishing his difficult essay in metaphysics, *The End of Existence*, I hope to draw attention to a writer who has not had the comfort or security that academic philosophers enjoy, and who has fought against personal difficulties of a kind that few philosophers have had to encounter.

Arthur Koestler left a small legacy to fund a 'Koestler Prize', to be awarded to the best piece of writing composed by an inmate in a British prison in any year that the prize can be offered. Garvin Rampersad's essay 'Mental Fight', describing the background to his life and thought, was awarded the prize in 2009, and readers will surely concur in the opinion of the judges.

Roger Scruton
Malmesbury, Spring 2011

Part I

Mental Fight: A Memoir

I will not cease from mental fight,
Nor shall my sword sleep in my hand
'Til we have built Jerusalem
In England's green and pleasant land.
W. Blake 'Jerusalem'

for Fiona Ellis
Friend, even in the pit;
and for thinkers, not tourists.

Preface

This is not an autobiography, it is a story of ideas and of a philosophy. I place it in a historical context, which is the context of my life, out of which these ideas emerged. The intellectual endeavour will gain potency, and so will the notions produced, when contrasted with the hurdles I had to overcome to give them birth. My life may, on one hand, be seen as tragic and, on the other, as a triumph over adversity. I hope it will ultimately be the latter.

The ideas are important in themselves, and it was for themselves that I approached the task of conceiving them. Hopefully, that is how they will be seen by those who read this book. But the life I here describe will be briefly portrayed. The persons who harmed or betrayed me will not be mentioned by name, as I do not wish to brood on grievances and give publicity to those people. The prisons I was incarcerated in will not be described, nor my life there. Mental homes will not be overly mentioned. The ideas that came out of these places will, however. They are the chief purpose of this book.

Of course, the type of life I have led cannot be recommended for most people. It seems an absolute miracle that I managed to live so long or produce anything intellectually worthwhile. But, as you will see, I have come not to believe in miracles or accidents. Because I infer that the world is necessary and ordered, I also believe in purpose: logical purpose. If the world was not as I portray it to be in this book, it would be as the existentialists claim it is.

Don't think that because the autobiography given here is so extended and devoid of anything philosophically original to start with, that is how the rest of the work will continue. This book is written for people who are interested in ideas, and then with how they emerge.

The best way to lead the philosophical life is not my way, but in the manner of the scholar who progresses through the educational system. Certainly it will be the safest. Something of the original spark may however be lost pursuing this path, but not every intellectual life has to deliver a revolution in thought.

Hope may be offered in reading the following account for those who lead unconventional lives in the pursuit of an intellectual goal. That is all I can give.

2006

1

Trinidad and England 1955-1975

As my life ends, I want to show that an intellectual pursuit can redeem an otherwise disastrous series of occurrences that could have characterized it. You don't have to have a career, or a family; devote yourself to acquiring money, to have dignity or self-esteem. You can save yourself from being destroyed by sexuality, disability, mental illness and imprisonment. This is said not boastfully, but in realisation that your life can still have purpose, shape and meaning, so that your particular life is transcended, and a relative happiness attained knowing that something has been done with and made of it. Finally, I hope that my parents could come to feel that their son was worth conception.

I was born in 1955 in Trinidad, the West Indies, and delivered in a hospital somewhere in Port of Spain, the capital. My father was Jerome Rampersad, a young journalist, and my mother was Mutrice Greaves. Both were Catholics and I was the second child of what was to be a family of four children – two boys and two girls – Mary, the eldest, myself, Mitzi and Gerald.

Trinidad was still part of the British Empire at that time, and had a population of about one million people. It is a relatively big island, as far as the West Indies go, about the size of Lancashire. My mother told me afterwards that we had at least one servant in the home, so we were quite well off. Though she did say that 'everyone' had servants at that time. I remember her helping my sisters with their Latin homework when we were later in England, so she was well educated, but I don't know what work she did in Trinidad.

My father was half-Indian and my mother, Negro. This means they brought together the two main groups that formed the island's population. 'Rampersad', I was in time to learn, meant 'food of the gods' in Hindi. I suppose it has the same roots as the ancient Greek 'ambrosia'.

My mother tells me I had asthma as a baby, which I outgrew, and that I was a very pretty child, which I also outgrew. I remember the taste of my baby food, as well as, later, the taste of the boiled egg I took to nursery school.

Childhood must have been a happy time, although my mother informed me that I had been a 'coward baby'. This probably refers to my attempts at walking. I sometimes stayed with my grandmother – universally called 'mother' – and we were later to live in England with her. She lived in a part of Port of Spain called Belmont – a dignified old woman and my mother's mother.

However there were omens for the future which occurred in infant school. Before the age of six, I felt and must have displayed feelings of a physical type towards a little Indian boy in my kindergarten, and towards a white boy, who I laughed and cavorted with. I remember a black boy burning me with matches – he must have seen something I had no name for and that others did not discern in me. That is how far back my peculiar sexuality can be traced, and I don't now feel any blame for it.

Something happened to cause my parents to separate, but not divorce, being Catholics, and in 1961 at the age of six I took the boat to England, with my mother, my siblings, my grandmother, but not my father, who stayed in Trinidad. I was not to see him until the early '70s, when he visited England for a short time.

It was what thousands of West Indians were doing at this period, when most of the islands were gaining independence from Britain. What would have my life been like if we had not done this? A lot different, and in many ways much more limited. The disasters that subsequently occurred would be possibly total, and redeemed by nothing. Surely for me it was a good thing we came then.

Arriving in England, we at first lived with a landlord called

Mr Singh, a Sikh man, and his family, whose children attended the same school as myself. It was St. Mary Magdalene's in Southwark, London. We lived in the same road later until I left secondary school. This was St. Thomas the Apostle, a Roman Catholic comprehensive which I went to in 1966. My sisters went to the same Grammar school, and my brother to a public school as a day boy on a scholarship. My mother taught secretarial skills at a college of further education.

I had a good schooling at St. Thomas's, coming first every year in the top class, until we were put in the 'grammar' stream in order to take the ordinary level exams at the age of fourteen and the advanced level exams at the age of sixteen – an age at which most of the boys left school. I got eleven 'O' Levels and three 'A' Levels, in English, French and Geography, though I only graduated in these exams with low grades on the most part.

In secondary school the seeds were sown for my future development. I was short and had worn glasses since the age of ten, so when I was unfortunately made a prefect at the age of fourteen, the boys simply would not obey me. I lost my temper many times and was laughed at mercilessly. Going home, and being alone in my room, I would weep copiously. Finally I tore my prefect's badge off and refused to be one any longer.

But good things happened. I studied classical music up to the age of sixteen and loved it, and listened to the classical station of the B.B.C. on the radio. In my later years at school, I obtained a Saturday job at a music library, which lent classical music discs. I went to the Opera in London. One of the best gifts my mother gave me for a birthday was an album of all Handel's Organ Concertos, which I had never come across before. It was a great pleasure of my adolescence to listen to these records repeatedly. At school I determined to become a composer, but later decided that you had to be talented and have an ear, which I lacked.

Earlier, and this lasted longer than my hope to be a composer, I wanted to write poetry. Poems of mine had won prizes in the local educational authority's competitions. As I grew older, the themes got darker and religious – the result of a Catholic school. Also, features of my later character began to emerge in the 'crushes' I had on various boys.

An unpleasant and life-long illness manifested itself as well, at the age of sixteen. This was epilepsy. I don't know what caused it, but it may have been the result of hitting my head on a goalpost whilst playing football. It was quite serious, though controlled with drugs, and expressed itself at different times in my life in different ways.

At the end of my schooldays, I did not know what I wanted to do, but I knew I wanted to do something 'great' with my life. It was an adolescent ambition, coming partly from reading a biography of Richard Wagner, and partly from reflections on my inevitable death, which I had contemplated for some time with foreboding.

Here is a poem, one of the last I wrote then, at least a part of it:

> What lies inside your armour, knight?
> The same as outside rolls.
> What do you seek?
> The Crystal Vault of Nothing is my goal.
> Your quest is foolish, well you know,
> For how can Nothing end?
> Tell me your deeper feeling now, my hollow friend.
> I feel an empty statue
> Sculpted in an absurd pose,
> And deep inside a squatting dwarf
> Who nothing sees or knows.
> Hollow Knight, where is your place?
> In the silent realms of Space.
> Hollow Knight, how are you feeling?
> My shape is burst, my skin is peeling.
> The atoms of my very being
> Spill asunder, fast are fleeing
> Far apart,
> And every region holds the pieces of my heart.

And so on. Depressing stuff, no? But I found from the poetry I was reading, that the modern kind did not rhyme often, and was a lot different from the type of verse I was writing. At last I came to realise that I would not have a place in poetry as it was now written. I dropped reluctantly that ambition.

But I managed to get admitted to university – Keele in the Midlands – one of only two boys in my year to go on to college. I went there though without a clear idea of what I wanted to do with my life and mostly for the reason of avoiding doing a job.

At the end of my school years and with the onset of adolescence, I started something which lasted many decades in my life, namely, voyeurism of women, who I gradually came to be interested in. I went to university in 1973, at the age of eighteen and this voyeurism lasted many years, eclipsing my homosexual feelings. I should have succumbed to these and entered a gay coterie at college; but as far as I knew I was alone, and certainly not proud. Homosexual sex had been legalized in the late sixties in Britain, but I was underage. I knew of no way to express these feelings legally.

I sometimes had followed girls around the streets when I was at school, but done nothing, and at Keele would slip into the girls' halls of residence to watch them taking their showers, I being safely concealed elsewhere.

But at Keele something momentous happened which would determine the course of my life. I entered university aiming to study English and French, subjects I had done at 'A' Level at St. Thomas's. At Keele though there was what was called a 'foundation' year, in which students would take courses for one year, before they began their degrees, in the humanities and a scientific subject. This was to ensure they had an all-round educational grounding to be included in their four-year degree courses. I opted to do, as one of my humanities, philosophy. I do not remember much about this year now, but at the end of it I had changed my degree to Philosophy and French.

Taking my B.A. in Philosophy, I met two men who would be important to me later: Jonathan Dancy, a young, bespectacled tutor and lecturer at the time, and Professor Richard Swinburne. Both men were to write books which I would subsequently read, under different circumstances.

Dancy praised an essay I had written in my first year in philosophy, the second at university, and I studied Lemmon's *Beginning Logic*, an excellent and classic introduction to the subject, covering everything, from propositional calculus – the algebra of whole sentences – to class theory – the logic of 'sets' or characterized collections. It ended with something I wasn't to comprehend for over a decade, namely Russell's Paradox, which Bertrand Russell himself said lay at the bottom of reasoning. Therefore I decided what I would do with my life henceforth. I remember saying to myself at the age of nineteen: 'I will become competent in this'. By 'this' I meant philosophy.

I had for one year a normal course in the various areas of philosophy: the Greeks, the Moderns – starting with Descartes, and proceeding along to Hume, with paradoxes in causation and induction, the latter being the logic of practical reasoning. We even studied Kant and were introduced to his ethical theory. I remember Dancy pointing to a copy of Kant's *Groundwork to the Metaphysics of Morals*, a slim little volume, and saying, 'That is one of the great books.'

Something however would emerge during my time at Keele which was to plague my life; it had happened in school during my unhappy time as a prefect and would dog me later. This was a proneness to lose my temper when I felt I was being mocked or was really being mocked; I came not to be able to tell the difference.

Continuing on more pleasant themes, we studied Wittgenstein, where he is contrasted with Plato, whose Theory of Forms dominated Western thought in various guises for many ages. The latter holds that things are the sorts of things they are by 'participating' in the perfect archetype that exists in a transcendent, more real realm. These archetypes are 'Forms'. Wittgenstein, in his posthumously published book, *Philosophical Investigations*, holds that things do not possess features that are common to all of their kind, such that one overriding 'Universal', which may or may not be real, is to be posited to explain them. They only have 'family resemblances' which are more or less strong, and by which we collect them into kinds.

I studied well and mostly enjoyably in Philosophy and French for the first year at Keele, and at the end of the third term took something I would have to take every year until the finals, namely my sessional tests in both subjects. On the morning of the philosophy exam, I awoke in my room in the halls of residence, early. I decided to go back to sleep. When I awoke again I found I had overslept and missed much of the exam, which I only managed to complete one half of. When my results came, I had failed the philosophy exam. I therefore had to re-sit it, but that would be later on and I had to return to my home in London to pass the time. Unfortunately my mother had gone on holiday to France and was unavailable to pay for my transport back to the Midlands. Contemplating the loss of my degree course and an inability to continue studying philosophy, I felt suicidal. I went to a local social security office to hopelessly plead for money to avert these disasters. The refusal made me cause a disturbance, which led to a tussle and, feeling enraged and in despair, went back to my home nearby and took a cricket bat and a carving knife, intending to cause as much damage at the social security office as possible. The police were called, and one of them, a big officer, wrestled me to the ground and tried to arrest me.

I stabbed him three times in the thigh and he limped off. His name was Ian Wheeler and I felt no animosity either to him personally or to the police in general and I feel sorry for the harm I did him. I did harm to myself, for I initiated by that action a lifetime of criminal implications, with the consequent imprisonment, further dealings with the police on the false premise that I had something against them, and homelessness and joblessness.

I was sentenced on a charge of grievous bodily harm to serve three years in prison, of which I would have to serve two years. This is a natural break for my history to take; at the age of twenty-one in 1976 I had laid the grounds for my education and direction in life, a life my mother told me in tears at the prison, that I had ruined. I asked her not to see me again whilst I was serving my sentence, and I faced the future alone. I continued suffering

from and being treated for epilepsy, and it is in prison that my
mental life would take a turn that might have been foreseen in
my university days, but at the time seemed to involve no definite
plan to it.

2

The Project: Prison 1975-1980

I started a process of self-discovery when I was locked in solitary confinement for some misdemeanour. Being allowed books again, I started to think and read philosophy. A book I obtained was A. J. Ayer's *Language, Truth and Logic*, which introduced the theories of the Vienna Circle to England in the 1930s. I enjoyed its style of philosophy, which was to argue for every proposition, give a conceptual reason why a statement should be believed. It became my own method in time.

But I remembered things I had encountered in Keele. One was the Ontological Argument for the existence of God, which was invented by St. Anselm, Archbishop of Canterbury in the 12th Century, and taken up by several rationalist philosophers in modern times, starting with Descartes. Descartes argued that one should think of God as a being who necessarily existed because he was something that contained all 'perfections'. Existence was one of these 'perfections' because not to exist would be to be less perfect than to exist. Therefore God, by definition, had to exist and he could not be doubted.

Variations on this argument, and on Anselm's version, which in some ways is more subtle and compelling, have been posited even in recent times by philosophers. But a possible refutation was offered by Kant in *The Critique of Pure Reason*. He maintained that 'existence' was not a real predicate. A predicate is anything said of the thing a sentence referred to and which describes it. In classical logic, one pointed to the world, indicating a particular item – the subject – and said something of it – the predicate. If existence cannot be a real predicate, and Kant offers examples of how it cannot be one, it cannot be a 'perfection' of God and the ontological argument is refuted.

However there may be alternatives to this which rescue the argument, and these have been seized on by other modern philosophers who want to accept it.

The ontological argument – 'ontos', the Greek for 'being' – is something that I am sure troubles many students commencing their courses, and it troubled me alone in my cell.

Again, there was David Hume's 18th Century scepticism on causality and induction. Hume held that no one event had to cause another because each fact was a distinct and independent existence. The necessary connection, which was the principal element in his analysis of the relation between cause and effect, simply was not observed. Also it was possible to doubt whether any object had to cause any other event and therefore it was possible because conceivable. If it was necessary that one fact had to be the cause of another, the negative would be inconceivable; but it was not, so 'causes' could not be posited.

But it was the problem of induction for which his scepticism is most famous. Induction is factual reasoning of the kind which argues from a particular instance of something to a general rule. This could be from experience of the past to projections onto the future; e.g. 'The Sun will rise tomorrow'. Or it could be experience from a limited region of Space, to a projection onward to all regions of Space. This type of reasoning is the basis of much science and common behaviour, and it is counterintuitive to doubt it. Logic however shows it can be doubted. The inductive transitions from the particular to the universal cannot be validated by deductive reasoning. In deductive reasoning, if an assumption is true, the conclusion is always true. But there is no reason of this kind to say that an inductive argument is valid. In inductive reasoning a true assumption may lead to a false conclusion. Our experience cannot be called upon to validate inductive reasoning, for it will itself use inductive assumptions. And since we can imagine the opposite of an inductive argument, or at least the negative of the conclusion, then it is logically possible that what we project does not happen.

I thrashed around in my mind trying to work these conclusions out. I could not accept them, yet I could not refute them. It is the position philosophy has found itself in since. 'The solution to the problem of induction is that it has no solution'. We have to use induction, but we cannot justify it.

I read what I could in my cell, and asked for notebooks, which I filled with my cogitations on these puzzles. If logic arrived at a paradox, then something must be wrong with the assumptions logic uses.

I conceived of something I called the 'exclusion arguments', that these assumptions must be radically revised: time, space, existence and identity. These I felt held the key to the problem. Then I recollected the vision of Bishop Berkeley, a philosopher who preceded Hume in the 18th Century. He denied 'material substance' in the world and he felt that things were just collections of qualities. He thought that those who proposed 'substance' meant by it 'being in general', along with the notion of its supporting attributes. But as he also rejected abstract ideas and thought that being in general was the 'most abstract and incomprehensible' of all abstract ideas, he said that those who proposed substance could attach no meaning to their words. It was as if things did not need 'being' to 'support' them and make them real.

Then I had very little to do to have the inspiration I had later on in my cell. I mouthed to myself: 'Things do not exist.' That I knew was the revelation the denial of which had been the essential fallacy in conceptual thought throughout time.

My mind was working overtime, and inspiration after inspiration flowed into it. What were things if they did not exist? Things were their natures. Things were how they are, not that they are. What was the meaning of 'existence'? At first, and for a long time afterwards, I thought that it meant 'universe membership'.

I determined to devote myself and my life to solving the problems of causation and induction, for these ideas were the key to the solution. Since things did not exist, they could not be distinct existences. If things were 'how' they are, then changes have to be 'how' they are rather than 'that' they are. They had to come about physically. If existence was removed from the world, so was the lack of necessity or 'contingency' it brought into the world. For what I called a 'physical description' of nature could not propound the lack of compulsion that attaches to existence because, despite the ontological argument, it has been almost universally held by thinkers that existence is not necessary. 'Whatever is may not be'. That is why the ontological argument is so paradoxical. And this argument is refuted if existence is not anything God could have.

I underestimated the complexity of the task, but I felt that this belief in existence was the reason for scepticism about causality and practical reasoning. I knew that I had in effect commenced with the solution to the difficulty and had to fill in the implications. I would not aim to get a job or have a career, because they would distract me in my goal; besides, my epilepsy would prevent that; and it was with single-minded determination, but with many diversions on the way, that I entered upon this lifetime's project. The purpose was purely intellectual, the solving of something akin to a mathematical problem.

When I came to leave prison, I had filled many notebooks with writing on these topics. Looking back, I marvel at how precarious this intellectual aim and purpose was. So many things could and did intervene subsequently to sidetrack me and cause my failure. Yet it was my source of strength: it has given my life motivation and a reason. In no way is it to be despised as an alternative to earning money and getting a home, for these things die with one but, if achieved, it attains nobility and can last.

I went back home and it was arranged that I fly to Trinidad to live with my father, who my mother had got to write to me in prison. My father, called 'Boyee' by his brothers and relations, was a stern, unhappy man, who had lost his job on the *Trinidad Guardian* for union activity, and had a job, a 'sinecure' he called it, on the local radio station as news editor. We did not hit it off, for I was also unhappy and silent. When he learnt I wanted to do philosophy, he told me that all I could do with it was teach.

Trinidad was not quite the intellectual backwater I had come to expect from my reading of V. S. Naipaul's travel writings, for I later found books by the logician W. V. O. Quine and others.

I came not to like my father, who lived alone in an apartment and never smiled. When I, demonstrating a tendency I had not outgrown, got into a quarrel at a cinema, and went back to the apartment to seize a cosh my father kept for intruders, I was arrested and injected with a sedative by a doctor and spent several days in a state of utter prostration in a mental hospital. Later, I went to a day hospital, and when at home got so much on my father's nerves that he threatened to call the mental home and have me sectioned. When I was in the day hospital the next day, I brooded on this threat and wished for my father's death. And got home in the evening and saw him lying on his bed. I went to my room. Friends and relations came as they often did, and discovered that my father was in fact dead. Later, we learned, it was of a stroke.

My relations paid for my return to England, where my mother got me a job working in a light-engineering factory as a general labourer, and she got me a place to live in a Y.M.C.A. hostel.

A quarrel with fellow workers about my homosexuality led to a second trial for threatening behaviour and possession of an offensive weapon. The police tried to make it more serious but a clever lawyer showed the jury that the more serious charges were concocted because I was known to them as someone who had injured a colleague.

Meanwhile, I had spent 3 months in prison on remand. I was sentenced to probation. Going home again, my mother professed herself surprised at the behaviour of the police, and my brother, who never liked my manifestations of homosexuality and my prison sentence, said I was 'corrupt', as he put it.

Several weeks later my mother told me that in three months time she wanted me to set myself up with a job. It was a reasonable request, but I took it as a signal that she did not like me. I gathered my belongings – books, notes and other things – in two suitcases and stormed out of the house; my younger sister, Mitzi, pressed a twenty pound note into my hands, and I never saw them again, since the age of 23, an age, I am sure, by which most children have left home.

I tramped the streets, homeless and destitute, carrying in two arms my heavy suitcases with my precious notes. Until they got too heavy for me, and I dumped one suitcase with my books from university but kept my writing books. I continued constantly to think about intellectual problems and would add jottings to my manuscript books of the thoughts that occasionally came to me.

I got to Parliament Square one day and was picked up by policemen. I was foolish enough to tell them that I had stabbed a policeman, and there and then they concocted a charge of resisting arrest and assault. I was bailed, but did not go to court at the appointed time, thinking the charge was too stupid even to contemplate. In a hostel run by a charity who took me in and gave me a bed, several months later, I managed to get into a dispute with another client who phoned the police. Arrested, I was taken to a police station, where my outstanding charge was identified, the one for which I was bailed to appear at court. I was again imprisoned on remand for about 5 months and found guilty at trial and given probation. So in five years since 1975 I had been imprisoned three times, though two were for periods of remand.

Even in prison I continued with my thoughts and had kept a manuscript book in the hands of a friendly probation officer – Arthur Ashby. I remember when I told him that I was solving the problem of induction and causality, he had objected, 'What about Entropy?' He also asked if my arguments in my notebook were in question and answer form; whether I made objections to them and replied to them. This, despite my reading of A J Ayer, was a tendency lacking from my work. There was too much pure assertion without a reason given for them.

A provisional title for my thesis was 'At Dreaming's End', a quotation from the translation into English of *Also Sprach Zarathustra* by Nietzche. The Midnight Song contains the lines:

I've slept my sleep
And now awake at dreaming's end...
I kept this title for years.

But towards the end of those five years, I came to reflect on the analysis of causation Hume had made. He included 'necessary connection' in the common idea between one event and another. Not only was it not observable, but logically it could not be shown to obtain since the denial of a causal relation was perfectly conceivable. I thought, and the idea stole upon me slowly, 'Of course things must be related or connected'. It was self-evident and intuitive, though these were not good enough philosophical reasons for saying why. In philosophy it is often very difficult to give logical reasons for the intuitive. I had however to do so.

The next few years, the years of the eighties decade, were to be characterized for me by association with the mental health system. Sometimes I went to mental homes as schizophrenia and anxiety evidenced themselves; this was in addition to chronic epilepsy, for which I took pills. In the next years I continued, with breaks, to do my saving philosophy, and it was towards the end to re-emerge in a much different and strengthened form.

Meanwhile, I was out of society since 1975, and had missed the Punk revolution in popular culture. I was no longer a virgin, but started going to prostitutes. They could handle my sexual weakness without mocking me, for I was, if not actually, almost completely impotent. I also consorted with men I met in public lavatories. If I had not met up with prostitutes, I would still be a virgin and I have always paid for sex with women.

This is a natural break in my narrative and the eighties form a distinct period in my philosophy's development and in my progress.

3

Years of Madness 1980-1989

Released from prison a third time, I was a homeless vagrant; I squatted in an abandoned factory in the Croydon area of London. I left my manuscripts in the keeping of Mr Ashby, my probation officer, who from time to time would write out small cheques from his expenses and give me money for a meal. Otherwise, I stole milk and bread left in front gardens. One night, in the depths of my desolation, I saw the moon shining, and it was very big. I lost awareness and the next thing I knew, when I came to myself, I found that I was in a place I later knew was Warlingham Park Hospital for the mentally disturbed. This was a place I visited occasionally for the next few years. Years in which I gained friends I met in the mental health system, though they were not significant in the production of my philosophy. Also I had a few jobs for brief periods, and of menial kinds.

After several months I was given a place in a half-way home in Kent for mentally ill, but recovering, young people. I had a room to myself then and could observe the world I had been out of for so long, on television. The Falklands War was taking place, but other things occupied my mind. Why were things necessarily related? The reason was, I was sure, because the nature of a 'world' demanded it. Merely by being parts of a world, and in order to form a world, things had to have access, one to another. It was conceptually necessary. A world would be impossible if things had no relations; so given a world, relations were necessary.

I called this argument by various names, starting in prison where it had originated: the 'universe' argument was one. This later became the 'world' argument. And it was one of the effects of existence that it separated things. If things did not exist necessarily, nothing else could make them exist. Existence was never in the nature of things – a reason why it was not necessary. So a thing could not be necessitated in its existence by another thing, or caused. This directly clashed with the 'world' argument, so either existence or 'world' would have to go. This was the foundation for my insight in prison that the belief in existence led to causal scepticism.

It seemed to me that the world, or a world, was self-evident. It also seemed a logical demand that a plurality meant that the elements in it had access to one another. Existence was to be rejected.

These ideas were generated over time and their development interrupted by a period of further incarceration in the mental hospital for a psychotic collapse.

The 'world' argument was to occupy my mind for the next few years. It was a time in which I got residence in several hostels for the mentally ill at different times and for different lengths of time. The longest was three years spent at one in the throes of and in thrall to anxiety. The latter involved panic attacks during which a nameless, unfocused fear would creep over me, and at its height, I would be rendered speechless, or at best, monosyllabic.

I, during the period 1984 to 1987, reached my nadir mentally. I was resident at a hostel in Croydon and recognized, as I had done soon after going into the first hostel in Kent, that I really wanted a university education. I felt half-educated otherwise. In Kent I had tried to return to Keele University, but they would not accept me. But later on in Croydon, I realised that I could not study at university level as long as I suffered from this terrible anxiety.

A psychologist at the day hospital I attended diagnosed anxiety, but said it would pass. Meantime, my despair caused me to attempt suicide, when I took a week's supply of epilepsy tablets at once. I passed out and was revived in hospital, but did damage as a result to my brain. I was unable henceforth to have more than what is called 'twilight' sleep. This meant that I could no longer get fully unconscious at night, but at best would dream profoundly.

I did however recover mentally, and the anxiety disappeared. Taking to heart the sense that my arguments in my philosophy needed counter-arguments, which could be met, I wondered if it was conceivable that the 'world' argument was wrong, for some unidentified reason. What if the world consisted of objects that simply existed and needed no necessary relativity?

My philosophy had been somewhat in abeyance during this latter period of my problems with anxiety, but it started up again with renewed vigour. Surely things in being real were also relatively real to other real things? But consider existence, which it was said caused this reality; not only did it lead to relevance to other things in a physical sense, but it also led to contingency, which meant independence. That was a contradiction. From my year of philosophy at Keele, I had learnt of the reductio ad absurdum proof, whereby if an assumption led to a contradiction, one could negate the assumption as false. Since existence led to a contradiction, it must be rejected, and something else should be responsible for things' reality. Therefore existence was not reality. Things were real, but they did not exist.

I spent a relatively short time working out the implications of this argument, and produced reasons to support it further. It proved causality because it proved it merely from the need for mutual relevance among real things. And it disproved existence by showing it was responsible for paradox. I came to call this chapter of my growing thesis, 'Paradoxes of Existence'.

But something was to occur towards the end of 1987, when I was recovering my mental equilibrium. I have always found I did my best work when I was most normal, and normality was returning.

In my reading that I was doing at that time, I came upon Russell's Paradox, which so baffled me since Keele. A class is a set of things characterized by common factors. To say a thing had a certain predicate was to say it was a member of a certain class. There are rules for membership of a class, one of which is to possess the relevant property. There are different kinds of set just as there are different kinds of thing. Some contain solid, real things; some are abstract collections. A set or class is thought to be an abstract object. The logicist movement among logicians and mathematicians, at the start of the 20th Century, held that all mathematics was reducible to logic, and one of the axioms it held was that for every predicate there was a class that exemplified it. Sets, or classes, are used in an advanced kind of mathematics, and numbers can be defined in terms of sets. What, Russell asked in his paradox, about the class of classes that are not members of themselves? Some classes are members of themselves, like the class of abstract objects; some are not – the class of rocks is not a rock. The class of classes that are not members of themselves, is a member of itself if it is not, and is not a member of itself if it is. Paradox.

For many years I did not understand the paradox, which, if valid, meant that every predicate does not have its own set. There could be no such set. To be a member of itself means to have the predicate it exemplifies. Not to be a member of itself means not to have the predicate that it is the extension of. What it was 'to be a member' was what baffled me. And the self-reference threw me.

Once I saw the reasoning behind the paradox, which meant that the logicist programme was overthrown, it did not seem so difficult to me. But it had been the starting-point of higher logic. If logic contained a paradox, something must be wrong with the assumptions of logic. Russell said this paradox afflicted the very basis of reasoning. Attempts to solve the paradox had been made ever since.

I was writing the Overview to my theories so far, in order to collect them together into a manageable form. I had used the definition I offered of existence, Universe Membership, and said that things could not belong, or be members, because of belonging; and this was an argument against contingency. Things could not exist just because they existed; things could not belong merely because of belonging.

Then I saw the answer to the paradox. In it membership was made the reason for membership merely by being the criterion for itself. It was its own reason. Membership and its negation, non-membership, cannot be predicates. Why? Because membership had no nature, it has nothing to characterize it. Not recognizing this became the essence of what I was later to call, the Membership Fallacy.

It was a great day for me when I discerned this. I knew I was on to something exceptional. For membership was a logical operator; it was part of the most exact part of philosophy – logic. I had discovered the logical basis of the existential fallacy. I could use logic to show that existence was invalid. For if membership was invalid, if it was also existence, then existence was invalid. Membership was not only a fallacy because it had no nature, but because it led to paradox. If membership was wrong, then the whole of set theory, or classes, was also wrong. My philosophy would be placed on a logical, nay, a mathematical footing.

At the end of '87, when my time at the hostel I had stayed at was drawing to a close because I was getting better, I was to be transferred to a half-way flat of my own before being given a council flat. There, just by chance, and in one of the most fortunate strokes of luck that could be imagined, I happened upon a final issue of an intellectual periodical. One of its articles was a fictional, comic account of a meeting at Cambridge between Bertrand Russell and Ludwig Wittgenstein. I remember something Wittgenstein is made to say to Russell, reclining in a deckchair: 'They came to the tomb and found it empty. That is the true mystery! Not how things are but that they are. Tell me Russell, why is there something rather than just nothing, why is there anything at all?' Russell replies: 'How am I meant to know? I'm a mathematician, not God almighty!' I had heard it said that God was a mathematician, and that the Universe was a mathematical object. Still, questions of this kind had been occupying me for years.

Also, I read somewhere in the magazine an advertisement made by the Open University. It was for a course, lasting eight months, in modern philosophy, called 'Reason and Experience': the continental rationalists and the British empiricists.

I applied for the course and was accepted, though I was on benefit, saw a psychiatrist regularly and was suffering from epilepsy. Every month the class would meet at the London School of Economics for lectures and otherwise study at home. I enjoyed the course and passed well. I met people there who were going to use that course at the Open University to get into other universities to do a full degree. My psychiatrist told me: 'Use a minnow to catch a whale'.

I opted for Birkbeck College, University of London, and a friend of mine, a former policeman, a young man called Paul Wolward, who I met at the Open University, chose the School of Oriental and African Studies at which to do a philosophy degree. Birkbeck was for mature students who paid for the degree course lasting four years, and had lectures in the evening. I was to get a charitable grant from an organisation because of my extreme poverty. All this I learned before I started the course in 1989.

But before Birkbeck commenced, and before I could move into my council flat at the same time, I got into trouble with the law again for carrying an offensive weapon, with which I had threatened a pornographic shop owner, who had mocked and 'rooked' me. I still betrayed a propensity I had not lost to brood upon mockery and insults. I was fined £20 and put on probation.

I got over this however and re-entered university at the age of thirty-four in 1989 to do a degree course in philosophy. There was also a move to a council flat, a bedsit. This was a place I was to stay at for the next five years.

Birkbeck was certainly a prestigious place; set in West London, near Tottenham Court Road, it contained some well-known philosophers, not the least of whom was Roger Scruton, professor of Aesthetics. I had read one of his books, an introduction to modern philosophy, whilst at the hostel. He was a well-known commentator on aesthetics, or the philosophy of art and beauty, and he appeared not infrequently on the radio and television. He was a political commentator and a right-wing intellectual who supported the Conservative Party, then in power for ten years. His doctoral thesis had been *Art and Imagination*, and I admired him much. This was not reciprocated, for my displays of homosexual tendencies, manifested in voyeurism at the college, seemed to alienate and repel him. He, at that time, was a tall man with a shock of red hair and glasses. His feelings towards me did not obscure his appreciation of any intellectual merit he might perceive me to possess.

There were others there: Professor David Wiggins, a noted ethicist and all-round thinker, whose book *Sameness and Substance*, argued for the re-introduction into Western thought of the notion of substance. And Samuel Guttenplan, who had written a best-selling introduction to logic on which our first-year course in the subject was to be based. He was an American, much admired by his students.

I had gone to university this time for the sake of my thesis, which by then had been collated in a thick manuscript book. The degree I was aiming for would be got by my research during the seventies and eighties for my theories, and by the original thinking I had done, which was extensive. I read during that time much theoretical physics and cosmology, because it was relevant to any metaphysics about the world and causation and induction. I also knew about – and had theories related to my thought – linguistic philosophy, which dominated the English-speaking world in much of the twentieth century. This philosophy rejected metaphysics as meaningless because unverifiable, but I thought the linguistic turn in thought self-referential and decadent. What I was doing was firmly in the tradition of Western metaphysics: it was about the world; but it had to make use of and not ignore, the developments made in philosophy in the twentieth century.

By the time the four years of my course were up, my theory would be complete and it amazes me now how much thinking I managed to get into it in those four years. Every summer I would revise my writing in a new, big manuscript book, and all the time I reflected. Roger Scruton came to like me, but he was a stern man who once said he tolerated homosexuality, but did not like it.

At that time I met and befriended Fiona Ellis, in the year above me, ten years younger and brilliant. She stayed my friend all through the nineties and even into the dark days beyond when I fell back into the pit. All these people, and others, were to help me in my thinking for my thesis. I shall indicate the ideas in and implications of my thesis, at least in part. This story is not meant as an autobiography but as a history of ideas. It is the tale of a philosophy and an explanation of it. The culmination of my thinking arrived in the nineties when, for the most part, all went well for me. So to this decade I proceed, but not forgetting the work done philosophically in the two preceding ones.

4

Redemption 1989-1999

Some of the ideas I mention here originated in the two years between 1987 and 1989, but I include them in the decade I describe. For many years I had seen existence as 'universe membership'; but a more exact examination of membership led me to change my mind. The universe was a world of physical things and these were, as I had said, *how* they were not *that* they were. Membership was a relation, and membership had to be of a class of some kind. It could not be of the class of physical things, which membership was not, but had to be of a class that ensured that membership had no nature. To ensure membership was pure it had to be membership of the class of class members. That was what existence was, for it likewise, had no nature. Membership would cause chaos if allowed to be a predicate or a reason for membership of a class: anything with it could get into any class whatever. So membership had to be quarantined and apply to a characterless class. But really, it was an impossible concept, with an impossible class. Just as membership was a pseudo-relation, membership of the class of class-members was membership of a pseudo-class. The elements in such a class had no nature, and so could not be collected.

I was able to show that membership was existence, logically. In class theory we expressed non-existence by saying that the class of the non-existent objects was 'empty', that is, memberless. So to express an object's existence we should say that its class was not-memberless. Thus membership was existence. Also, asserting belonging to a determinate class was predication.

The pre-condition for determinate belonging and the pre-condition for predication were the same. The pre-condition for determinate belonging was pure belonging, and the pre-condition for predication was existence. These were identified. And since membership, existence, had no nature, it could not belong to anything; so membership, existence, implied non-membership, non-existence. This was the source of the long-held belief that existence was nothing.

Another long-lasting dispute, from the beginning of Western philosophy, was the monism-pluralism debate. Monism held that there was one thing, and pluralism that there were many. This was resolvable if existence was membership. Having no nature, members could not form a class, because there was nothing in virtue of which they could be related or connected; so members were isolated and distinct, utterly. But a nature allowed things to be collected and classed. A class of both members and things with a nature would be isolated in terms of members and, if these members were also nature-possessing, collected. This was a contradiction of external relations, relations that were not inherent to the things related. Pluralism maintained such relations, so the dispute between it and monism was resolved in favour of monism. Atomism, the belief in individuals that were simple and isolated from each other that went with pluralism, was refuted.

I later came to see this argument meant that in a world without membership in the form of existence, things had to transcend pure particularity and be non-particular as well: they had to have universality. This was a way of establishing induction, for the problem of induction required us to see things as atomic individuals with no possibility of allowing general, universal statements being made of them.

The membership fallacy caused the fallacy of existence, and it caused others. I showed this by examining, over a period, logical, linguistic, even mathematical paradoxes. The Liar paradox was suspicious; it looked just like Russell's, and it did not take long for me to see that Truth too was membership, therefore had no nature and was an impossible notion. It goes like this: if we say, 'This statement is false', then we can derive that if 'this statement' is true, it is false, and if it is false, it is true. All theories of truth are susceptible to the Liar paradox. Truth is reduced to absurdity by the paradox; and so is, of course, falsehood.

So what was Truth? I determined that to say a sentence was 'true' was to say that it 'belonged' linguistically. The physical situation described by a sentence was supposed to belong in reality to the world and thus it 'belonged' and existed. The sentence reflected this by reproducing the physical state of affairs and reproducing its belonging mediately, by means of language, both to the world and purely. I could show that truth, membership and existence were identical: if an object, any object, 'fell under' a concept, then one, a concept was 'instantiated', two, a concept 'was true of' an object – understanding 'F is true of x' to be equivalent to "'x is F' is true" – and three, an object 'was a member' of the extension of a concept. The quoted formulas said the same thing. For a concept to be 'instantiated' was to assert existence. Other historico-metaphysical arguments were found.

These paradoxes were examined in the years of my recovering from anxiety and going to university again.

The membership fallacy ran through the whole of philosophy. Cantor's paradox, named after an important 19th Century German mathematician, was solvable. It was solvable if classes were rethought. They could not contain real things and yet be abstract objects, but had to run over ideas, sub-ideas, if they were to retain their abstractness. And these sub-ideas mirrored sub-classes; they replaced them. Members were to be excluded.

I examined paradox after paradox, some linguistic, some mathematical, all in order to express and fortify the point about the membership fallacy, which in some way was responsible for them all. Because classes with membership contained real things and were real objects, they could contain themselves. What was called 'self-predication' was always going to be possible with membership; and it was directly responsible for Russell's paradox and the others. But in solving Cantor's paradox, I had rethought classes as containing sub-ideas derived from 'originals' or real things outside the class. At the top of the abstractive progression that was the class was the Notion or Intension. Classes can be seen theoretically as a collection of objects, or as the meaning, the 'intension', of the concept or predicate that those things are collected under. This is in the conventional theory of classes. I had a 'notional' or 'intensional' theory. Sub-ideas, or sub-classes, were included in classes and within the class itself, a notion could only identify with itself. It could not be included in itself or have itself as a predicate. This was because the Notion or class was at the top of the tree, in terms of abstraction, so could not itself be one of those things it was abstracted from. It was self-identified.

My thinking was getting more metaphysical now, but I was still able to include the membership fallacy in it. Things were not existent, but the reason why they were real was because they were how they were, because they had a nature. Not existing meant, not that they were nothing, but that they neither 'existed' nor 'not-existed'. They were beyond both, like the God of the Sufi mystics. When existence went, so did non-existence. Neither was possible.

My thought had gone far from being a simple examination of cause and induction, but I was able to bring it back for a while. The world was not a collection of particular individuals. Collections meant members, and the world did not have membership in the form of existence. This meant that the world, without membership, must be a systematic unity. I was able to solve inductive and causal paradoxes at a stroke. Things were connected of necessity and they transcended particularity, so any description of them could not break them up into isolated bits, either of space, time, or instance. A rule for a time was a rule for all time.

The world was what I called the 'qualitative' world or 'descriptive' world, being a thing containing items that were how they were. A charge in events had to be how it was. That is, it had to be physical. It did not just come into being but was brought about: it physically arose; there was a reason for it. That was 'cause'. But was it necessary? Here, going to Birkbeck and encountering sharp minds proved useful and essential in the development of my ideas. I had long said, Yes: if that was how something was, that was how it had to be. If the colour Green was green, it had to be green. Fiona Ellis pointed out to me when I said this to her, 'But it's trivial'. It was a tautology, something not really applicable to the world.

I went away to cogitate about this, for I knew I was right in the end. I saw that when the criterion of necessity to exist was applied to my arguments, they failed. But when the world no longer existed, but was how it was, the criterion for necessity could not any longer be the necessity to exist, but was the necessity to be how one was. And things in the world satisfied this demand. Red could have existed instead of Green, but in its nature Red could not have been Green, or any other thing. A triangle was a geometrical form; Red was a wavelength of light. Things had to be how they were in the descriptive world; they were necessary. The criterion had changed. Tautology was avoided.

This meant that physical events, causes, relations, and so forth, were necessary, being what I named 'descriptive'.

The changes, causes, that happened had non-particular aspects. When it was observed that A was physically followed by B, this could be expanded into a rule that A was always followed by B, non-particularly. This showed induction to be a logical, not a psychological practice. But of course, epistemological impediments arose in these cases: we could always get the relationship between A and B wrong; but the point was that Induction was established as a logically valid practice even if inductions could not be so justified.

The 'descriptive' world needed attention given to itself. One could hardly reject a concept as wide-ranging as existence and not say what the concept that replaced it made the resulting world like. Because the world did not exist, it was not brought into existence. It was not created. Also, because it transcended being and nothingness, it did not have the possibility of being nothing. It must be something; but that meant be descriptive and nature-possessing; and it was necessarily real since being descriptive was the only possibility.

There were difficulties that arose in my mind concerning the things in this world. These difficulties concerned change, which I had to explain. Things could not come into being or go out of being. Associated with Change were problems about Identity. I defined two senses of the word 'identity'. One was as 'uniqueness' in the sense found in such sentences as: 'The nations of Europe should retain their national identity'. The other was more problematic, in the sense of relational identity or sameness, as in: 'A is identical to B'. The latter seemed to be a predication of something of itself. It seemed to be a self-predication.

I was able to see the first sense and the second in existential terms, when the membership fallacy operated. Uniqueness was a product of the isolation and distinctness of members from each other. Relational identity was a self-predication of a class to itself. When a thing was unique, it was like a universe or set, and the only thing it could belong to was itself. But we had seen that self-predication was illegitimate, and replaced by self-identity in logic: it was another way of expressing self-identity. So both senses of identity were definable in terms of existence and membership. And I had to re-express identity in the manner of descriptivity.

Another way in which the membership fallacy appeared was in the ancient idea of Substance. All the features of substance were explainable by membership. It was a form of membership. Indeed, all the concepts that lacked a nature had to be the same thing, for only in virtue of a nature could they be different.

I went back to Necessity, and saw that, because the descriptive world was real, its necessity could not be in an abstract form, but identified with how things were, with situations themselves. Reality was Necessity. Old questions like, 'Why is there something rather than just nothing, why is there anything at all?' which Wittgenstein had asked Russell in the comic and fictional debate, were answerable. Because things were beyond being and non-being, Necessity was now necessity to be how one was. And the question was not: 'Need the world be?', but: 'Need the world be how it is?' The answer was 'Yes'. The world was necessary, but not necessarily existent; it was necessarily how it was. The way things were was necessary. Things, the world, were not created.

I saw that the old philosophical dictum that experience gave one no idea of necessity, was wrong. For experience of reality was experience of necessity. We knew if and how something was necessary by knowing that it was real.

These were deep areas, and my thought grew more and more metaphysical as I progressed. I had thought that analytic statements were necessary, like thousands of other thinkers before me. 'Analytic' statements were statements where the concept of the subject contained the predicate of the sentence. But I had rejected 'truth' and replaced it with 'analyticity'. I contrasted it to self-contradiction – a natural opposition – and that replaced 'falsity'. Meanings were objective, and things gave the subjects of sentences their meanings independently of ourselves. There was however the problem of necessity. In the existential world, any description of it would be contingent. So how could an analytic statement describe it if it was necessary? This occupied me for a long time; then I saw that the nature of the world gave sentences their necessity or contingency: their 'modality'. In respect to analyticity or contradiction, these were neutral in terms of modality. Depending on the 'world' one accepted, an analytic sentence could be necessary – the Descriptive one – or could be contingent – the existential one. It was a great revolution in my thought to grasp that analytic sentences could be contingent, that analyticity and self-contradiction could be modally neutral.

The membership fallacy manifested itself also in the concept of reference. Asserting reference, for instance, for subjects of sentences, was to assert existence; and asserting failure of reference was asserting non-existence. But existence and non-existence were membership and non-membership; consequently asserting reference or its lack was asserting membership or its negation. The argument was more complex than this, but it was essentially simple. Reference was membership. But if that was so, self-reference was self-membership, which was self-predication. If the case, then in the intensional theory of classes, it was illogical, and though possible in membership, was ultimately wrong because membership was fallacious.

Reference was linguistic, and of course membership appeared in other areas of philosophy like metaphysics and logic. But reference was a way of acquiring meaning; and self-predication was similar. But if talking about something outside the sentence was the ultimate way of meaning acquisition, or talking about the world, then talking about oneself, as in self-reference, implied meaninglessness. This must be the final solution to all self-referential paradoxes: they were meaningless.

In Godel's Theorem, which destroyed the logicist programme, it was stated that: in any system of logic that can express the mathematical truths, if it was provably complete, it would not be provably consistent, and if provably consistent would not be provably complete. That is to say, for such a system, if it could express all the propositions of maths, it would have paradoxes in it; and if it didn't have paradoxes, it would not express all the propositions of mathematics. However, in the proof of this theorem, Godel used quite essentially a self-referential formula. This meant that it was meaningless. It was outside the scope of the logical system; it was not a possible formula within that system, so could not say anything about or affect that system. Possibly, one impediment to the enterprise of reducing mathematics to logic was removed.

I reflected some more on the nature of philosophical inquiry. What made abstract concepts and abstract arguments apply to the world? Why should we believe them? I saw that my arguments, say for causality and induction, applied to my concept of the world, and only if this concept mirrored the real world was it likely to be valid. The order in the world generated conceptual thinking, I believed, and there were reasons for believing in order; an order conceptual thinking emerged from and pointed back to.

I considered an implication of appreciating the membership fallacy was that it meant that the world was innately self-ordered. And indeed worldly order was a prerequisite of reason. In a sort of transcendental argument, I said, if one asked 'Why?' and replied 'Because...', you could not accept the answer if it was possible that anything whatsoever could be the case, that your conclusion could be falsified. And this was what happened in a Chaos. Reason was founded on the premise that there was no chaos, that the world was ordered, so could not be employed to prove disorder. This was what in effect was attempted in the arguments that 'proved' the problem of induction.

The argument for innate order was an argument against the argument from design, which proved the existence of God. The latter was used to show that the order in the world required an Intelligent Designer; but I showed that order was logically necessary. The lack of creation showed the needlessness for a creator. And the ontological argument was refuted because things did not exist, even God, so could not necessarily exist. Kant said that all the reasons for the existence of God finally came to rest on the ontological argument. But that did not, in my mind, show that, though all the reasons for believing in God were refuted, we could only accept atheism. Spinoza, the rationalist philosopher, spoke of 'Deus sive Natura': 'God or Nature'. Why he used this proposition, I do not know; it may have been a definition in one of his proofs; though it is a weakness of Spinoza's method of argument that you don't have to accept the definitions. But if God was nature, and nature was descriptive, then God could be real. Indeed, God was Reality.

Again, if the world was a mathematical object, and the hurdles to reducing mathematics to logic represented by Russell's paradox and Godel's Theorem were removed, then the world was ultimately a logical object, and it was accessible to logical analysis. This was however only speculative.

Then finally, I brought together Relativity and Descriptivity, and could show how the latter reduced to the former, how Relativity explained Descriptivity.

I had for many years, compiled a manuscript book of my thoughts during each of the summer breaks whilst at Birkbeck. In 1992 I showed Paul Wolward, my friend at SOAS, the thesis. I had rewritten it completely, from a literary point of view, that year, and had decided to exclude uncouth locutions, sentences that began 'It is...' or had the form 'The...of...'. I expressed my thoughts in simple words, short sentences and relatively short paragraphs. For my work avoided mystery or mock-profundity, and it did not reduce the world to the human mind. Paul told me I should get it typed, which, after some months and with some difficulty, I managed to do. By the end of the year it was complete.

David Wiggins had examined the whole of the third chapter, the 'existential fallacy' I called it, which included the membership fallacy and my discoveries about existence. He made detailed criticisms and told me, to my surprise, that there were people who thought that things did not exist. They were called the 'predicativists'. Fiona had spoken of the 'quality of his mind'; that was one of the reasons she so admired him.

Then when my thesis was typed up, and David Wiggins had said it was beautifully written, I remembered something my father had said, all those years ago in Trinidad. He told me that when you submitted a manuscript for publication, it must be typed. Several times during my career I had said as I reached what I thought was a termination to my intellectual enterprise, 'Now I can die.' But I had discovered some new objection and consideration to my thoughts and for my mind to reflect on and solve. Now however, I felt I should get my typescript published. I had not formerly even conceived this.

When I graduated in 1993 it was with a good upper second. I had not done the reading and had forgotten how to study, though I missed none of the lectures. Scruton told me when he was my tutor in the second year, that I could get a first. I told him I would not for just those reasons.

Other students had been speaking of 'when' they got their degrees; I had thought 'if' I got a degree. I honestly thought I might fail or get a third. But after the finals, an exam that was a 'federal' degree, the same papers being set for all the London colleges, and before I knew the result, I said that I had not done brilliantly, but I had not done too badly. When I got my degree I said to myself, 'Who would have thought the day would come?' After all those years of prison, epilepsy, mental home, insanity, homelessness and unemployment, I had done what others in my situation could not do. I had met several people, in the years of madness, who had been to university, even the best universities, and had their courses cut short by mental illness. Most had planned to go back; none would or could be imagined doing so. But I had. And that was not the end. I was aiming to get a book published. My ideas would not die with me.

In the years after graduation, I moved out of the council bedsit I occupied for four or five years, and into another flat. But it was unsatisfactory. Something however happened at that time. Because I was an epileptic I was eligible for further social welfare benefits. These, taken with the others, meant that my income rose by a great degree. I was able to save money and go on a holiday to the continent, a thing I had not done since boyhood.

I got a private flat because, in a relatively short time I had amassed enough money to make the down payment. I had thousands of pounds in a bank account.

At the same time my intellectual enterprise met its zenith and I my nemesis. I started going to a strip-joint featuring young homosexual men and fell in love with a wild, working-class boy, a beautiful youth, who worked as a dancer and a prostitute. I was in awe of his virility, and was addicted to his company. I even took him back to my new home. But when I told him once I cared more for philosophy than sex, he howled. One day he said casually to me, in an off-hand way, 'I hope you get AIDS'. That was like him; he took and sold drugs and was casually cruel, out of control.

I got scared, for I had a terror of AIDS all through the eighties and was terrified now. I had been trying to publish my thesis for four years since graduation, but had not succeeded, or found the acceptances unacceptable. I now sent off the typescript to

Cambridge University Press, who did not take me up, but with advice I took to heart about my book, told me to go to an independent academic publisher of which they gave me the name and address, saying they published good material. I sent it off to them and several months later, in 1997, my thesis was accepted for publication. Making some additions and alterations, my book was published under a different title from the one I had used all these years, but still of my choice; it was now called: *The End of Existence*. That was in 1998.

I basked in the glory of my success, replete and content, with my intellectual enterprise becoming finally independent of myself and transcending me. But in the next year presage of my future personal destruction took place, in my being taken off all my psychotropic medication by an over-confident psychiatrist, and quickly having a nervous breakdown, something I avoided for over a decade, and being sectioned. Then in the following year, after a dispute involving payment for sexual favours, my author copies were stolen by the prostitute in the presence of his friends when I was absent from my flat. I overrated the disaster this was, but bought a knife and stabbed one of the friends of the prostitute who had been in the flat at the time.

He was wounded and I was charged with wounding with intent, a charge which led to a life sentence when taken with my previous offence of this kind, against the policeman, Ian Wheeler. That was in the year 2000. There are those who say that my book caused my downfall. I disagree. It was my salvation; it gave my life purpose, hope, meaning. The existentialists say that the world is absurd, but you can give your life meaning individually. That is not how I think, but they may have a point. And in intellectual terms, I succeeded. For the result of my thinking expressed in that book, far exceeded my original aims. The book was excellently written, and it was a triumph. I no longer control it, and my thoughts are known by academics on three continents. That is my vindication. That, and above all the intellectual achievement.

5

Past and Future 2006

Past

I did not do my philosophy to be published. It was not done for widespread fame, nor to gain wealth. In fact, I never earned a penny from it. I did not hope to become, in solving the intellectual difficulties, a holy man, or a great man, revered and respected. I did not become wise or good. The problems were solved despite the impediments to my progress in life. But it might be claimed they were solved because of those very 'hurdles', for I gained at least the leisure to apply myself to continuous thought. The impediments of prison, chronic epilepsy, mental home, mental illness released me from the ability or need to work.

The project was to solve an intellectual or logical problem, and that alone; for no gain other than that end. That was done to my satisfaction, and in excess of my expectations.

We are illogical creatures thrust into a complex, logical world. That is the absurdity of our condition. Accidents caused me to achieve my aim and to suffer the drawbacks. What can be learnt from this? Maybe we can understand the world: but can we understand ourselves? Or in understanding ourselves, we fail to factor in the world. Our predicament is absurd, yet the world is not. Holy men grasp, and even transcend, human nature; clever men grasp the world, a world that we may ultimately be only tiny parts of, and thereby redeem themselves from the incomprehensibility of selfhood and lose themselves in the total history, the developing universe.

Time, science tells us, is the fourth dimension of this

world. There may be other worlds in other dimensions, with different physical laws. But metaphysics says what must hold in all possible worlds; and the study of it releases us from any particular universe and gives us knowledge of the mathematics of all worlds.

How must we feel when we are emancipated from the ties of time, world, dimension? Like a disembodied spirit. It is not our natural state, and we are not comfortable with it. Hume got it right: 'Be a philosopher, but in the midst of all your philosophy, still be a man'. Remember the lines in the poem I wrote at the age of seventeen, before I started my quest? I spoke of the 'hollow knight' who found himself lost in the 'silent realms of Space'. The poem ends in lines I did not write at the start of this manuscript:

My place on Earth I have just found!
Want nothing but the ground!

Have I then spent my entire adult life journeying to comprehend something I dimly knew before I attempted the mission? That may be so. But I vaguely knew that things did not exist at the start of the enterprise. But it was knowing why that constituted the reason for going on. Knowing why gave me knowledge of the metaphysical world. Achieving this in the end gave me a quiet joy. That may in a sense outlive me: my body, mind, but it may be my eternal, disembodied spirit. It will not be, I hope, alone; it should join the ranks of the contributors to thought and be part of the living flow of ideas.

My work is done and is free of me. I don't matter: my thought matters. I will suffer, grow old, and die. My ideas are pure and perfect. They continue to amaze me still in their perfection and my inability to correct them for the better.

I want now to reflect on the person and places these ideas were the children of. They did not come out of a study in an academy, surrounded by libraries and civilized, intelligent people. They came out of prisons, hostels for the disturbed, and sometimes conditions of real homelessness. The mind that produced them lived in the company of the poorly educated, was attacked by periods of mental breakdown and prolonged mental incapacity. It was not a gentle, decent mind, but managed to remain, in despite of everything, a logical mind, in love with concepts, and this love saved it from its destruction long enough to complete the task it set itself.

All this goes to demonstrate that the academic mission is not solely achievable in the academy. Look: many of the great ideas were not produced by professionals working to earn a living by academic drudgery. It has only recently become the norm. So the worth of someone's thought is not to be evaluated by the mode of its presentation. Convention and conformity have deadened and laid waste the world of philosophy. It has become a job, a career; something done for the principal aim of gaining money. My father, back in Trinidad, said all you could do with philosophy was teach. I never felt that. The philosophy I was doing was to be produced originally. Can every thinker do this? Maybe not. But one should not say that the possibility of original thought, certainly in the present day, cannot arise.

Could I have done my work if I had become, as I determined in Keele at the age of nineteen, merely competent? If I had become, say, a teacher, and had not had the social and mental difficulties I subsequently encountered? I think not. My mind would have been lost in the complexities of scholarship, and I would have ended up concluding that 'the solution to the problem of induction is that it has no solution'. I would never have had the audacity to conceive of and maintain the existential fallacy and the membership fallacy. Too much that I had learnt would have to be unlearned, and whole systems and histories of thought that I grew up with in the academy would have to be abandoned. I would be left with no ground to stand on. Did Nature then pick the unlikeliest candidate to be the channel that millennia of civilized error was corrected through?

The value of the work is the only promise I now have that it will grow and thrive. But it must do that independently of myself, for, through the illogicality and irrationality of the self, I have fallen into the pit. Neither a good man nor a bad man would have attempted or achieved it. A man torn between both conditions was the vehicle for success. But now that the work is done it is plain that it was a benign obsession.

Future

My end draws near, but I do not look back on the past with longing, as some are wont to do. I recognise my coming demise, and that it may be in personal ignominy and darkness. I hope though that the product of my life survives even if my name does not, for it was always the content of the work that was my concern.

The world is of infinite complexity, but not chaotic. It may seem disordered; that though is only because we cannot discern the ultimate order. We may never be able to do this. I will disappear into time, and so will my lifetime's work. I will be forgotten; maybe however my intellectual contribution will influence other minds, other work, and finally and at last change the ways we think. That will be gradually.

I am glad my work is so succinct, so clear. This will help others who want to think along the same lines. It will of course, and I hope, be developed, and surely I have got many things wrong; so change is in the offing. Not, though, by me. The point is that my life was useful, productive, even if I am unknown. I take pleasure in this. It is less than the great, but more than the mediocre. I was doomed to this by my nature, but I have been rescued from myself by my intellect and by circumstantial accidents. My life was more than most people's and less than a few.

Because I am locked into my subjectivity, I necessarily hope for ultimate achievement and recognition before I die. That is the same as hoping that one can live forever; but I do not believe this now. It is impossible however to be free of this irrational aspiration. The self cannot be free of awareness of selfhood. Not while life or consciousness persist. The self cannot imagine the lack of self, but the reason can. One should not, if one is not to be blown hither and thither by the forces of circumstance, surrender to the person. One cannot be purely rational, unfortunately.

Looking back on this narrative, I am struck by how humourless it seems. But my life was not so. My life is not what I recount; it is the unfolding of a philosophy through the life. That life was tragic, trivial, ridiculous, desperate, lost and found. Like some lives and unlike others. The pattern was not discerned until near the end; but the end has not yet arrived, and illumination and blackness inevitably await me.

Part II

The End of Existence:
Membership and Metaphysics

Foreword

Questions raised by the varieties of doubt almost immediately claimed my attention when I first engaged seriously in philosophy, as could be expected. The attitudes adopted by those who were most inclined to scepticism and were most comprehensive and acute in it troubled me greatly, for their arguments, whilst displaying a correctness and strength all would wish to imitate, led to conclusions which the behaviour of the world and intuition seemed to refute. One could only assume that the premises both sceptics and their opponents accepted were mistaken.

Hume's causal scepticism appeared the most profound formulation of a doubt that is no longer taken as method, but as a desirable viewpoint, as a conclusion rather than as a medium through which one passed to achieve positive knowledge and not awareness of the magnitude of our ignorance. Those, I feel, who hold that position do so not only out of a sense of logical compulsion but out of an emotional attraction towards scepticism, thinking perhaps that it is close to a proper open-mindedness. It may also have a cultural basis.

Not only do I not feel attracted to a negative doubt, but my honest common sense, which in philosophical matters I have a great confidence in, stands opposed to it. I feel that anything in which I, and not only I, believe as instinctively as the inherent orderliness of nature, having as much evidence on its side as it does, will have reason on its side as well. Nevertheless, I make no appeal to common sense in the following essay – indeed I go against its grain; that is not a legitimate method for a philosopher. Also I recognise that the errors of scepticism as it applies especially to causality would not be so widely accepted philosophically, even by those who do not wish to admit some of the uncertainties it forces them into accepting, were not the doubts legitimate ones in view of our conceptual models. If these last lead to results which contradict the behavioural patterns of the physical and seem moreover to serve no useful scientific purpose, since sceptical beliefs hardly lead into or justify the practices of the sciences, then it appears that scepticism is proof of the failure of our philosophical premises, which consequently need a major revision.

However, so large an undertaking as reforming primary beliefs in general was not my original aim, it was rather the intellectually fascinating denial of causality's rationality that interested me. Hume's definition of it was such that what he called 'causality' was so different from our normal idea, lacking as his analysis does in the attribution of inherent, objective necessary connection between events, that he effectively, and explicitly, held it to be absent from the world.

This assumption of causality is essential in our reasoning about the world, and its Humean treatment inspired a reaction of defence, renewed investigation, clarification and re-establishment of the whole notion. I am confident that we do know the reasons why we should believe in causality as a matter of logic, and I aim to make this knowledge explicit by attempting an optimistic, frontal attack on relevant and important metaphysical puzzles.

In a widening spiral these reflections encompassed topics related to causality, not only subsidiarily, but which were major logical and philosophical principles in their own right, and causality was rather an aspect, an implication of them. However logical investigation is not my main theme; more finding and examining principles necessary for treating scientific enquiry conceptually, and indeed ordinary practical life, owing to the scope of causality. Philosophy of science does not simply provide glosses on current scientific developments, following behind the scientific theoretician: the philosopher of science is an axiomatist who unravels the consequences of his discoveries concerning the basic and most simple in our concept of the universe, which, being purely conceptual, remains untouched by science.

Simple and powerful ideas last longest and send out the most distributaries, so to speak, and my arguments will be simple. Curiously though, the further my thoughts were developed the less complex, the more lucid they became. I shed the moribund, involved, conventional standpoints and attempted to grasp the simple but difficult, because radically strange, elements of a system which will no longer leave science hanging in the air, self-supported, and finish the disjunction between deductive, positive philosophy and empirical enquiry in that respect, thus be of service to all methodical but 'unjustified' sciences. But what follows should be seen as a basic hypothesis, and my arguments as no more than that: arguments, not proofs.

That scepticism should be so much in vogue in an age which has seen such domination by the empirical sciences seems paradoxical and reprehensible. But, given the ideas we start with, the questions raised, the positions held, are legitimate and useful in that they prompt their refutation, deepening our understanding thereby. If refutation is achieved by attacking notions which, though not themselves sceptical, yet lead to conclusions which are, then we can feel confident that we shall ultimately benefit.

Whatever one's attitude to the sceptical triumph, in whatever spirit one takes it, it remains a major failure for the speculative endeavour. However, I believe our perceptual equipment and our conceptual abilities are strong and sensitive enough, that the raw material is sufficiently informative for us to be able to found the logic of empirical enquiry: a metaphysic and logic underlying scientific methods, not clearly understood or expounded by them, but intuitively assumed. I want philosophy to justify scientific practice and provide more lucid and flexible notions for it to start from.

The narrow concerns of analytico-linguistic philosophy hinder this aim. Steeped in and overwhelmed by a logic which insists that it is the only kind of necessity, this philosophy has been taken to extremes by its practitioners, as were the philosophies derived from Descartes. These, to the detriment of philosophy, arrived at idealism, which science simply ignored. Analytic philosophy instead seems to have led to a new age of scholasticism in which the subject is self-fascinated and emasculated. We have now swapped the veil of ideas for the veil of language, with language deemed the basic study of philosophy. To do this is like advising an astronomer to investigate the eye, and not the stars.

It may be the cause of my unconventional philosophical idiom that I do not believe in many of the results and methodological premises of contemporary analysis, but this will not, I hope, detract from the content of what I here propose, and this last will not be called a parody of philosophy.

1978-1992

1

Necessary Connection:
The 'World' Argument

Introduction

Those practically engaged in the world cannot found their conception of it on the philosophical premise that one thing just happens after another.[1] Yet no absurdity is felt by the thinkers who propose this. One would say that since they believe an almost infinite number of types of event could be associated with any particular one, the regularity in the world's behaviour indicates the operation of some Agency; but of course they do not allow this. There must be a mistake somewhere in the assumptions of their arguments, leading as they do to so unsubstantiated a conclusion, and their fallaciousness must be exposed now.

To begin with I must draw attention to the unallowable progression that has consistently been made by sceptical commentators on causality which has irretrievably doomed their investigations at the outset. Though explicitly initiated by Hume, it was tacitly accepted by his rationalist opponents, his predecessors, contemporaries and successors. The error is to confound the purely philosophical examination of Causality with the practical study of causes. This can in brief be called the cause/causality error. Because we cannot indicate necessary connections between particular events, neither perceptually nor ideally, it has been inferred that we cannot prove the concept of

---

[1] A J Ayer: *The Central Questions of Philosophy* (Weidenfeld & Nicolson 1973) p.183.

necessary connection. 'The power, by which one object produces another, is never discoverable merely from their idea ... cause and effect are relations of which we receive information from experience, and not from any abstract reasoning or reflection.'[2] The author passes from the level of particular causes or necessary connections to that of the concept of Causality without realising that at these different levels the term, 'cause', changes its meaning. Causality is the conceptual precondition for causes and does not concern itself at all with what causes what. Causes are the reasons for events, whilst Causality is the reason for reasons for events.

The point to be grasped is that causes are physical and particular whilst Causality is purely conceptual. Scientists and lay people want to know causes, but philosophers want to know Causality. Necessary connection, or more widely, Causality, is known, as I shall show, not directly from the world or from psychological compulsions, but from applying various concepts to the world we encounter.

There was a time when I thought that it was not Hume but his successors who failed to distinguish between what is strictly philosophical – necessary connection – and what is practical – necessary connections. But I see that he did make this mistake, though he does attack the problem in purely a priori, and therefore philosophically acceptable ways as well. 'Reason can never show us the connection of one object with another.'[3] This epitomises the confusion of the physical and conceptual aspects of the question; in what follows I show by argument that there is a connection between object and object and that it is of a causal nature. Here I speak quite abstractly and do not presume to undertake the task of an empirical investigator. But it is right to say that reason cannot by itself show the connection of objects – *a priori* – in a manner that is of specific, practical use. Because the above quotation telescopes two ideas, makes the phrase 'the connection

---

[2] David Hume: *A Treatise of Human Nature*. Book 1, Of The Understanding (Penguin Classics 1969) p.117.
[3] *Ibid*, p.140.

of one object with another' apply at two levels, the conceptual and the worldly, and unconsciously so, and thereby encapsulates at those different levels two separate meanings, the contention is superficially plausible, but hopelessly confusing and confused. There is conceptual connection between the concept of 'objects' in the plural, but not between the real, physical objects. Between the latter is a physical connection.

I repeat: I address myself solely to the metaphysical issue here: why there must be reasons for events. To be explicit, I cannot and do not attempt to determine whether from the 'idea' of a baseball bat and the 'idea' of a ball that when one strikes the other, one must move. Nor whether from the idea of a lump of sugar and that of a cup of tea, the sugar must dissolve when put into the liquid. But I can decide, conceptually, if from the general notion of an object, leaving out its specific nature, there has to be a causal relationship between it and another, without making specific inductions. The 'idea' of an object, which is no more than a Humean withered impression, denotes something with a special nature. The general concept of 'object', by which I mean 'worldly object', treats of no specific nature, but deals purely in the conceptual field where causality alone is to be found.

Because this distinction is ignored in the sceptical analysis of causality, that of causes and causality, particular and conceptual, the strategy is flawed at the start.

Only through the following thesis that I present can I hope to sufficiently demonstrate precisely how causality – and induction – may be rationally justified and explained, without having at the same time to justify or consider causes and inductions. I say this because the cause/causality error is ubiquitous and subtle, and one cannot at one blow, as it were, disabuse people of it. Much of the ensuing work can be seen to be a purely abstract, conceptual establishment of Causality. But I must not be understood to be saying that causes are conceptual relations: it is causality which is one. Causes are material relations. To know the reason for reasons for events is not to know the reason for any event. Therefore it cannot be an objection to a theory which establishes causality that we cannot say what caused what; with the appropriate substitutions the same holds for induction. That we cannot conceptually show an induction to be justified does not mean that we cannot justify induction.

The Concept of 'World'

'Taken in itself'[4] an object makes no reference to any other particular object and does not allow us to infer beyond itself. This has been urged as a powerful argument against the connection of objects such as would be required to establish the notion, as it is commonly held, of causality. But can an object be 'taken in itself'? Here we start our investigation into the concept of necessary connection.

To take any object in isolation and not in a context is to load the dice in favour of causal scepticism. We arrive at the impossibility of such a conception by considering the notion of a 'world'.

My present environment constitutes my 'world'. Everything I am directly acquainted with at least is part or maybe all of my 'world'. Anything, if there is nothing else, is a world.

And a world logically requires the relativity of its components to each other. It does not matter what the world is conceived to consist in, whether in physical objects or in sense-items, the concept of a world transcends such disputation; and once it is admitted we must also identify it with a necessary relation, in the most comprehensive sense of 'relation', between the things in it. A world at least requires some kind of access between part and part, otherwise there would properly speaking be no 'world' at all. Anything in our universe, merely by being so, cannot be separate from the other things; and this is not simply a contingent fact: the very concept of a 'world', the very meaning of the word, imposes the necessity to be interrelated upon the 'things' therein, from a conceptual viewpoint. The 'thing in itself' is therefore an impossible vision incapable of realisation given a world or universe.[5]

4   *Ibid*, p 35 & p 189.
5   A J Ayer: *Hume* (Past Masters O.U.P. 1980) p 61.

If things were really isolated and separate from each other, had no kind of access amongst themselves, one to the other, they would literally form different, inaccessible worlds, each of them, and moreover complexity would be impossible. If they are not in the same world, they are not related, so, if they are related, they are in the same world. Other worlds do not appear to be a conceptual possibility since if they had any kind of relation they would effectively be a superworld, and the possibility, of their 'otherness' surely indicates that they can be related and compared in some fashion. In addition the very meaning of the words 'world' and 'universe' appears to exclude other external things; they signify the widest possible domain. However I shall investigate other worlds since some thinkers believe in them.[6]

The concept of a world requires relativity of its objects; togetherness is entailed by the concept of a world. An object could not be conceived to pass from one world and to appear in another, one, because there would be no space and time relations if things, worlds, were genuinely isolated, and, two, because the possibility of the relation of identity could not survive real separateness. The common identity of one thing in both worlds would be a point of contact, hence relativity between the two worlds.

Expressing things differently, something's being part of the world logically requires that it is in no way absolutely separate from all and any of the other components or constituents of the world. This lack of absolute separation and absolute lack of separation between things is called 'connection' and, for the given reasons, is necessary. Relative access is necessitated if there is to be a world at all. I am not saying that contemplating a thing by itself renders a necessary relation to others, but that granted a

---

[6] Most pure philosophers seem to use the idea of other worlds in the sense of 'possible' worlds, a notion which derives from Leibniz. They use it most often in respect to questions in modal logic and counterfactual conditionals and thus it appears to be metaphorical. But those philosophers who take interest in cosmology and theoretical physics do, sometimes, seem to envisage them not merely as possible, but actualities in other dimensions.

world a thing by itself is impossible, and contemplating a thing as being part of a world, as being a 'thing-in-the-world', enforces relativity. The 'thing by itself' and the 'thing in the world' are two different kinds of thing, and once a world is given, one has a thing in the world for which isolation is impossible. And since other worlds are completely unrelated to this one they are wholly irrelevant and do not have even to be considered.

Can the inseparability of things as they are conceived and as they are physically be interpreted as genuine necessary connection, which would entail causality? For several reasons the answer is yes. Since, given the concept of 'world', things cannot logically be contemplated as apart and isolated, they are, in the light of their being constituents of the world, inseparable. This means that they are not ultimately distinct. Material things, objects, events, cannot be understood as materially distinct, therefore they are joined or connected. The logical inability to be apart entails a necessary union, and, as they are conceived, physical objects must be admitted to be necessarily connected to each other physically.

In the real world the relations that events necessarily and indubitably have must be concrete, for these relations must be meaningful to physical things and would fail to be so in a material world if they were not material. They would not be relations in such a world if they were not concrete. So lack of separation must be interpreted physically and is then lack of absolute physical separation.

Now is it possible that objects can only be 'related' but not exactly connected? This, it might be suggested, would or could be the case if the only relations in the world were spatio-temporal ones between physical things. Certainly, those who analyse causality in the Humean manner do assert this. But are space and time relations enough to express non-separation, and can essential lack of connection accompany 'mere' but necessary relation? There is in reality no such thing as 'mere' relation in the physical world, if that is allowed to mean essential independence for things from each other. Relation needs to be physically manifested amongst worldly things, and this will mean that so far from space and time relations being neutral, somehow immaterial, they must also be physical connections or expressions of physical connections, being relations in a physical world. Separation is antithetical to togetherness and consequently impossible in a universe. Real separation and relativity do not mix. Spatio-temporal relation must be an aspect of lack of separation, of physical connection, contrary to the supposition. These dimensional relations do not separate but show the physical togetherness of events. If they had no time and space relations they really would be apart, and the logical connection of things appears in physical guise as dimension relations.

However, the problem is wider, for some philosophers believe that the only kind of relations are in the end 'external'[7] ones, and the above supposition of 'mere' relations comes under that term. Given what I say about the concept of 'world', can there be such relations? I said that if there was no relativity amongst things there would be no 'world', so a world necessitates such a relativity. Of what kind? It cannot be external relativity because of the necessity of relations. The 'thing in the world' is internally related to other such things. Things, being necessarily related, cannot be taken out of context and examined or conceived of 'intrinsically' or alone, or atomically.

Therefore those who suppose external relations are deprived at one stroke of their necessary concept and subject of discourse: the isolated thing which has non-essential, external relations only. To suppose this externality is to beg the very question against which the world argument is deployed: the possibility of the 'thing in itself' or the thing 'taken in itself'. Externality presumes therefore rather than proves extreme pluralism.

Because we cannot abstract some thing from any context whatever, and insofar as we use the concept of a world, relativity, because of its necessity, is ultimately innate to the concept of

---

[7] External relations are those which are not necessary to the things involved in them. Things' natures do not depend upon the relations they have to others if those relations are 'external'.

the thing. So far as it has an intrinsic nature, the thing must be conceived to be relative. In any case, the formation of a 'world' is inevitable for a 'thing'. There is finally no difference between them: either a thing is part of a world or it is a world itself. Only one thing is needed for a world, and the worldless thing is inconceivable.

One may argue that a possible exception to a universe which entails relativity would be a single-object universe. Now, it is the effect of relativity that it makes the constituents of the world into a unity, when that relativity is necessary. This is what a one-object universe is. In both cases we have, effectively, one thing: a single thing and a necessarily interrelated universe are indistinguishable. Again, if our one – object world endures through time, we may then see it as a relativity of its various temporal stages; that is, it would be related by self-identity.

Am I guilty of a modal shift fallacy in all this? Am I saying 'All things are necessarily connected' when I should be saying 'Necessarily, all things are connected'? The 'things' I am speaking of are 'things-in-the-world', whose necessary interrelatedness makes the first formula correct. In this case, it seems that the second formula has just the same force as the first. I start with and retain the 'world' vision, not the individual-thing vision. The 'thing' then is seen as the 'thing-as-part', and a 'part' is necessarily, of its nature, connected to other 'parts'.

Necessary connection is established on the premise of a world, therefore it seems to be a relative necessity. But if a world is inevitable when we have at least one thing, necessary connection is likewise inevitable and is to all extents not relative but absolute. In addition, it is simply impossible to assert a multiplicity and deny a world: togetherness is presumed in the act of recognising a plurality, a group. We could not talk about 'other' things if we doubted their relativity; and everything is in some sense related. Imagine one thing thought to be utterly isolated, alone: it is plain one could not at the same time think of other things any more than if one thought of everything and attempted to conceive of extra things. To conceive of more than one thing is to relate those things.[8]

Our world's interconnection or system of relations is inclusive of time. The world consists of temporally distributed events; its building-blocks are in part temporal, so the world is so too. To be part of such a universe requires necessary temporal connection. We cannot then suggest that the world of say twenty years ago, or an event that occurred then, was not part of the universe, that is, is not related to the present universe. This is prefigured in the passage concerning dimensional relativity, and 'relation' is to be understood in the widest possible sense. The 'universe' has to be seen as a historical term as well as, and not merely as, particular stages in history. All of the stages are in the total system we call 'the world'.

Because in a physical world 'relation' must be seen as connection, and because connection is inherent to things, and concrete, in every aspect of its behaviour, every single event is related of necessity, as a thing, to every other, and so is caused by all other events; for to be connected of necessity is to be caused.

Causality, it must be remembered, is in the process of being defined here as well as demonstrated; I am not approaching the subject with the preconception of priority in time of cause to effect and adjacentness in space and time.[9] Indeed, I am not even considering 'cause and effect', only necessary connection, which when put in a physical guise must imply physical influences passing between thing and thing. 'Cause and effect' is a hackneyed term and it shall emerge in this essay that the notion of just one thing standing in a causal relationship to another is untenable. The notion that causal relationship is one between one thing alone and another helps to engender the belief that the

---

[8] Leibniz's "windowless" monads fail for precisely this reason. They are absolutely removed from each other yet can be conceived as a plurality – by Leibniz at least. There must be, in order for this to be possible, a transcendental dimension for them to be collected in (Leibniz: Monadology 1714).

[9] See Hume *op. cit.*

philosopher's concern is in any way one about special causal relationships, that is, it promotes the cause/causality error noted at the start. Posing the question as concerning 'cause and effect', which has the explicit overtones of a necessary concomitant to an event of a certain type, is responsible to an extent for creating the illusion that the philosopher is engaged in indicating our special causal beliefs about what causes what. Also, starting from the vision of the causal relationships as a one-to-one affair is partly, I would say largely responsible for our failure to perceive the world argument, which is, when one thinks of it, stunningly obvious. Thus far we take causality to operate universally and not at a special level, and for the present I can hold that it is merely conventional to believe that only one thing causes another, for as we see anything is necessarily and physically related to everything else.

Consider the case of a bat hitting a ball and the ball flying away. We can at least say that in some way the bat's behaviour must have been physically connected with the ball's behaviour, as things and events, since they are parts of the same world. But then, so must every other thing. Causal behaviour does not happen in a vacuum, everything in the cosmos and over time participates. Though we lack the ability to pin-point any particular cause, we would in common parlance call a causal sequence those events deemed to be most closely connected. Causes cannot be identified with deductive precision.

The supposition that something could 'come into existence' or 'begin to exist' without a cause is incoherent given what has been said. To be causeless is to be physically dissevered from the environment in space and time. But for as long as an event lasts and is part of the world it must be connected to the events with which it is at least contemporaneous. Whilst it happens it has got to be related to everything, for no part of the universe is not necessarily connected to the rest. But this will not satisfy those who agree that the existential commencement of events has no linkage to temporally prior events. Some things, they object, will have no connection to situations that preceded them. Since worldly relations are nevertheless concrete ones, it must be admitted that even though events are not contemporaneous in many instances, they are still temporally related, therefore materially linked, and this is all one needs for necessary connection or causality.

Again, events have to be conjoined to their contemporaneous contexts, some of the constituents of which endure before others 'begin to exist'. In this way there is overlap through time and a new event is indirectly connected to a previous state of the world. That is, since events are connected at least to simultaneous events, through the identity and continuity of some of these last, events are connected to earlier ones mediately. If there was not an overlap, a new universe, unconnected to the old one, would come about every time any new event happened 'without cause'.

The universe consists of physical events. One important feature of events is their temporality: they have a temporal content or component. Therefore they must be related to other events in a manner inclusive of time. Since events comprise the universe, it has an irreducible temporal aspect and not only spatial but temporal distribution is part of its nature. To be part of such a world for an event, consequently, must involve connection in time, over its history. A historical universe requires its elements to be interconnected materially and historically.

This identification of the universe with its history means that if being without cause is equivalent to being part of the universe and yet disconnected historically, then such a supposition is indeed self-contradictory.

What we have discovered so far allows us to reject the applicability of the argument to the universe that if things are distinct they are separable. 'Distinctness' in a universe can only amount to 'difference' – a less strong term. Things have access to one another of a physical kind and can at most only be 'distanced' but not totally apart.

Establishing the physicality of connections and their necessity enables us to discover further things about the causal interactions between events. One may argue that whilst connection in general is necessary, the manner of connection is contingent. What does the 'manner of connection' mean? The phrase may be misinterpreted: it might be understood as the sort of mechanism whereby two or more things are linked. This is not what is intended. What is meant can be expressed in a very basic way by saying it is the way things behave in relation to another. An improved expression would be 'quality of the casual relationship'. Instead of any two uncharacterized, abstract 'events' being taken as necessarily physically related, we ask: Is the quality of that union or mode of connection amongst things necessary? The mode of relationship includes the natures of the things involved in it as they behave, as they are. We do not doubt that there is a necessary relation between things, but does that necessity extend to the natures of the things related? Do things have to act in the ways they do *vis-à-vis* one another? For instance, does the ball have to fly off after it is hit by the bat, and does the contact of the swung axe with the tree have to be followed by the cleavage of the wood, or was something else possible? Yes, necessarily things modify each other, but do they have to modify each other in the ways they actually do? The basic answer to this lies in regarding particular types of associations as togetherness, which is necessary, made qualitative. Essentially the difference I am concerned with is the necessity of causality and the necessity of causes, which are two separate questions.

Since all events are necessarily connected to each other, then how they are connected, which is a practical issue, is the character of this necessity of connection. How each set of events are related is an expression of a particular mode or form of necessary connection. Things must be connected, and this necessity is not taken away, only transmuted, when we describe interactions: necessity remains, but is particularised and rendered qualitative. In the universe, necessity is made physical. Connection is both necessary and physical because in a physical universe necessity cannot be abstract: it must mean something materially. But the physical always and only appears as a mode, sort or kind of thing, so that the quality of the connection expresses this necessity, embodies it. I am not saying that we see what causes what, only that we must conceive the world as possessed of a concrete necessity. This is a very important result and this approach to the problem has consequences that go beyond this area of theory: it is a way of defining and introducing natural necessity. Worldly events are not blank and characterless: they have qualitative natures, they are 'how' they are. The particular manner of an event is that event. Because events are connected, the manners or modes of events are necessarily physically related: how one is will be related of necessity to how others are, meaning that finally there is no contingency concerning events' natures. Put another way, there is a necessary connection between the behaviour of one thing and the behaviour of another, there is an interdetermination among the characters of things. Necessary union between objects becomes union between their natures, so that each, in some way, 'causes' the natures of the other, to some extent.

Necessity of connection is allied to the characters of causal relationships. Firstly, the 'how' of connection, its mode or form, is brought up to the non-contingency of connection. Next, necessity is brought down to qualitative level by being made physical. Lastly, connection is revealed between the natures of events. So we have the 'how' of necessity, the necessity of the 'how', and necessity between the 'how'. The 'how' means the qualitative nature of objects, events or situations.

Since there is a direct qualitative relationship between the character of one thing and that of another, we can expect different things to differently determine the natures of others. Connection is physical, therefore various, and this leads us to modify what was held earlier, that it was conventional to say one event caused another. Linkages are different: the presence of a massive body may 'cause' something about the motion of a ball that is struck, but the instrument that strikes the ball will be connected in another fashion to that ball's motion. The instrument will then cause the motion in its particular way, all connections taken to be different, and we are allowed to speculate as to the cause, the particular cause, of any event. Recognising the variety of connection, it is a short step to accepting that events 'cause' or contribute to one another differently.

We have had an intimation of a necessity in the universe that is physical, and can make general statements about the character and possibility of what philosophers have long guessed at, those at least who were not satisfied with a sceptical position regarding causality: natural necessity. I think I can safely say that it cannot be tautological or to do with language, and this means that philosophers steeped in logic and conceptual necessity have no idea of what it would be like. I fully realise that what I say here is provisional and until I enter a new area of theory relevant to necessary connection I cannot require natural necessity as it will be defined now to be accepted unreservedly. Indeed this whole 'world-argument' is provisional. Until I produce new material the following must be taken as a partial establishment of a non-logical necessity.

In Nature, necessity of connection is transformed. Relations are expressions of the natures of things. Instead therefore of imagining them as 'necessary' connections, think of them as 'natural' connections. When put in the context of a physical universe, this is what necessity, of connection, becomes: it is physicalized. Relationship between things in Nature is one involving the natures of things, so relations are natural. In the world 'necessity' becomes 'what is natural'. For the function of 'necessary' is taken over by 'natural', and 'necessity' becomes 'naturalness', except that in the world things must be made unabstract, the world being unabstract, and 'naturalness' is 'what is natural'. Necessity literally identifies with whatever is natural, that is to say, the physical. This necessity is not imposed from above like rules, but identifies with what happens. And this is what one should expect of a physical necessity: for the physical is the natural, and events themselves contain as part, as an aspect of themselves, necessity. Events are necessity. Naturalness is the force for and heart of necessity in the material world. That force identifies with whatever happens, whatever is natural, so it is not external to events.

One may not be clear as to how the transition from 'necessary' to 'natural' is made in the foregoing, but if one recalls that all relations deserving the name in a concrete world are necessary and are not external, one sees that they must at the same time be natural ones, and the natures of things interrelate. Therefore, whatever is a natural relation is a necessary relation, and if anything is a necessary relation then it is a natural relation, and so the natural is the necessary: naturalness is necessity. Insofar, I have said, as objects have intrinsic natures, these must be relative; and to apply this particularly, the special nature of the thing is its particular complex of relations. Now, the innate or intrinsic is both the natural and the necessary, and so the last pair identify inseparably. Put in another fashion: the internality of relations is an expression of their necessity; but internality expresses also innateness, and what is innate is simply the nature of everything. Hence the identification of nature and necessity.

This is the source of the assumption we make of natural necessity, but this is not the only manner of approaching it in philosophy. We are not told much about it by a priori reasoning, but we can attain some sort of understanding of it thereby. At least we recognize it, and we also define it though we do not give its content. For securing it fully however we shall need to make investigations in a relevant field which could prevent its acceptance: the concept of existence. In establishing causality this will be my major task, and it is prudent not to undertake it before other issues have been inspected at least.

What has been written so far enables me to make certain observations, deductions, which are of great importance for the theory's development. One is that I cannot hold descriptions of events in this world to be contingent. So to regard them is disconsonant with necessary connection and irreconcilable with natural necessity. Another important inference is that because we do not observe how things physically follow from and are connected with other things, but only that they are conjoined, juxtaposed, the world must have an unobserved physical dimension which things operate in and have access to. This is of consequence to natural necessity and for the limited study of epistemology that I will allow myself in this thesis. One of my firmest contentions is that theory of knowledge should not have a prominent place in establishing causality, we can do without it and causality has incidental implications for it rather than otherwise, except in the area of induction. This hidden world is of importance though in philosophy and other use and proof will be made of it. Theory of knowledge has always sought to discover this realm, but within its own field, and has failed.

The most consequential implication of what has emerged so far is that if being a 'matter of fact' or existing means that things are essentially separate from each other, then things, being in the world, are not 'matters of fact'. If worldly things are not factual, what being 'factual' means requires adequate determination first in the context of the world argument. This will be attempted.

Experience then, shows us what is necessary – though not all of it – and contingency has no place in the world. All events are inherently relational and we cannot determine what a thing is like in itself, if 'in itself' means 'by itself'. But if 'in itself' recognizes a context, relativity, then a thing is what qualities are proper to it even when these are imposed on it, to a large extent, from outside.

I repeat that the arguments in this essay so far I regard as only provisional; a more radical treatment will follow.

The Counter-Concept

I now turn to the crucial, outstanding problem that confronts every philosopher not satisfied with a position of causal scepticism, and which is the foundation and unacknowledged source of it, namely the relationship of 'existence' and 'fact' to causality, and in this particular argument, to the notion of the world. To begin with, I have to define unambiguously my use of the term 'fact'. Because this is a philosophy about the world the term shall be defined in respect to its worldly manifestation, and this will result in a more limited usage than possible, but this will be all to the good.

The essential element in the 'fact' is that of existing. One may conceive of all kinds of situations, attach all sorts of predicates to all sorts of subjects, but unless the situation exists in the world, it is not a fact. I do not even have to know the nature of something to ascertain whether it is a fact or not, all I need to know is whether it exists or whether it does not. If I know that something is, I know that there is a fact. Of course, the nature of 'something' important, but as regards factual status, it is secondary to existence; so I may say that a fact is the existence of a situation.[10] Objects 'are', things 'exist', in order to be facts. Facts are 'that' they are. I think common usage justifies the existence of an object being called a fact. If readers are unhappy with the word 'fact' they don't have to suppose it as essential. 'Existences' or 'what exists' express my meaning; but I do not see any good reason for not using 'fact'.

We must distil the essence of the 'fact' out of it, to discover why it is important and how much so for causality. Those who have read what I have written so far will feel that I have grossly avoided mentioning a certain quality that attaches to statements made about the material world: their syntheticity. They will be annoyed, impatient with this omission of statements' syntheticity and would point out to me that it entirely subverts my a priori establishment of the causal concept. I agree with them. But can statements about the world's behaviour be synthetic? Should they be, and if so, why are they like this? So far it is a philosophical consensus that descriptions of the course of worldly affairs can only be contingent, and here I would like to break with tradition by refuting this. What makes such statements contingent and synthetic?[11] I would hold that it is the concept of existence. Existence is the culprit, the germ of causal scepticism.[12]

Existing makes situations or objects matters of fact. The existence of matters of fact, their existential component, is

---

[10] Compare L.Wittgenstein *Tractatus Logico-Philosophicus* (Routledge & Kegan Paul 1961) Paragraph 2, p 5.
[11] Contingency and syntheticity have been, until recently, almost seen as nearly equivalent. In what follows I conflate the Leibnizian, Kantian, and 20th Century definitions of syntheticity, though they differ in important respects.
[12] Here I must be seen as penetrating to the heart of the metaphysical reason for causal scepticism, not re-presenting previous analyses.

commonly held to be contingent. The situations do not have to exist – they are contingent. If this is the case, their verbal denial is possible without self-contradiction. This being so, they are synthetic statements which assert them. Matters of fact all have the contingent existential element, therefore statements or descriptions of such worldly things are 'truths of fact', factual propositions, which is the same as saying that they are synthetic. So schematically: existence is contingent; existence makes fact; facts are contingent; descriptions are statements the truth-values of which are contingent: they do not have to be as they are because the situations they describe do not have to be; so worldly statements of fact are synthetic: their denial is logically possible.

Contingency at the factual level is responsible for contingency at the prepositional level because the factual level precedes the linguistic level; and existence is contingent. Propositions can only reveal and not make for the contingency of facts. The statement of the nature of an event such as 'The bat hit the ball and the ball flew off', that is, the meaning of words designating the nature of an event, does not include existential assertion or denial, for existence is outside of nature, it is external to the character of a situation. So this purely, shall we say, qualitative aspect can be entertained apart from the conditions which make the situation a fact. To assert the proposition as a fact is then to go beyond the meaning of the sentence describing this qualitative, merely possible, event; and so the factual proposition is, because of its existential element, synthetic and contingent. The statement is not true or false merely in virtue of its meaning alone, but because of what exists. The meaning captures only the nature of the event, not its existence.

One might say that such a statement as 'Apples cost 30 pence a pound in the market' is synthetic simply because the cost is not part of the 'meaning' of the word 'Apple'. But this is incorrect because as I say propositions merely indicate and do not cause real contingency and therefore syntheticity. A purely logical, conceptual proposition can derive its necessity from itself, but one about the world can only derive its contingency or its necessity from the world. Because existence is not part of the nature of a situation, the situation's existence is contingent. The situation can be logically denied without self-contradiction. We determine syntheticity from the whole sentence, we do not analyse parts of a sentence; but the whole nature of the event described by the statement is seen not to allow existential assertion or denial.

Apropos of the quoted 'synthetic' statement, one notices that whilst the concept 'Apple' has essential attributes such as say, being organic, the 'apples in the market' are real things and not concepts, so that 'Apple', the concept, does not equate to or mean the actual natures of real 'apples in the market'. So no analysis of the concept 'Apple' is going to be sufficient to appraise one of the contingency of physical apples or their attributes, or of the syntheticity of statements made about real apples. Therefore it may be in the meaning of 'real apples in the market', which the concept of 'Apple' does not equate to, that they cost 30 pence per pound. To assert that this situation exists, that it is a fact, is to go beyond the meaning of the description of the situation, of its nature, existence not being part of the natures of things. Thus existential qualification makes for syntheticity.

Factual assertion should be seen like this: 'The situation: the dog barked, exists.' Factual denial is: 'The situation: the dog barked, does not exist.' The content of what is existentially affirmed or denied does not vary. What does vary is the existential qualification. The final clause in each sentence makes for the syntheticity on the basis of externality of existence to nature, hence to necessity.

A statement like 'The bachelors in this room are men' is a factual statement, and so contingent whether *de re* or *de dicto*. *De re* it is about a contingent fact. *De dicto* it can be analysed so: 'There are bachelors in this room' and 'Bachelors are men'. The second sentence is necessary. The first is contingent because it is existential. So the conjunction as a whole is contingent, one of the conjuncts being so. The fact there are bachelors in this room is what makes the sentence *de re* contingent as well.

The whole foregoing passage and state of affairs has the result that if any matter of fact is existentially contingent, can be the case or not be the case, then, given this freedom, its existence cannot be necessitated or brought about. Certainly not innately or internally at least, and if the contingency is thoroughgoing, not externally. What this leads to is that we must admit individual matters of fact to be independent of one another in respect of their existence, and hence in respect of their natures and behaviours: if a situation's existence is independent of another's, the situation itself, its character, is so too.[13] How contingency makes for internal existential freedom is clear; externally or relatively it may not be so clear. If it is not in the nature of something to happen at all, because nature doesn't include existence, the existence of something else cannot make it in the nature of the first event mentioned to exist either, if nature is separate from existence. It can never be the nature of a situation to exist, whatever else happens or exists. Each object is a distinct existence. Take this analogy: the nature of water is to boil if it is heated over a certain temperature. The nature of one event is to exist if another event exists. The second sentence is denied because the parallel between it and the first is not legitimate: existence is not in the natures of things.

Plainly this cannot be reconciled with the outcomes of the concept 'world' that we have relied upon in this essay to produce causality: one takes away what the other gives. How are we to resolve this tension?

Attempts at accommodation

I have said that the very notion of a world requires relativity between its parts and that if facthood means unconnectedness in essence to other facts, then things cannot both be in the world and be facts. Some hold that the world is the totality of facts,[14] and as this stands we have a dichotomy owing to the very concept of the world. What can they mean? It seems obvious. Can it be all that is required for the items in a world simply that they exist, are

---

[13] See L Wittgenstein *op.cit.* 2.061.
[14] *Ibid*, 1.1.

facts? Doesn't there have to be a further requirement that they be related of necessity to one another, and is this compatible with factual status? Or does facthood precede relativity? One outcome of necessary interrelation is that the nature of one thing brings about, determines that of another. But if things do not have to be, being matters of fact, nothing compels anything else to exist and to exist in a certain way.

Anything not impossible in itself can come into existence, and if anything does – but indeed nothing has to exist at all – it is quite free to be as it is independently of the behaviour and nature of another thing. Things are in themselves absolutely independent of one another if they are facts.

I am not saying that in themselves things have necessary relations to others, but that the concept 'world' imposes this on them by making them things-in-the-world and denies the very possibility of things in themselves. If existence requires their independence of each other, these concepts cannot be harmonized. To say 'things do not have to be parts of the world' is pointless, for it is not ultimately a fact that worldly things participate in necessary connection: the very concept of a 'world' imposing necessity of connection on them cannot be based on fact, on existence, because we would have the contradiction that it would be contingent that things are necessarily connected to each other. Things are not connected by a reason that springs from a matter of fact, but conceptually, not from a contingency but from a non-contingency, and this means that facthood and world are irreconcilable, antithetical. We have a choice between two seemingly obvious but mutually exclusive propositions: there are facts and there is a world. Some have doubted the latter,[15] and this is why the necessary connection argument up to now is provisional. We need to prove the invalidity of existence. What I propose is that we trade Existence for Causality because of the contradictions the former leads us into and because in the conduct of practical life, in our relations with the world of every

---

[15] Russell at one time.

sort, it is more important to use causal reasoning and to assume causality than to retain existence.

Perhaps the existence of things is contingent and their relations are necessary? Once it is made clear what this involves it cannot be maintained. Consider that whilst being contingent facts, things could determine the behaviour and other features of each other under this scheme. The bat would have to be a cause of the ball's motion, have to be somehow relevant to it, yet, if they were facts, firstly, they would be independent of each other and what one did would be irrelevant to what the other did. Both would be the mere matters of fact, 'brute facts'. One event either could or could not have come into existence; it would not be compelled to exist; it would be free. Because of the qualification of independence derived from the contingency of facts, they are essentially isolated and interaction cannot obtain and is meaningless to them. The attempt to reconcile facthood and necessity of connection results in a contradiction.

As was said, between fact and fact is an insuperable gulf, meaning that they are different worlds entirely, absolutely without any linkages. This though is refuted by there plainly being a world in which things are together: so things as they appear in the universe cannot be facts.

Maybe there is a middle position: there could be relations, but 'factual' ones only. This possibility is dispelled at once when we reiterate that in a world things must be related: it is all or nothing. If there is no necessary relativity there is no world, and no contingent relations are possible. The idea of a world must be eschewed by those who accept 'factual relations': these would only be the illogical products of those who were under the illusion of togetherness when really there were only unconnected existents. Things involved in such relations would be involved in no intrinsic way; relativity would be illusory, meaning nothing to existences, and this is quite unacceptable given the character of our experience.

Possibly, one may imagine, there is a world involving the pure existences of things alone, and omitting their natures; and it is based on the still-valid contingency of existence. But that very contingency destroys this possibility, for it means that nothing has to be, that the existences are independent of each other, enclosed worlds in themselves. Being existentially independent they have no existential access to one another and so cannot form a world. At the existential level they have no common field or background. So we see again that the existential aspect makes facts essentially worldless.

Facts are islands, incapable inherently of being affected by what is beyond and outside themselves, and because togetherness is manifest only a metaphysical interpretation of the world or of things can dispel it. That interpretation is the metaphysic of existence. Separation is separation: no common forum is available to things, no access, no kind of relation therefore, external or otherwise, is possible. This is one reason why existence in the end must be a misconcept. Existence negates relation, 'factual' or necessary, and the only alternative is to posit a world and deny facts, existences.

May there not be a quite comfortable fit between world and existences if we allow the world only to mitigate but not destroy contingency? The antithesis spoken of is between the effect of a world, which is necessary connection, and that of existence, which is separation. We could see the separation between facts as a kind of relative contingency. That could be abandoned in favour of an overall, global, absolute contingency. We could allow a necessary connection between worldly events on account of their being worldly, but maintain that, absolutely, the whole world does not have to exist. So whilst one event must cause another in a given way, the whole world could just go out of existence rather than the given event should happen. The grounds of this is that no one individual thing in the world counts as a thing, for the thing is by definition a creation of or involvement with the rest of the world. The world cannot be abstracted from the supposed individual, making its nature as it does. So for one thing to cease existing it is necessary that the whole world ceases to be. Only the whole world is a 'fact', then. So we could maintain contingency and necessary connection, i.e. if the whole world is annihilated one cannot expect the necessary concomitant of a given event to exist; but if the world does continue, then the concomitant must happen. Both contingency and necessity are mitigated and combined. Is this feasible? Can existence thus be saved?

Consider how we arrive at our antithesis. We do not presume either the connection or apartness of objects. We apply existence to them, and, through contingency, we get separation. We apply 'world' to them, and through its very concept, we connect them. So left to itself, existence produces one result and, left to itself, 'world' produces the opposite. One must keep in mind that I presume nothing about things: we do not covertly unite or distance them by surreptitious use of either concept, and we have an antithesis. On the basis of not assuming either concept, existence and world, we have this contradictory situation. In addition, my point must be conceded, for in the scenario I envisage here as an option, the concept 'world' deprives its components of facthood: there are no facts in the plural in the world.

There seems to be three choices: a world and no facts; no world, but facts; and fact and world, where the only 'fact' allowed is the whole world. The first defeats causal scepticism and existence; so too does the second since it is counter to experience and since a world is unavoidable, given at least one object; and the global existence and contingency allowed by the third does not defeat causality in any serious way and cannot be accepted by the causal sceptic. Indeed 'fact' and existence are rendered impotent, which he cannot permit.

That things can evidently form a world proves they are not essentially separate, and this leads to the conclusion: worldly things are not facts, or facthood does not mean separation, in which case it is quite redundant since independence is one of the main qualifications of the factual. Whatever it means, the notion of 'fact' stands in need of a considerable revision.

Introducing Induction

The theory has reached a stage, I feel, where we can introduce the topic of induction and treat it, albeit in a primitive and cursory way. My main subject is causality and it is only secondarily that induction will appear in these essays, and I believe this is the proper order: induction is a problem that should be tackled only in the context of causality and causal induction is the sphere to which I limit myself.

An error, similar to the one noted at the beginning of this essay, when we contend that because necessary connections cannot be proven or observed, necessary connection is beyond our powers to prove as well, is made when certain philosophers argue that because inductions cannot be deductively justified neither can Induction. For the method to be inductive and do its proper work, some say, it cannot centrally involve deductive elements. The error lies in confusing the inferential form with the inferences.

The form is not itself an induction but an argument type founded in metaphysics, and is completely a priori, whilst the applications of the inferential form are, though involving, as we shall see, certain conceptual features, not conceptual in a decisive way. Induction is not an induction. The lack of a priori certainty at the latter level is no guarantee of a similar lack at the former. Inductions are justifications for types of empirical statements, but induction is the justification for justifications for types of empirical statements. In the same way as the reason for reasons for events, causality, identifies with its justification, so induction identifies with its validation. Empirical argument-types are legitimated by a philosophical argument, which can be called their 'form'. Giving content to this form is where practical difficulties arise. Induction is not so much empirical reasoning as the validity of that reasoning; not the various methods of inference, but the reason is why it is proper so to reason. Induction can be conceptually justified, and inductions can be justified by the canons of what constitutes good inductive argument, that is, from within.

We admit that modes of connection are necessary; and they will remain so. If we reject contingent fact and existence from our picture of the world, we cannot permit correct descriptions of related events to be synthetic: they are propositions concerning natural necessity. The course of nature stays the same and time will not alter this physical necessity: types of union will theoretically be repeatable. This is because it is not as empty numerical 'individuals' but qualitatively that physical things are associated and inter-determinating, and physically similar events have the same relationships with other resembling events. That is to say, because it is the characters of events that have necessary connections with each other, and because it is innate to the characters of events to be unlimited by those events' numerical particularity, can spread beyond a single instance, in the way that, say, a given colour may appear – like green – in leaves, grass or paint, those characteristically necessary connections are universal, unlimited, repeatable. So if it is natural that events of a kind should be associated with those of another kind, then it is necessarily and universally so.

Each individual object has its own qualitative identity: the only identity it can have. Therefore when one says 'this object' one speaks of a special sort of qualitativity. Other things having different histories may yet resemble an object characteristically, and these properties determine, are necessarily linked to, how other objects behave. If the characters are initially similar, if initial situations resemble, the behavioural relationships should be the same or similar. But what may not be done is to blankly, numerically individuate the description of a material object or event. This is done when particular things, individual times, are illegitimately chosen to qualify the natures of objects. Consider the case of a bat striking a ball and the ball flying off: the instrument connects with the ball as a bat, not as 'this' bat and 'this' ball, at 'this' time, and 'there'. To distinguish such numerical identities is not to describe physical qualities of events; one fails thereby to recognize that physical objects naturally fall into kinds; such indications are not qualitative constituents of physical things, and do we not distinguish qualitative from numerical identity, with the former not limited to individual instances?

Associations are unalterable over time because times are

irrelevant to them qualitatively. If we imagine salt not dissolving in water, we plainly are not imagining salt and water as such, not imagining their known and necessary properties. For something to 'change its nature' is plainly for that thing not to be itself – a contradiction – and one imagines it and its nature as matters of fact. Anyhow, things are not contingent. But we are not completely aware of how events are connected and scientific statements are not, as the philosopher would define the term, wholly certain.

The conceivable is held to be possible because what makes the impossible conceivable is ignorance as to the natures of objects and the qualities of connection springing there from. Because science is not 'certain' and philosophical, its statements are deniable without knowledge of self-contradiction. If we do not know a thing's full nature to begin with, then of course we can affirm a multitude of things about it. If all we were told about a square was that it had four sides, we could, knowing only that about it, imagine all sort of properties that would be incompatible with its other features. This is the position we are in when faced with many empirical propositions. The properties are not conceptually assured but have to be discovered. Given that necessary connection obtains in Nature, the status of objects as being extra-conceptual is what places particular causal laws outside the scope of a purely conceptual analysis. We know of natural connection and natural necessity, but we do not know how they translate into special causal patterns of behaviour. We have an a priori insight into their form though not into their natural content a priori. They have to be speculated about, though that does not mean there is inherent lack of necessity in Nature: it means there is uncertainty in us.

We do know that Nature is not contingent because our arguments are ideal and deductive. We even know there is physical necessary connection in the world: how can it not be directly perceived as the abstract kind of necessity is? The world is apparently in part somehow occult, and if we had the right kind of faculties necessary connections between things could be observed. Physical necessity it seems can only be approached through abstract, philosophical reasoning, and the laws of Nature are only suppositional so far as we can know them. Perhaps though natural necessity in its content can be observed by us, but not intellectually. Since natural necessity equates directly to what is natural, namely events, and since we are phenomenally aware of these, we are aware of it. We also observe it through the compulsions it imposes on our bodies. In a way, we are 'sensitive' to it, and so is everything else. We participate as objects in natural necessity, and this must mean openness to, awareness of, in a broader sense than usual, what is natural. We 'know' it because we are part of it, otherwise we would not be in the world at all. The influences of natural necessity are felt by us, only sub-intellectually.

2

Paradoxes of Existence

My reasons for rejecting existence are not merely pragmatic, not simply to permit Causality a place in the conceived world, but because I genuinely believe it is not a valid concept. The following examination of its contradictions comes out of the necessary connection argument, but is singular enough to be taken by itself on its own merits.

Perhaps we should abandon for the time being and for the sake of argument my contention that a 'world' demands connection. Maybe that thesis is not decisive enough as it stands and is misconceived for some reason I have not recognised. Things do exist, and my idea of what a 'world' means is not the only possible one, let us say. What if things simply exist and the plurality of such existing things constitute the world, a world without any kind of necessary relations? I cannot in this case appeal to the concept I had of the world, but must approach the problem by asking what is entailed by things 'existing'. However I must first crystallize what the use is that I make of the word 'fact'. To repeat, the prime element in facthood is existing; a fact is that something is; a situation 'is' in order to be factual.

In existing or being facts, things become 'real'. This implies that they are real to each other, relatively real, so they impinge upon or are relevant to one another. Thus, amongst facts, relevance means some kind of accessibility; they must be meaningful to or be capable of influencing one another. A fact cannot have no bearing on another fact. But if being factual implies a lack of connectedness, derived from the contingency of existence, amongst existing things, facthood cannot mean 'reality to' or relevance and the concept involves a contradiction. This suggests that what makes the world and the things in it 'real' is not facthood, existence, but something else, for a reductio has been achieved from it.

Bearing in mind the vision of an existential, non-connected world, we may consider the description of the world as a 'totality' of facts. If the items in that totality were not real to one another at the existential level, they would effectively not be part of any 'totality'. A collection requires that the components be relevant in the sense of having access to the members of the group. At least something, in belonging to a group, adds to it: that is one kind of access. But if the members of a totality are not relatively real they would be insignificant to each other. Any such 'fact' would indeed be outside the sum of facts: it would not contribute to the collection. Facts must be mutually meaningful at the level of existence in the world defined as their totality. Yet the common philosophical use of the term 'matter of fact' separates them. This, if one likes, can be seen as a reformulation of the world argument, but I am not taking it as a proof of necessary connection derived from the notion of 'totality': I use it to expose contradictions inherent in existence; at least that is my intention at this stage, though it will be developed later.

This inconsistency is encapsulated in our quasi-philosophical utterances when we say that something is 'just' or 'merely' a matter of fact, which hints at its contingency and lack of involvement with any other thing, and when we say of something that it is a 'fact', is real, solid and significant to other things.

First, I will examine the connection between existence and independence among facts. Existential contingency I submit is the ultimate cause of this. Matters of fact do not have to be, neither innately nor externally, therefore one is existentially uncontrolled by anything; they cannot be brought about, and are not necessitated: whatever happens is 'just' a matter of fact. This is also the source, as I have indicated of the syntheticity of factual statements. Facts are existentially independent and existence is the prime element in the definition of the fact. Briefly, if it is not in the nature of any thing to exist, it is not in the natures of any two things to co-exist in the sense that it becomes part of the nature of one to exist when the other exists. The concept of a son requires the concept of a father, but neither as objects necessitate the existence of the other. Alternative reasons can be proposed for the consensus among empiricist philosophers that facts are independent of each other logically, though I think this one noted lies at the bottom of them all. Indeed, logical independence is a form of contingency.[1]

A philosopher, for instance, arguing for complete externality of worldly relations will propose that any property of any individual whatsoever is contingently had, any action one that did not have to be performed; thus no relation is ever going to be definitional, partly, of the individual, hence not internal, therefore only external. If he says that though a relation is one something did in reality bear to other things, yet the contradictory of it is not self-contradictory, merely 'false', then he is really admitting that the relation is a mere matter of contingent fact. The contingency of the relation, when seen as the existence of a situation, founds its lack of internality to the individuals involved in it. A given relationship is contingent if another relationship could have been possible. This is so because the former relationship does not have to exist, though one of the terms in it can still exist and that relationship not obtain. No complex fact has to exist, so no part of it has to exist. Since worldly relationships between matters of fact therefore are only external, the existence of any one object is logically independent of the existence of any other.

Part of the concept of the matter of fact seems to be that it is independent. Certainly causal sceptics maintain this, perhaps without knowing precisely why. At the very least, independence is associated with, if not written into, the fact. But the admitted reality of the fact compels us to concede its significance for other facts, which, from whatever source the independence comes, plainly reveals an incoherence in the doctrine of the 'fact', which consequently cannot be maintained.

---

[1] See 'The Existential Fallacy' (Chapter 3, Part II) where I discuss the reasons for atomism.

Asserting 'relevance' or 'materiality to' as a result of the reality conferred by existing on the fact is extremely comprehensive in its implications. Consider any two facts: in the world these will be events, the behaviours of objects, physical objects – they will be the existence of these at least. One behaviour's existence is a fact which is significant, in factual terms, to another's. This factual determination must mean that one fact literally 'makes' or influences something in or about another. If a behaviour's existence is relevant to another behaviour's existence, then the former is relevant to the nature or form of the other behaviour. Responsibility and significance for the existence, in part, of another behaviour or event carries along with it control of some kind over the form the behaviour takes qualitatively, for existence and nature are wedded in the fact.

We can distil out of this the proposition that since the fact is the existence of a situation, inter-factual relevance must mean responsibility for, sensitivity to, and control over the actual existences of each other. If what exists is significant to what exists, what exists is significant to what exists. For one, if something could come into existence quite free of the controlling influence of another fact, then there really would be irrelevance or indifference between fact and fact. The main element in the fact is the existential part and materiality to a fact must be materiality to its existence. Even if we have only one single fact which is real we do not need the existence of other situations already given, other actual facts, for relevance at the existential level to be in operation. To be relevant to the existence of something else means that something else does not have to exist yet or first before the solitary fact has some influence over that other's existence. We can say that 'fact makes fact'. For a fact to be real to another when both are physical objects is for a physical object to modify, influence or bring about some aspect of the other physical object: that is part of the meaning of its 'materiality to' the other.

All this is contradicted by the orthodoxy which says that things, as mere matters of fact, are irrelevant to each other's existences. This is the view of the predominant causal scepticism.

As matters of fact they have no connection;[2] as realities they do; hence the tension that splits apart the philosophical concept of the fact, the existence of a situation or object. This contradiction springs directly from the notion of existence and is surely a good argument against its validity.

The preceding paragraphs have implications for existence as it concerns causality, but I will set that aside for the moment and will consider examples of relevance in the physical world and how facthood can be used to prove contradictory theses.

One example of real things' relevance to one another is that it is not possible for a thing to do anything it likes given the presence of other things. Take something I thought to be indubitable: that only one thing could occupy the same place at the same time. I must admit to having been surprised to discover it was controversial, but it is in keeping with the tendency to reduce the physical world to a chaos characteristic of analytico-linguistic philosophy that this should be so.[3] Two or more things coinciding in space and time seems to go against intuition, but intuition is not enough here and arguments need to be produced against its possibility. Obvious objections are the following, though I have to make it clear that by 'objects' 1 mean individual objects.

Supposing two objects could occupy the same spatio-temporal location is not self-consistent. If a given spatial extension was filled with a body with a specific characteristic, say a certain colour, it could not also be filled with another body with another incompatible characteristic, another colour, that is, at the same time. The separateness or individuality of these objects would be forfeited and would have to disappear; there would only be one

---

[2] In Hume, causality is the relation which connects objects in our reasoning about the world, but he holds that the necessary connection, which is the principal part of it, firstly, is not observed, which is important given his impressions/ideas epistemology, and secondly, can be contradicted, which is the conceptual part of his atomism. Here however atomism is established on the basis of existence's character, because neither the Humean epistemology nor his logic is adequate.

[3] R. Harré: *The Philosophies of Science* (1985 O.U.P.) p.112 p.135. Norman Swartz : *The Concept of Physical Law* (C.U.P. 1985) p.22.

thing there in reality. Two or more things, as a plurality, could not coincide in this way and remain individual, being mutually exclusive. And the idea of an individual filling an extension completely would have to be maintained as inconceivable, for complete occupation and filling in the ordinary sense carries with it the character of exclusivity: this is, naturally, the negative meaning of 'filling'. Also, if objects modify one another in occupying the same location in time and space, as it seems they logically must, relevance is demonstrated between real things and the objects are not deemed absolutely independent.

This though does not tax my philosophical inspiration and all the foregoing is possibly refutable. A better and more complete reason comes from considering the conceptual consequences of coincidence if it were to be accepted. This is an indirect argument that makes use of our notions of space and time and individuality.

The state of any spatio-temporal location as being occupied by an object would not bear upon another object, and this could occupy it coincidentally. The condition or state of any spatio-temporal location as being occupied by an object would not bear upon any object whatsoever so that the same object could occupy different space-locations at one time. One may object that all the locations are relevant to the objects which occupy them; but this does not make these locations exclusive to these objects, they are not their sole and proper territories. Indeed, as far as the singularity of space-time location goes, of one object claiming exclusively one location, this condition is irrelevant to objects, even the one that occupies the location included. One object cannot claim one space/time location solely, and this operates both ways: two or more at one space and time; one at more than one position at the same time. Coincidence means no exclusivity in the dimensions, and the absurdity of this consequence reveals the fallaciousness of the premiss. Space and Time must mean something to objects since physical objects are spatio-temporal. To fail to be meaningful and relevant, if this is a consequence of coincidence, in this way, would demonstrate the doctrine's impossibility.

Perhaps my argument is not lucid enough. Its general point is that, under coincidence, location and ordering, spatio-temporal, break down and become meaningless to physical objects with results that reduce the coincidental hypothesis to absurdity. Objects and events are spatio-temporal and the dimensions are in part orderings of events and objects. Things can be said to be at places and at times, that is, to be spatio-temporal. So much is conceded. But under coincidence there is not a special, owning relationship, a one-to-one, one object-one space/time location relationship holding between object and location. Location is no longer 'special' location, so an object could be at other places at one time as well as several other objects being at one place at the same time.

Things under coincidence cease to have private locations: privacy, in locational terms, does not obtain. Nothing has a special location, its own. One cannot maintain coincidence and deny that one object could be at several places at one time because the former situation contains the logical conditions for the latter, through locational lack of specialness. The logical bond of specialness between object and location is cut. Not only would ordering go but logic as well. The transitive relation of one ring being inside a second, and the second inside a third, making the first inside the third, would be violated if a situation could ever arise where the first was elsewhere at the same time, and so outside the third. More colourfully, if I could be in two different locations at the same time, I could have a boxing match with myself and simultaneously win and lose it. If one object, one place, one time does not hold, one object could be at several places at one time.

One can proceed to make use of my example of relevance if these arguments suffice. Now this denial of coincidence is rich in possibilities for much more than relative reality between already existing things. I believe that the very existence of a thing controls the existence of another. Consider that if something exists we can at least deduce that another thing cannot exist in its exact space/time location. That another thing contains a contradiction in its nature is not so much what prevents it from existing at a particular location, as that the mere existence of a certain object at that point excludes the other existing there. What stops anything that is not impossible from existing in such a situation? Not non-coincidence primarily, because something has to exist first in order to exclude anything, and existence is the more fundamental concept than non-coincidence: only through existence can non-coincidence be a reality. Two chairs for instance are not impossible objects in themselves, as are spherical pyramids, but if one exists anywhere the other cannot exist at the same place at the same time. Consequently, one existence prevents, controls, is significant to the existence or non-existence of other things.

The existence of things is not entirely unconstrained therefore, and facts, as facts, in their existing, are not independent and are significant to each other. This goes against the received opinion among empiricist philosophers:

"... the existence of any one object is logically independent of the existence of any other."[4]

"From the existence or non-existence of one state of affairs it is impossible to infer the existence or non-existence of another."[5]

The first is overthrown by consideration of mutual existential relevance and lack of independence coming from the impossibility of dimensional coincidence. A rubber ball thrown at a brick wall, which continues to exist, cannot behave as if it – the wall – was not there. The second by recognising simply that I can indeed infer from the existence of one object to the non-existence of any other in that same spot at the same time. This may not seem like much but it certainly breaks a hole in what had been an impenetrable barrier between logic and facts in the physical world.

These results do not establish anything about existence other than its contradictory nature. I do not, remember, even believe in existence. But when we contrast the lack of existential independence amongst facts with the 'necessity' of their independence, we obtain a contradiction derived from the concept of existence which expands the original formula of 'reality to' or

---

[4]   A. J. Ayer.
[5]   L. Wittgenstein: *Tractatus Logico-Philosophicus* (RKP 1961).

relevance, for in this case, the non-coincidental one, only one fact needs to be given and considered for its relevance to the existence of others which do not yet actually exist to be elicited. Prevention of existence is but one instance of relevance.

In case one regards this existential sensitivity as merely applying to possibilities of existence, we need only reflect that what does come to be is what can come into existence given other things' facthood. What can exist is limited and regulated by the existence of other things, so what does exist is likewise controlled. What does exist is not entirely free.

One must bear in mind that we are not discussing the existence of a thing purely, in itself, here. For one may argue that whilst one can say the existence of something at whatever location one chooses determines other existences, one seemingly cannot contend that the existence of something, pure and unqualified, controls that of another thing. Considered absolutely, anything may be: everything has an equal chance that is not impossible. But in this section we are not investigating existence in itself; we are dealing with it in relation to other things that exist or that attempt to. Locational exclusivity is used to exemplify lack of existential independence and, more generally, it is existence and independence that this essay is given over to. Contradictions that emerge from these two concepts are what concern us and they will certainly say something about our use and understanding of existence. But even so, one contention of this essay is that independence indeed derives from existence. People have severed the existence of one thing from that of another, but we can show that under certain circumstances this is not possible. Surely this contributes to our judgments on existence, its status and validity?

The existence of any two things is never 'pure and unqualified' in the universe, since it will involve relationships. So when we consider existence, we understand it in some context. Nothing whose very validity we question can be examined outside of its implications. To take existence out of any conceptual context is to accept it, but the contexts show it to be mistaken.

Non-coincidence does not place so light a conformity upon

existence as has been indicated so far. It can be taken further because it can affect the configuration of situations and happenings which we call 'the universe.' Things must exist 'outside' each other; facts are real to others that are beyond them in space and time. In itself the fact is only real; but because only one thing can occupy one location, to be 'real to' something must mean that this other thing is not where the 'merely real' thing is. And if relative reality crosses distances so to speak, perhaps there is no reason why it should not operate temporally as well as spatially.

From another angle, the totality of facts consists of members which must be significant to one another; certainly mutually accessible; and if this totality is distributed across both spatial and temporal extensions, facts in the past must be relevant to facts in the future, otherwise there would not be a historical totality. Wherever and whenever facts are found, they matter to each other, all of them. The requirement for relevance is plain reality then: every real thing is real to every other.

Earlier I said that in being material to each other events must be understood as contributing to each other to some extent: facts make facts. If one objected that first the things had to be real, to exist, before they could become relevant in any way, I would point out that this would indeed make for irrelevance, existential indifference, since whatever was influenced in no way, bore in no way upon, whatever else was. We would have independence. Co-existence is not necessary for relevance; existence is. But as I have previously indicated, to be relevant to things described as 'the existence of situations', facts, means that the very existence of a situation is influenced, and this can only be seen as a form of creation, of significance to a thing in its very existence. Facts literally bring each other into being without the need for each of them already to exist. And as we have exemplified it, only one thing needs to exist for it to be relatively real to others' existences. If existences are controlled in some measure, then existences have an origin, a cause as such. If control is exercised by other existences, these others are responsible for existences they control. So 'relevance' is such a comprehensive term that it can mean not mere 'significance' but 'causal power.'

The only interpretation that can be given the supposition that several things must exist 'first' before being relevant, must be that it is an inferential proviso. Given that they do not exist simultaneously, or even if they did, their 'existences' would be needed if we are to infer that they were significant to one another because in this essay we say that existence generates relative reality. Existence guarantees relevance logically and deductively: we deduce the latter from the former: in that sense things must 'exist' before being relevant. This is not a statement about the universe, but about logical inference. The 'before' indicates existence's status as a logical premise for relevance.

Relevance therefore requires that what exists should control what does and will exist, which is nothing other than an expression of causality: so paradoxically we have been able to argue for causality from the premises of existence and relevance. Dropping for a moment these clumsy existential formulations, I can say that real behaviours and real events must express their relevance to each other by a mutual modification. This is nothing less than causal interaction. Fact producing fact is a pretty un-illuminating type of causality, but it can be broadened by reminding ourselves that if any sort of fact could occur, there would be genuine immateriality of existent to existent; so the character of a fact is created, one can say, by another existing event. If what exists is significant to what exists, what exists is significant to what exists.

The counter-argument to this position is that things in themselves and absolutely do not have to exist: whatever is may not be. There would be existential freedom if this were allowed; but we could always object that the existences of things cannot be taken in themselves and absolutely. They are relative things and their existences 'bounce off' or recognise one another: a plurality of existences form a community in which they regulate and determine each other. If there are any good anti-relevance arguments they merely serve to expose the contradictory nature of existence by denying what seems a logical outcome of that concept. Even if one insisted that the relevance arguments depend upon the hypothesis that there is one fact at least, making the existences of others in absolute terms contingent, one has done no more that score a trivial point since contingency does not apply in every circumstance. We should at the same time remember the context of the discussion, namely, does contingency apply in a plurality of facts, and more importantly, do separation, indifference or independence apply? We are not concerned with the existence of one thing, but of several, with a world.

What I have called 'reality to' and 'relevance' is exemplified in cases where non-coincidence obtains; but can non-coincidence, which demonstrates what can only be said to be 'significance' in an existential way, really cause events? Consider two objects on a collision-course, or consider one moving into contact with another. Given non-coincidence, this situation – say a rubber ball is being thrown at a wall – has to be responsible for what happens subsequently. Inability to share the same space/time location determines that a new existential situation, a change in events, has to take place. There are several possibilities as to what shall be the nature of the change, but there has to be a change: change is not contingent. The continued existence of both objects, meaning a change of behaviour for at least one of them; the cessation of both; and cessation of one – all these are possible and one is necessitated by the constraints of non-coincidence. Existence is certainly regulated and cause is part of this control.

By considering existence relatively we contradict the orthodoxy concerning it and discover paradoxes. Even if contingency did not originate independence, relevance would destroy contingency. My present aim is not to prove the orthodox position on existence incorrect, only to argue that its denial is tenable and therefore that the concept should be rejected as it generates contradictions. Also, I show that many of the premises causal scepticism relies upon do not have to be accepted, as they concern existence.

Independence is a fruit of contingency, even a form of it, and when independence goes, contingency suffers. Existence's lack of contingency indicated above shows existence not only to lead to the contradiction of being contingent and not being so, but, if non-contingency amounts to denying existence, then existence denies itself in the end, and another reductio is effected. One does not only have to consider the antithesis between relevance and independence, but that between relevance, which leads to existential regulation, and contingency, to see how generous in paradox existence is.

But still, the objection is possible, what about existence seen absolutely? Taken in isolation we have the received maxim: whatever is may not be. Surely I have not tackled this problem which should lie at the very heart of any critique of existence? But I have alluded to it. It was not the intention of this essay to take existence in isolation, to examine the existence of things in isolation from others. I have taken existence and its contingency in various conceptual contexts in order to refute the generality of the maxim, which by itself seems correct, but which in relation to other concepts is not.

I have said moreover that it is not at this stage desirable to comprehend or criticise the concept of existence pure. Mostly, it must be treated contextually among concepts or amongst things. I say that a plurality of existences cannot be consistently conceived as if each one was isolated, as we tried at the beginning of this essay to suppose. Applying to the concept of existence notions like those of causality and non-coincidence attacks its very validity, and this is a deeper investigation of the concept than one which accepted it and only tried to define it and properly apply it in that light. Anyway, the formula 'existence – reality – relevance' is a pretty 'isolated' study of existence, of existence by and in itself. I will later give a definition of existence positive and pure, and when I say that it is not desirable to comprehend existence by itself, I mean this within the strictures of this essay, which is essentially a conceiving of existence in a multiplicity. The definition of existence I shall give will not be one which leads to its acceptance as a valid notion; and I can also note for the time being what I alluded to earlier: the separation of 'existence' from 'reality'. That will be useful later.

3

The Existential Fallacy

I   Physical Objects

Sceptical reasons for denying Causality as I understand it rest on such widely held beliefs which approach almost to intuition, but which I have found to be mistaken, that the following is forced to be a negative statement of my case. To begin with I must expose an error I realize to underlie all causal and inductive scepticism, and much else besides, and which is I suppose the greatest fallacious premise in all thought.

Unlike some efforts which treat existence as it appears in statements, linguistically that is, my approach is to examine it, at least to start with, as it impinges upon things in the world, for if it is genuine it must mean something recognizable to things when they are credited with it or it is said of them. Unless one does this one begs the question in any examination of the subject, a question that ought to be asked: whether existence is valid; does it mean anything to things? However, I have come to the conclusion that I should do this in an indirect, broad, conceptual manner, as is natural to philosophical enquiry, for I do not believe that existence is a 'thing' like other things to be found in the material world.

Some incompatibilities between the concept 'existence' and that of the world with its attendant necessary connection have been briefly investigated, and the pronouncement has been made that insofar as things are worldly and necessarily physically related they cannot be matters of fact, they cannot exist. These statements need expansion and further investigation from other angles. Introducing existence into the formula of necessary connection creates contradictions: things are necessarily related to one another, but if seen as matters of fact, are completely independent and apart. Consequently, an event's nature is necessarily linked to another's, yet nothing has to happen and anything not impossible in itself can happen if things are seen existentially; so an event's nature is not necessarily linked to another's. Understanding physical objects as constituents of the world cannot cohere with their interpretation as matters of fact. This suggests that the notion of what it is to be physical is better understood by itself to see if we can in any way ally existence to it. I call all worldly things 'physical'. So we will suspend our determinations thus far and attempt to study physicality from a fresh viewpoint. But before abandoning every relevant conclusion we have made concerning these matters so far, it might be worth mentioning that the hidden dimension we have inferred consists at least in part of the necessary connections, the powers, operating amongst things. Therefore physicality is associated with power and this, seen as necessary connection, is irreconcilable with existence.

Not only has existence been attacked from the conceptual vision of a connected world, but it has been assumed and placed in a pluralistic, atomistic context and contradictions have emerged from it. Now I believe a more direct attack can be resumed which will lead to the solution of the causal problem by considering the notion 'physicality': what it is for a thing to be physical.

This kind of investigation can take many guises, but since causality is the framework and existence is seen as the pivotal notion upon which the problem turns, it will be in relation to these two concepts that the task will be undertaken. I propose to do this in as general and as conceptual a manner as possible, but though employing the minimum empirical input, plainly we must have recourse to the discovered and evident world in forming any opinion on what physicality consists in. Although an important part of the following analysis will need to be empirical, the conclusions will be reached deductively. I cannot afford to present any decisive material as pure insight or intuition. My route lies in examination, not of physical things, but the structure of the concept 'physicality'. Since they are connected I can pass cautiously from the abstract to the material, and conversely.

In part, a general description of physical things is their qualitativity. So the concept physicality is composed partly of qualitativity, and how extensive this dimension is in the concept needs close study. Physical qualitativity breaks down into the categories in the evident world of types of light-colours, of sound, of smell, of taste, and of feeling. Also, it may be expressed in terms of charge, motion, solidity, fluidity; it may be organic, forms of energy, forms of extension, crystalline structures, states and processes. This information we receive directly or from scientific knowledge. The qualitative dimension cannot be omitted from any account of physicality.

I can clarify the terms 'qualitative' and 'qualitativity' that appear above in several ways. Things are to a large extent composed of descriptive properties: they are clusters of adjectival characteristics. To speak figuratively, their actions and histories may all be comprehended 'adjectivally'. So I introduce a term to suggest and capture the notion of qualitativity: things are 'how' they are. Physicality's conceptual structure has this dimension.

Physicality has been thought to possess, besides a descriptive aspect, an accompanying dimension: that of existence. Commonly, we allow existence into physicality because we can ask ourselves: if a thing did not exist, would it be counted as physical? Since the unanimous answer is no, existence is a dimension of physicality. What qualifies it? Existence is not qualitative; it does not partake in descriptiveness, though I am not saying, trivially, that it is not a 'quality'. 'Exists' does not share in the 'epithetic' aspect of the concept of the physical – superficially this is a reason why it is not a predicate, though the ultimate reason lies in its definition. Existence is not 'how' things are. So this means there cannot be modes of existence, 'ways of being', that is, qualitative lack of qualitativity. Something's existence is also not an event, for it gives no description – in the sense of a 'nature' – that an object lacks when it is merely qualitatively expressed. Yet unless the object 'exists' it will be absolutely nothing. Existence must be a radically different dimension in physicality from qualitativity. While we can say that through the latter a thing is 'how' it is, through existence a thing is 'that' it is.1 Existence is applied somehow individually to each thing but yet is not defined into anything's attributive nature. Is this conceptual arrangement workable and helpful? I hold it is unhelpful and clumsy: it dogs clear, logical thinking and is the essential error made on both sides of the causal divide historically. Let us then make a preliminary study of its nature in its role as part of the conceptual structure of physicality.

I have said that 'existence' is not to be 'found' like any other thing in the universe, and this has led some people to say that it 'adds nothing' to things as they appear in the evident world.[2] The object and the object-as-existing are not to be distinguished.[3] We have already established the qualitative nature of objects called 'physical' and have indicated that these objects are thought, if physical, to exist. Now if no addition is indeed made and no distinction is to be elicited between the physical object and its existence, then we do not seem to have much choice as to our inference. Existence is not a thing that objects have like a physical property, but since they are qualitative and since existence is identified with the object, existence must identify with the qualitative aspect of physicality. But we have already said that existence has no descriptive nature, so either the foregoing schema is wrong, or, 'adding nothing', existence is itself nothing – nothing significant to physical objects, hence to physicality.

One can deny the claim however that existence 'adds nothing' to objects, for it makes the objects credited with it, as we have

---

[1] I am at present not attempting to define existence itself and do not assume any previous analysis – like, say, taking it as a quantifier – but I engage in a cautious examination of what it involves. The 'how' and the 'that' characterization of physicality could be seen as the conventional 'essence' and 'existence' dichotomy.

[2] See Hume: *A Treatise of Human Nature*. Book 1. Part II. Section IV. P.115 (Penguin Classics 1984).

[3] *Ibid.*

seen, contingent matters of fact which have the possibility of either being nothing without existence or something with it. It makes these objects independent of each other in addition. It amplifies objects, hence physicality, only not qualitatively.

People express the supposed inability to expand a subject to which existence is applied by saying that existence is not a predicate. But this does not render existence non-predicative; lack of ability to be descriptive of the thing credited with it has this effect. In classic analytic statements the subject is not expanded, yet that does not mean the predicates in them are not genuine ones.

Rather than take it for granted that existence is no predicate, I can at this stage say there is a categorical difference between statements of existence and non-existence and those qualitatively descriptive ones. If one describes something negatively one always tacitly asserts something else positive, for a negative predicate cannot denote a property. But if one existentially denies something one absolutely denies the whole thing, no subsumption of a positive characterization is offered. Similarly, one absolutely asserts something if one does so existentially, whereas one merely expresses what can be called a non-absolute modification of something if one describes it positively. This absoluteness that pertains to existence bars it from predicative status.

Thus physicality must be, to resume, a fusion of two distanced sub-concepts at least: existence and qualitativity. My endeavour is to see how and whether such a fusion is possible.

Let me use the analogy of a cube, firstly, to illustrate relations between the sub-dimensions of physicality. The cube is partly composed of plane surfaces, partly of volume: it occupies dimensions. We have said that physicality occupies at least two dimensions: howness and existence. But while I can say that the two-dimensional surfaces of the cube do not have volume, I have to say in respect of the 'thing' that its qualitativity is existential as well, that these conceptual dimensions overlap and interpenetrate. But existence is not qualitative. So whilst volume is rightly kept separate from two-dimensionality, non-qualitativity is said of qualitativity. The 'dimensions' of physicality cannot be kept apart by any stratagem: in an existential world the qualities have to exist if they are to be anything at all, rendering themselves non-qualitative. This analogy does not presume the complete separation, only the distancing of qualitativity and existence. If this is not done, as we see it is not, we have an incoherence and a contradiction. Therefore some formulation must be found to accommodate, the two aspects of physicality satisfactorily. Maybe though this cannot be done so as to allow both to cohabit in the existential metaphysic, and the latter must be abandoned.

But how is distancing to be achieved since everybody agrees that a thing would not be physical if it did not exist? Some authors indeed have identified the whole of physicality with the existential aspect: they call the resultant worldly object a 'being'. Consider one such on the notion of existence (though the 'being' postulated here is a somewhat different concept than that of a physical object):

"That idea, when conjoined with the idea of any object, makes no addition to it. Whatever we conceive, we conceive to be existent. Any idea we please to form is the idea of a being; and the idea of a being is any idea we please to form".[4] Also: "The idea of existence ... is the very same with the idea of what we conceive to be existent."[5]

The writer here seems to identify the idea of 'existence' with the idea of 'object'. What the author is saying is something like, I suppose, that if 'x is red' is followed by '... and is red', nothing that has not already been stated is conveyed by the second qualification of x: a literary tautology.

But, I will ask, is it all or part of the concept of physicality that is existential when existence is treated in the above way? Is the existential dimension co-extensive with the qualitative dimension or, as I have said, need they be kept apart? This consideration furnishes us with an argument against the existence of the physical, against the supposed need for what is physical to

[4] *Ibid.*
[5] *Ibid.*

be qualified by existence.

Assume that existence is a part of physicality, that physical things exist, that is. It cannot be merely a dimension or part of physicality which is existential for, conventionally and theoretically, if something is said not to exist, the whole thing goes without residue: not even the qualitative, as qualitative, remains, for annihilation is absolute. So one must infer that the whole of physicality is existential. But part of this whole is qualitative, which existence, hence the existential dimension, is not. Not all of physicality is qualitatively blank as is existence: so the whole is not existential. Again, if things exist, then it is only part of physicality which comprises this existential dimension, for insofar as physicality is qualitative it is not existential. But all of an object goes, if existence goes, so that only part of physicality is existential cannot be the case. Therefore things do not exist: physicality has no existential dimension.

The dimensions' inability to be together and their necessary interpenetra-tion demonstrate the fragility of existence vis-a-vis the concept of physicality. A reductio is produced. The theory of physicality as a fusion of these dimensions is not sustainable.

The conventional notion may be salvaged if we consider that perhaps both existence and qualitativity are necessary elements in physicality: they are two props supporting each other in the conceptual structure of the physical. If one is subtracted, the whole edifice of physicality crumbles and nothing remains physically. That is why the subtraction of existence from the object appears to destroy the other aspect: what it eliminates is physicality, not the other element of it. Likewise, if the attributive dimension were taken away we would have nothing left of physicality conceived as a union of dimensions. Thus existence and qualitativity are essential to physicality but do not intermingle: they form a higher synthesis; the physical.

This manoeuvre fails because we categorically say and must say, given the existential metaphysic, that a thing's qualities, or rather its qualitativity, exists. That means we regard existence as not merely 'supporting' non-existential qualitativity, but as pervading it to its core. Existence is said of the qualities a thing has. We cannot say that existence, partly defined as lacking qualitativity, is qualitative, but we do say the qualitative is existential, meaning that existence suffuses all the concept of physicality and yet, because we deny existence's qualitativity, we deny this ubiquity. This is the point of the whole/part reductio. In the existential world and metaphysic, everything exists, otherwise it would be nothing: "Whatever we conceive, we conceive to be existent."[6] Not only does the qualitative exist in order to be physical, but the qualitative exists in order to be qualitative.

What about the qualitative aspect? What if that goes? I am starting here with the assumption of the qualitative and existential dimensions in tandem and am not supposing the purely conceptual omission of the dimension, that is, that the physical thing is nothing other than its existence. Isn't there, as in the case of existence, nothing left? And if so, isn't all of the concept of physicality limited to the qualitative? But if we had begun here with the vision of physicality as fusion, and not used the anti-existential version of the whole/part argument first, we could argue that the physical did not have a qualitative dimension since we could add that existence is not qualitative, so that the whole of the concept of physicality is not qualitative, and that is a reductio of qualitativity. Therefore the form of the whole/part argument can be used against qualitativity as well as existence. Nothing is solved by saying that physical things are evidently qualitative at least, for to most people they are just as self-evidently existential.

But applying the whole/part argument against qualitativity suffers from a telling flaw. Its assumptions are revealing and fallacious in a peculiar way. In a dimension that is of its nature existential we can only speak and conceive in an existential way. For something, in the whole/part argument, to 'go' is an existential notion. It means to cease being, to be annihilated. Existence and non-existence are wedded together, parts of the same concept-system. Only where we can conceive being can we conceive non-being. But where there is no being, there is no non-being,

---

[6] *Ibid.*

and that is the case in the physical qualitative dimension. Of the qualitative we can only speak qualitatively. We can describe, we can say 'how' things are, and that alone. Therefore we cannot existentially assert or deny what is qualitative when speaking in that mode, hence we cannot positively or negatively qualify the qualitative dimension existentially; neither annihilate nor existentially posit what is in itself outside being and non-being.

Thus one can speculate about the non-existence of a thing in the existential dimension, but not about the 'loss' of qualitativity in the qualitative dimension, because 'loss' is annihilation and has existential significance. Qualitativity in itself cannot be 'lost'.

To be more exact and careful, the existential aspect of physicality can only have existential considerations applied to it. When speaking of it we may only use those concepts and that discourse appropriate to the general existential concept, which is broad enough to include existential assertion and negation. This discourse cannot properly be applied to the qualitative dimension of physicality; we only conceive it qualitatively, say how it is, but do not allow the concept an existential content by asserting that the qualitative aspect of a thing is or is not.

In fine, when speaking descriptively we cannot speak existentially: we can only describe. Existential and descriptive discourse are distinct. One can absolutely affirm and negate in existential discourse, one cannot do so in descriptive speech. This is not merely a linguistic but a metaphysical distinction. Because these modes of speech are essentially mutually exclusive, one can grasp the metaphysical exclusion of the existential from the qualitative. Because qualitativity has its own special character, as qualitativity it cannot suffer negative or positive existential qualification. Qualitatively, it is enduring and eternal and can only be susceptible to description. So of its nature it is beyond and indifferent to existence or non-existence, and physicality cannot be a fusion of qualitative and existential sub-concepts.

But if something does not exist it is not real, it is not a thing! So one may object. This is where a hitherto neglected corollary in the qualitative and existential dichotomy needs to be introduced.

It does not 'not exist' either. In short, it is a thing which does not require existence to be a thing; its reality is not dependent upon existence. What it depends on we shall shortly see.

I do not, in what I have said, assume that existence and qualitativity cannot fuse; I only point out that existence and qualitativity have in themselves, innately, their own special characters or 'natures', and to these we must be faithful. In the 'how' dimension we can only say 'how'. In the 'is' dimension we can only speak existentially, and saying 'is' or 'is not' is part of existential discourse, part of the vocabulary of existence, which is inapplicable in the 'how' dimension. We cannot totally negate in the 'how' dimension: negation is existential.

Putting the matter somewhat differently, if existence adds nothing qualitative to the qualitative, non-existence takes nothing qualitative from the qualitative. Therefore the qualitative of itself is beyond and independent of existence and non-existence. Not being affected by existence, the qualitative loses nothing when it is said not to exist. Nothing is lost because only descriptive characterizations can be made of it and can affect it. There is no qualitative nullification. The qualitative must be, as such, eternal and indestructible. It cannot be, or not be – be nothing – for that matter. So finally, because existence cannot trouble the qualitative dimension of physicality, physicality cannot be said to be a fusion of these dimensions.

Obviously, since existence and qualitativity cannot mingle, we have to revise our notion of what it is to be a physical thing. The content of the world is evidently qualitative, and existence is irrelevant to it, thus it cannot 'be'. Therefore we can define the status of physical objects: things are how they are, not that they are. And saying conventionally something exists is to state 'that' it is.

Existence is banished from the physical world and this means that materiality is wholly defined in terms of qualitativity. Beforehand we noted a separation between existence and reality, and when these concepts cease being identified, reality becomes qualitativity, things as their descriptive natures, even when the natures or things are 'imaginations' or 'thoughts'. Since qualitativity is physicality, physicality is reality. The three terms are, in the world, synonymous. Things are 'real' but not 'existent'.[7]

What 'Existence' Means

But what is the solution to the conundrum of existence? What can we mean when we say that a physical thing 'exists'? For though we have now excluded it, it must have meant something special.

We say that the physical is always 'descriptive', always a sort of thing: it spins, is coloured, is a sound, is massive, but it never 'is'. And I have defined existence in several negative ways, saying that it is contingent, i.e. lacks necessity; that it, through contingency, confers independence on things that have it of other things; and that it lacks qualitativity. By now it should be becoming plain what exactly is the status of existence. To say that something exists is not only to give information about one thing – it is hardly even that since one does not describe that thing at all thereby – but to give information about an environment and its constitution. The idea needs a context. Common parlance and analysis have made the mistake of not perceiving that existence is a relation. Existence is a relation, the relation of membership. Membership does not identify with the whole or part of physicality, but is the outcome of the relationship between the thing and the world set up by the physicality of the thing. Because it is physical the thing is said to 'belong' to the world. The relation of pure membership expresses existence.

Now, being a relation-word, membership must be 'of' something, and always 'of' some kind of collection or class. What class is that? Not membership of the physical universe, since to be a member of that is to be physical or qualitative, which I have shown existence not to be. Membership of the physical universe, if understood as the definition of existence,

[7] Joseph Owens: *An Interpretation of Existence* (1985) p.4, n.5 (D. Williams and J. McTaggart).

would make the error of confusing reality and existence. In order that membership be pure membership, the class has to be quite unspecific. Therefore the class is the class of class-members. This can be abbreviated as the class of members, it being always understood that membership is of a collection of some type.

I did not merely intuit this definition, but I considered that once one removed the qualitative aspect of the physical object from any part in determining existence, what have we left to express, signify or symbolize the presence of this object? Nothing, plainly, but the membership of the thing. The membership is of a universe in which other things' qualitativity has been stripped away too, so membership is not of the qualitative universe. This relation is external, the grandfather of external relations.

Some light must be cast on this belonging relationship. By having some property or characterization things 'belong'; but membership is not itself a characterization; in the world, not something qualitative. The 'characterization', that which determines something, gives it a characteristic, is equivalent in worldly terms to qualitative determination. One belongs because of being somehow, not because of belonging. Membership is then outside characterization: in the world, qualitativity. Being immaterial and unreal, it cannot contribute to physicality. This external relational definition of existence explains how it can be 'said of something and yet not identify with that thing even in part, that is to say, make the thing into a 'being'. Things can only participate in membership, an unreal therefore pseudo-relation, verbally, and thus be said to 'exist'.

Consequently we shall find that descriptions of physical events have in philosophy failed to be precisely physical descriptions. Whenever the event is described, no part of it, nor it as a whole, must be described or conceived of as existing. In what I call the 'physical description', stressing 'physical', can the real expression of the causal process be found. When events are understood as 'how' they are and not 'that' they are, a proper account can be given of them. Previously, descriptions of events have been what I term 'historical'. To be 'historical' is to include any existential element as being essential in the description of events or the schemes of events, to treat the event as a matter of fact and give a factual account of it. Events become released from the tyranny of the fact, from contingency, and accounts of them from syntheticity once they are wholly regarded as physical and no nonphysical term is used to denote them. When they no longer exist they have to be the ways they are; they cannot be otherwise.

In case membership is interpreted as something real, we do better to see it as a conceptual device expressing a merely convenient but misleading 'relation' without making any physical comment about anything. Membership, existence, is qualitatively zero; it cannot affect by its presence or absence the qualitative realm that has emerged as the only realm in the conceived world. Membership is a qualitative blank. A thing does not have or do it. Through qualitativity a thing is material or real. The route to the error of existence is to claim a thing belongs to the real world through its reality.

Existence is a purely linguistic convenience. Existence is not 'concreteness', for the later is physicality. Existence is ghostly and certainly not anything self-evident. Neither is it something transcendental,[8] for it would at least be agreeable to qualitativity if it were, not antithetical to it. It is nothing immediate, but inferred and strengthened by habitual usage. Reality is immediate, but existence is a misconceived hypothetical leap, and quite unreal.

II Membership

Though it was my intention primarily to examine existence as it impinged upon the concept of physicality, and by implication, upon physical things, the nature of my positive definition of existence leads me to realize that it has important logical implications as well. As we shall discover, the existential fallacy is but one of a group or family of fallacies that issue from a single source: the fallacy of membership. *This* provides the reason for

---

[8]   In the sense of applying to all things regardless of category.

rejecting existence finally, not the arguments reached through treating the existential dimensions: contingency, independence and lack of qualitativity.

The membership fallacy appears in a pure form in the logic of classes. With classes in logic, something 'belongs to' or 'is a member of' a class because it has a certain characterization, a determination, or because of being somewhat. But as I said, belonging, that is, membership, is not itself a characterization, a condition for membership, only a result of or inference from characterization. Belonging is always outside characterization, its own conditions. There will be no things that have the common property of merely 'belonging to' a class, being purely 'members'. A chair belongs to the class of chairs in virtue of being a chair, not because it belongs to that class. Membership then cannot secure itself, be its own criterion as regards classes.

Why should this be so? In answering this question we illustrate and solve the membership fallacy as it appears in class-logic and other realms: semantic and metaphysical. I sketch the solution first, then amplify it. When class theory is expressed in all the authority of symbolism we are apt to forget its metaphysical basis; but it has one.

The solution is that membership is devoid of a nature, invalidates itself consequently, and a word that denotes that concept has as a result no meaning other than as a misconcept.

Let us consider the class which needs only membership to belong to it, that is, let's suppose that membership is a property or predicate and that there is a 'member-class', a class of class-members. Membership, e, is seen as a 'primitive predicate'. Well, we treat it as such and see what emerges. A member of the class of members is one solely on the ground that it is a member. A cat is a member of the class of cats; but as a cat it is not a member of the member class. As a 'member', divorced from its feline nature, it belongs to the latter. Belonging is the sole criterion.

The reason for this is that if something belongs because of belonging it can only belong to the member class for otherwise class-specificity would collapse.

If 'belonging' were the property of anything with a determinate nature, and since the 'property' of belonging applies to classes, the property of membership would be all that is needed for belonging to a class. That 'character' or 'property' would give it the entrance key to any class whatsoever, thereby allowing, say, a cat to be a member of the horse class, which is to allow a cat to be a horse, which is absurd. One has a class, any class, and any class is as much a class as any other. Then one has something with the general property of class-membership, and any 'member' is as much a member as any other. This thing can therefore belong to any class. And this belonging because of belonging happens when membership is treated as a predicate or property. The class of horses is indubitably a class as well as being the class of horses; and insofar as it is a class my point is that anything possessing the property of class-membership will not just be able to enter it, but actually will be in it, so that the difference between classes is obliterated when belonging gets something into them. I believe this applies to the null-class as well. Class-membership would destroy the distinction between this class and the others.

The chaos this would leave class theory in is checked by constructing a quarantine zone as the location of the class of class-members, the 'member-class'. So if anything belongs to that class it has to forsake its determinate nature, indeed its nature, for 'nature' is always determinate, specific. Specific chaos is the result of allowing membership to be a property of things, that is, specific. The denizens of the member class are thus purely 'members' with their specificity, cat, horse, and so on, being abandoned. If specificity were not removed, members would be class-members. If anything specific gets into the class of class-members it would be because the specific thing had the property of class-membership. But since class-membership is not a property, it isn't a property of specific things, so specific things can't be in the class of class-members. Saying that a cat can be a horse if membership is its own criterion is inexact. What is meant is that class distinctions vanish. Membership has to be transcended in order to attain specificity.

This tells us that 'belonging' is not to have a special nature:

belonging defeats specificity and so cannot be a property, and it is outside characterization. The inability to specifically qualify, its creation of class-disorder, the solitary locus of the class of members, which is the result of shifting membership away from the domain of properties; all these mean that belonging or membership has no nature. Since the specificity of classes is destroyed by membership, the nature of members is obliterated, and if members have no nature, their class cannot have one. Moreover, if the elements have no characterization a class cannot be created out of them. They cannot be collected and cannot belong to anything. So really there is no member-class at all, and a 'member' is a member of nothing. Removing membership from the realm of classes means that it is no longer membership and that membership cannot make sense. Given what 'membership' means, if members are not class-members, they are nothing. If there is no property such as 'class-membership' there can be no 'class of class-members'. If membership cannot be class-membership, what members are members of cannot be a class. Belonging as a property and as a non-property defeats itself. And this has consequences for the concept of membership. A thing is a member only if it is a member of the 'member-class'. Most other concepts do not have or involve membership in their meaning. But pure membership, the concept, having to mention a class in its very meaning, since membership is always membership of a class, involves an impossible class. Therefore it is an invalid, impossible concept. Because of its effect on class-specificity, membership has to cease being 'class-membership' and become 'member-class membership' as its conceptual definition; so it is not a real concept, since the 'class of members' cannot be formed.

Holding that the simple, unconditional property of 'membership' would get anything into any class whatever is quite correct; but one can formulate the disruptive effects of treating membership as a predicate in a different way. If membership by itself could get something into classes, any object that had it as a property would belong to any class at all and so there would be specific, class-disorder. Therefore, in itself, membership is as a property revealed as anti-specific, thus anti-natural and non-characterizational by the effects it has once it is treated as a characterization like any other. This formulation is conditional unlike the argument in the preceding paragraphs which states categorically that chaos would result from the membership property. Here I say 'if membership alone could be a determination ... etc', exemplifying the naturelessness of membership from its effect on classes. Both approaches are valid, only one is more indirect.

Membership's naturelessness is brought out by another consideration. Take an 'arbitrary' class of members, one in which the elements kept their determinations but only needed membership to qualify for membership of that class. Such a class would be nothing but a collection, and in the case of the largest such class, the arbitrary class qualified by membership alone, containing everything, determination in respect to all other classes, which we could say were sub-classes of the overall arbitrary class, would be accidental. The sub-class containing cats would be one whose members happened by accident, and without any kind of condition for membership other than membership, to contain cats alone. What I call 'specificity' is nullified by membership. Felinity is not required, only belonging, and characterization is rendered irrelevant.

The largest 'arbitrary'.class containing members that had no other common denominator than that they were members is effectively this hypothetical member-class.[9] This class would contain everything imaginable: pure class-members, specified members (like cats), classes, and even sub-classes (which would be members of power-sets). Class distinctions disappear. So a class of five members would be represented in the member-class by (a) the five members, (b) the class itself (seen as a member of five-membered classes), (c) the sub-classes (including the null-class).

Now the domain outside the member class would be what

---

[9] Not the class of class-members.

we ordinarily call classes, i.e. the Universe class, or maybe the class of classes. And this should effectively be the power set of the member-set. But this power set[10] of the member-class would not be numerically greater than the member-class as it should be, and the conclusion we draw is that there is no such class as the member-class, consequently that there is no such property as class-membership, and that implies that membership has no nature since it is not a property.

Part of what it means for membership not to have a nature is that it is not a predicate. The chaos in classes resulting from treating membership as a property means that insofar as something is a 'member' it cannot have a determinate nature, and insofar as something has a determinate nature, it cannot be a member. On the supposition that membership were a property, everything would have it, we should bear in mind, everything would be a 'class-member'.

These arguments should not be controversial, for it must be apparent that specificity is beyond membership and vice-versa. Merely to belong to a class gives no information about the sort of class one belongs to, the sort of thing one is. If you consider an object which, like all objects, is a member, and say that by being a member it belongs to a special class, a determinate class, the logician would interject: But what property does it have? Membership alone is not enough. The query of the logician reveals that he doesn't regard membership as a property. No-one doubts that having the general so-called 'attribute' of belonging is not enough to get anything into a special class, and that alone discovers the characterlessness of membership. To be a member is not to be a sort of thing: membership is not a property.

Seemingly, a good reason for saying that membership does not characterize is that everything is a member and so there is no difference in this respect between one thing and another. But, of course, everything is not a member of the member class; that is the real reason for anonymity, not that everything else is

---

[10] That is, the set of sub-classes.

such a member. Consider that one characterization is 'V' – the universe class, the class of everything, the widest domain. Since membership is extraneous to characterization, it is outside 'V', outside everything and beyond class. Membership is completely void. If one does not belong merely by belonging, one does not get into the universe class by membership, but by being something. This means the exclusion of membership from the realm of thinghood and class, the most comprehensive realm. So it is completely null, nothing.

The member-class, the class of class-members, is not, as some might think, co-extensive with the universe class. The latter has a nature. Of it one can delimit various sub-classes: sense objects, geometrical objects, physical objects, abstract objects, and so forth. There is no variety permissible for the contents of the member-class. Variety would, as we saw, destroy specificity, for variety is the possession of a nature. The universe class is indeed the realm of the specific.

If someone contended that perhaps at some level everything is a member, consider that though some classes contain virtually indistinguish-able elements, they, the elements, nevertheless have a character, as do the classes themselves. So the homogeneity of such classes is limited and relative since there will be classes that differ from each other. The anonymity of the members of the member class, would, if everything at some level was a member, be absolute, universal. In characterlessness membership would be unqualified and unrestricted. If I call someone a footballer I have not specified the team he belongs to. At that level of description, team-distinctions do not appear. But there are things that are not footballers, and the anonymity of that description is limited. However if everything imaginable is a member, and nothing is not one, the anonymity of membership is total, and at that level specificity is completely absent. That 'property' of membership lacks any specificity whatsoever and thus lacks a nature.

Membership obliterates nature, but not in the way that membership of the universe class reduces everything to a constant. Membership is antithetical to nature, which is always specific nature. To allow 'belonging' as a specific nature is no more valid than allowing indeterminacy as a determinate quality of something. Belonging, by destroying class-specificity, shows up the erroneousness of postulating it as a peculiar class-determination. Simply recognizing that literally everything is a 'member' demonstrates membership's lack of determinacy, lack of specificness, hence its complete lack of a nature. Members are not limited to a hypothetical 'member class',[11] but every other class except the null-class has them. Therefore membership cannot be called the property of a determinate class, meaning it is not something that can be captured by class-specification.

Membership is commonly supposed to be a relation: a 'two-place predicate', and it should be a relation if it is to be anything at all. But the foregoing pronouncements disqualify this interpretation. If it were a relation it could belong to a class: that of relations. Therefore it would be involved in its own conditions, involve characterization, that is, it would not be entirely external to characterization as it should be, for characterizations specify, unlike membership. But more broadly, if membership were a relation it would have a nature: this cannot be permitted from what we have learnt of it.

If membership cannot characterize, be a characterization, or be a genuine relation; since, as a property, it creates specific chaos, and as a non-property, it is not membership; and since it is outside the universe class, its emptiness, its nullity, is complete and thoroughgoing. It cannot play any role in philosophy or logic, and can only produce paradoxes and contradictions, where it is treated seriously, and anything is based on it in any form it takes: logical, semantic or metaphysical. It cannot refer to or attain itself: its nullity precludes this. To do so is to treat it predicatively and give it a nature.

Membership is a pseudo-relation, a seeming-relation, which cannot sustain self-reference. Moreover, membership is conceptually invalid and impossible. Membership is a

---

[11] Where 'membership' is seen as a property of everything, not a non-property.

misconcept, and in its form of existence is also a pseudo-relation, the generator of paradox. We shall remain in the field of class theory however for immediate illustration of this.

Because of what I have said of it, membership is something classes should do without, being a misconceived piece of verbiage indicating a superfluous, unreal relationship between the class and the thing with the property. Membership, in the form of existence cannot, like any form of membership, be the reason for itself, any class-characterization involving it is destroyed thereby, illegitimated.

The Class Paradox

Consider the class of classes that do not belong to themselves: it belongs to itself if it does not and does not belong to itself if it does. Many who have attempted to resolve this paradox stressed or were struck by the reflexive part of the formula, how it talks about itself, and rightly so. I can only at this stage introduce the general solution for the paradox, given what has already been said. I will be brief. The essential error of the paradoxical formula lies in including membership or belonging in a characterization. Still more importantly, membership's nullity and naturelessness has been exposed by this paradox, which is consequently a *reductio ad absurdum* of membership, not only in the field of classes, but in others where it appears.

Though 'membership of itself' is denied in the characterization, nevertheless membership forms the heart of the characterization, thus membership is made a criterion for itself, allowed to attempt to secure itself. Membership cannot be responsible for membership or non-membership, and non-membership cannot be responsible for non-membership or membership. Membership is generally invalidated by the contradictions stemming from it, including this one. Behind illegitimate usage of membership as a characterization, allowing it to attain itself, lies ignorance of membership's emptiness, the ultimate reason for the paradox, and why it cannot characterize.

This is far from the complete analysis of the causes of the

paradox, I repeat, only the general reason. I shall tackle the paradox in more detail when I come to enquire into what classes must be like if they are to be exempt from the distortions of membership.

Some say the class paradox shows that not every predicate determines a class. What they should say, in this case, is that membership is not a predicate and that asserting membership is not predication. Predication is a way of saying 'how' a thing is, and one should not mean by it that something 'belongs' to something else, whether an object or a class. When we speak of 'properties' this is an easy move to make, for it suggests ownership, belonging. Terms like 'attribute' and 'has' also exemplify this danger of misconceiving predication. Saying something about something is not to make the second belong to the first.

Existence and Membership

I can now introduce considerations which support my claim that existence is membership, and everything detrimental to membership is detrimental to existence. Not merely that membership is beyond nature, but that it is absurd and invalid as a concept; and if existence has no nature it cannot be a predicate at any level.

There are strong connections between existence as it appears in metaphysics and membership as it appears in class logic.

We express non-existence in class logic by saying that the class of the non-existent objects is 'empty', that is, memberless. By a simple deduction, if we wanted to express the existence of an object we would say that its class is not-memberless. (One object may be found in several classes, so we should say that all the relevant properties it has will be represented by classes which are not memberless). If I wanted to say 'The Yeti does not exist', I could say 'The class of Abominable Snowmen is empty, memberless'. If I wanted to say 'The Yeti exists' I could say 'The Class of Abominable Snowmen is not-memberless'. So membership expresses existence in class-theory. The class's nature does not alter, but when existence and non-existence are affirmed of an object or a kind, membership varies. Therefore to say of something that it exists or does not exist, we say that it 'is a member' or 'is not a member'. And membership equates to the existential quantifier ('some'), which in predicate logic expresses existence. The memberless class contains as its main idea that of 'not-something' or 'nothing'. Its negation, the class characterized by membership, contains as its defining idea that of 'something'. Therefore membership contains as its main idea the existential quantifier, 'some', that is, 'at least one'.

Some have defined existence in the following way: "to say that something exists is always a way of saying that some predicate is satisfied." And plainly the synonyms for 'exists' – namely, 'is satisfied', 'is instantiated' – equate to, on reflection, 'is a member'. Do not think that when I say 'things do not exist' I am merely talking about 'things' and the day can be saved for existence by pointing out that it is a property, not of things, but of predicates. I deny 'existence' itself in any form: concepts are not 'instantiated'; predicates are not 'satisfied'.[12]

In what follows one must note the membership I speak of is pure membership without regard to the specificity of the concept of whose extension something is a member. I am considering membership as such.

Instantiation, satisfaction, express putative relations, as does membership, between a concept, predicate, or the extension of a concept, and an object. 'B is instantiated, is satisfied by A', says nothing other than 'A is a member of the extension of B'. Where we concentrate upon the specificity of the concept, we express predication. When we focus upon instantiation, satisfaction, membership, without regard to conceptual specificity or nature, we note an equivalence and we express existence. For some concept or other to be instantiated is for some object or other to be a member of some concept's or other's extension. And non-instantiation, non-satisfaction, non-membership are the same and

[12] A. J. Ayer. *The Central Questions of Philosophy* (1973) p.204.

mean non-existence.

For an object to instantiate or satisfy a concept or predicate comes to the same thing as for a concept or predicate to be instantiated or satisfied. If a predicate is satisfied, an object satisfies a predicate. If an object satisfies the predicate 'is a horse', at least one horse exists. If no object satisfies it, there are no horses. Similarly, if the predicate 'is a unicorn' is satisfied – by something – unicorns exist; and if the same predicate is not satisfied – by anything – unicorns do not exist. Something satisfying a predicate and a predicate's being satisfied express the same thought. But 'x is satisfied by y' or 'y satisfies x' are both equivalent to 'y is a member of the extension of x'.

In the above, we draw a connection between concept or predicate and object in respect to instantiation and satisfaction. Then we clearly see that instantiation involves an object which is plainly a member of the instantiated concept's extension. Satisfaction and instantiation are pseudo-relations not second-order predicates.

For something to 'fall under' a concept, any concept, is for a concept to be 'instantiated'. For nothing to 'fall under' a concept is for that concept not to be 'instantiated'. So for nothing to 'fall under' the concept 'Martian' is for that concept not to be 'instantiated', for Martians not to 'exist'. But to say that something does or does not 'fall under' a concept is to say that something 'is or is not a member of' the extension of that concept. Therefore we see the equivalence of 'instantiation' with 'membership' via the locution 'falls under'. It would be wrong to object that my use of 'something' already contains existential significance; for that 'something' means 'there is an x' depends upon your foisting on me more than a logical formulation, but a metaphysical position, namely, that to assert or deny 'something' is to affirm or deny existence, and that is a metaphysic I dispute. 'Something' thus should be neutral between an existential or non-existential metaphysics. To eliminate troubling mention of 'something' and 'nothing': 'falls under' implies 'is instantiated' and 'is a member', whilst 'does not fall under' implies 'is not instantiated' and 'is not a member'. For a concept to have the 'property' of instantiation is for an object to have the 'property' of membership. And since the concept's being instantiated means that an object exists, an object's being a member means that the object exists too.

Instantiation is membership seen from the concept's point of view. Membership is instantiation seen from the object's point of view. I ask that the nature of the concept not be focused upon, that concepts be seen as a genus, nor the particularity of the object, so that we discern that we deal with pure membership and pure instantiation. A concise expression of my argument which incorporates the 'quantifier', which is what 'some' is, for those dissatisfied with its omission, is that a concept, say F-ness, being instantiated, means or is equivalent to 'something' being F. Thus instantiation carries the same force as the existential quantifier (some). But since instantiation and membership are equivalent so are membership and the existential quantifier.[13]

'I am loved' means, and must mean, 'someone loves me'. Now a person may say 'x instantiates C' and 'x satisfies F' presume the existence of x already because the two sentences are predications of some property or other of x. That would be wrong. These sentences are not predications owing to their equivalence to their counterparts 'C is instantiated by x' and 'F is satisfied by x', which are commonly taken as statements of existence, not ordinary predication. Though 'x instantiates C may seem to have the form of an ordinary relational sentence, it is not because of the nature of 'instantiation'. Just because it is used passively in one context and actively in another doesn't alter the word's meaning. If the 'instantiation' of a concept isn't an ordinary predicate in this

---

[13] This is why in the preceding paragraphs, where I seem to concentrate on 'instantiation' being equivalent to 'existence' and not 'some' being equivalent to it, I am really not ignoring the quantifier. But 'some' does not, as I shall indicate later, have to be seen as only capable of being an existential quantifier, therefore to commit oneself to 'some' as expression of existence cannot be safely done. Thus 'instantiates', 'falls under'/'satisfies' capture 'exists', and we shift the burden away from quantification. When 'some' is not existential, it is not equivalent to 'membership'.

case, where it means that something exists, it cannot be different just because it is used actively and said of an object. 'Love' said of you towards me, doesn't change significance when I speak of my being 'loved' without specifically mentioning you. Because 'satisfaction' and 'instantiation' are relation-terms we have to remember that the satisfaction or instantiation of a predicate or concept are incomplete expressions. We should really mention the objects. C is instantiated *by* x, a concept is instantiated *by an object* are fuller expressions of what is often taken to be a formula for existence. We can make 'x satisfies F' signify that a property is had by an object by adding specificity to, and concentrating upon the qualitativity of, F. But the primary thing that is said by 'x satisfies F' is that something exists, for it is commonly held that predication presupposes existence. Any predicative statement asserts covertly and prior to the qualitative predication that something exists. Tacitly accepting and suppressing the existential assertion allows one to express the thought that an object has an attribute.

Following on naturally from the above, my next connection of membership and existence is the recognition that the member/ nature division in class theory we have unearthed, exactly reconstructs the existence/qualitativity dichotomy in metaphysics that we commenced this essay with. Membership, like existence, has no nature; both concepts are anti-qualitative, not conferring a description on objects. If existence has no nature, nature has no existence. To assert belonging to a specific, determinate class is predication. What one presupposes the other presupposes, and these identify. Predication presumes existence. Belonging to a determinate class presumes simple belonging or member-class membership. Such a belonging as the latter is belonging, as we have discovered, to the indeterminate, or indeterminate belonging. Everything that belongs to a specific class has the more general 'property' of unspecified belonging, member-class membership. Therefore existence identifies with pure belonging.

I can put the argument in a slightly more expansive way. To assert belonging to a determinate collection is predication, and many have identified the qualitative with the determinate, the specific. Belonging to the indeterminate, or pure belonging, is the precondition for specific belonging; belonging to that which has as yet to be made determinate is the presupposition for specific belonging. Indeterminacy is beyond property, and so 'membership', thought to be a predicate, is the only 'property' something has that belongs to the indeterminate class. Since to assert belonging to the determinate is predication, the precondition for belonging to the determinate is the precondition for predication. Belonging to the indeterminate, unspecified class is the precondition for predication. Existence is the precondition for predication, so existence is belonging to the unspecified class, which is, to repeat, pure belonging or membership.

Remember though that the general class of the determinate still identifies with determinacy, so that to assert belonging to it will always be predication, not to assert existence. General determinacy must be distinguished from the indeterminate. Existence is not 'universe membership' but 'membership of the class of class-members' – pure membership – for the same reasons that the member-class – the class of class-members – isn't the universe class. Membership of the universe is membership of the physical universe, which is to be physical. Membership of the class or universe of members is to exist. The universe of physicals has a nature; the universe of members has no nature.

At a more circumstantial level, I can point out that both membership and 'is' have a copulative function, and when used on their own after subjects of sentences fail to be predicative since they lack a nature.

Extending the range of my argument, 'there is', in its most general sense, fulfils the role of 'belongs to'. In the metaphysics of existence we perplex ourselves over the existence but non-reality of certain fictional things. These may be possible objects that are not actual, impossible objects, mythological objects. Though these things are unreal, they belong to classes, and in membership they exist. Therefore there is a 'level' at which anything may be said to exist, even if unreal – and reality isn't existence – and this has been contended by writers who nevertheless do not know the reason why.

Membership exactly mirrors existence in the instances encountered metaphysically when we try to explain how a thing cannot 'exist' in the real world, yet somehow seems to 'exist' in another. The answer is that it 'belongs' to a class of unreal, may be imaginary objects. If we substituted the word 'belongs' for 'exists' we see our way out of the difficulty. 'The golden mountain does not exist,' ceases to bother us when we recognize that though it does not belong to the class of concrete physical objects as a mountain and as golden, yet it belongs to a class of imaginary things with imaginary members. It 'exists' and does not 'exist' depending on the class we specify. But since the golden mountain finally does belong, it does in the end exist. By this illustration we see the emptiness of the concept of 'existence'. I will say more about this kind of paradox which is called a referential contradiction.

The round square belongs to the class of absurdities, and though its nature is impossible, incoherent, its existence is not. And the merely possible objects 'exist' through 'belonging' to the class of non-concrete, non-absurdities. Seeing how membership is indifferent to the coherence or incoherence, possibility or impossibility, of nature, we note its indifference to nature in general. This is reflected in existence being indifferent to impossibility or consistency of nature. A thing's nature may be impossible, but its existence will not be. Impossibility, possibility, and necessity indeed refer not to the existences of objects, but to their natures. Existence is judged the widest and emptiest concept. We have seen that exactly the same can be said of pure Membership. The latter is empty because it is natureless and this explains the tendency of ontologists to say that pure existence is nothing, if we identify it with membership.[14]

Membership, like existence, is used to 'establish' objects, but without in itself describing their natures. To say that something

[14] Joseph Owens, *op.cit.* p.4. n5.

'is' is to establish it. Objects are fixed, placed in a context by existence and membership, only when, as in the case of existence, literally everything has it, everything is the class, membership appears to lose its relativity and is not seen for what it is. It ceases to seem derivative and unreal and dependent and is not viewed as 'membership', but as something felt to be active, positive and absolute, and to be applicable to individual things without any need for a context. This is because sheer membership, though it suggests a context, given what the concept means after all, has not got one itself, since there is no class of members. 'Establishment' and being 'fixed' at that level seems like an absolute and positive determination, empty though it is. And membership's pure and unfettered blankness makes for its absoluteness well. So where membership is pure, contextuality paradoxically disappears. But we can only say that a thing 'is' when we can locate it,[15] say where it is. This should have provided a clue to existence's apparent, though in the end pseudo-relativity.

Existence and membership qualify things proper but do not identify with them; they are 'said of' but do not enter into things. Things 'exist', but cannot, we see, be 'existents'. And things 'belong' but cannot, insofar as they have natures, be 'members'.

If something 'belongs' because it belongs, divorced from any other reasons, and if a thing 'exists' because it exists, then they are effectively uncontrolled in belonging and existing. Membership and Existence in themselves are 'contingent'; they rule themselves and are inexplicable in their own domains.

Some of these assimilations, if they work, justify the divorce of existence from qualitativity, in a logical fashion.

The definition of existence as membership, generates, I now believe, the reason for all the dimensions of existence I have examined so far. Because membership is null, natureless, it cannot be qualitative, that is, be part of the nature of things; so it is external to thing's natures and therefore things' membership is contingent; because membership is contingent, the existence,

---

[15] Existence is the ultimate act of location.

membership, of one thing is independent of that of another.

The Class as Collection

There is a better reason though for independence: because members have no characterization, a class cannot be formed out of them. Therefore members are logically isolated. Contingency is not needed to explain apartness: naturelessness suffices. One cannot even conceptually compare, connect or collect things that have no nature; hence the conceptual apartness of members, existents. There is nothing in virtue of which the natureless can be related or linked (as, for instance, the extended can be connected in terms of dimension). Similarly, one cannot conceptually link the natureless, membership, to the nature-possessing. Membership, positive or negative, for non-membership can only have meaning if membership has meaning, is thus independent of nature. Anything with a nature can at least be classed: not so members. So the argument of the first part of this essay is vindicated. When, however, elements have a characterization, they are collected into a plurality, a group, exhibiting external relations between each other. What collects them is the characterization; what isolates them is the membership. Membership alone has no characterization to bring the members together, so they are utterly apart. The double-feature of being brought together by a nature and kept isolated by membership is an exhibition of the contradiction of the 'external relation', which characterizes atomism. This double-action engenders the classic plurality called the 'class' as it is commonly understood up to now: the group or collection. So the class seen as an extension contains a contradiction.

This capacity of membership to explain and generate the existential dimensions is a good reason for identifying the two concepts.

These assimilations and connections turn what was largely an intuitive insight into something much more substantial. Because membership is spurious, the class calculus must be based on premises which do not involve it. If classes cannot function without membership, classes are invalid, though I do not think anything so drastic needs to be seriously considered. All we can do is describe things in their qualitative, physical relations with other things and not introduce such empty, unreal relations as 'belonging' and 'existence'.

The Liar and Truth

In the paradox of the Liar the same fallacy that appears in the class paradox operates, namely, the membership fallacy. The Liar paradox may be formulated in this way: 'This statement is false'. If it is false, then it is false that it is false, so it is true; but if it is true, it is false.[16] No real statement is made here, just as the class paradox formula is not really a valid predicate in the class logic. For in the same way that membership cannot achieve itself, truth-value cannot be responsible for itself. But this is what is attempted in the paradoxical statement.

The similarity goes much deeper than this for there is a conceptual linkage of a most intimate kind between membership and truth. Both are sham predicates: they cannot procure themselves. Something has membership by dint of character; something else has 'truth value' by dint of the relationship between the nature of the statement and the world: a class or totality. Membership and truth-value cannot function significantly by themselves. They are pseudo-relations conjured up by our logic and language, revealing their emptiness when the attempt at self-establishment is made. In the class paradox the characterization contains belonging; in the truth paradox the meaning of the sentence contains its value.

Not only in both these paradoxes is the same strategy attempted, but the same concept is involved. Membership and Truth should be abandoned if we are to solve the paradoxes. Statements are 'true', but statements which contain their own

[16] Another form would be: 'I am a liar'. If I am lying, I am telling the truth; but if I am telling the truth, I am lying. Lying, that is, the deliberate assertion of a falsehood is not itself important; but the telling of a falsehood is, particularly this statement.

truth-values and thereby refer to themselves, are not so. Things with characteristics are 'class-members', but membership cannot be one of those characteristics and thus be its own condition. Membership's and Truth's vacuity one is led to suppose causes their inability to achieve themselves.

Just as membership needs something with a determinate nature, so truth needs a qualitative assertion, one which describes, says how things are, that is beyond evaluation. This implies that in itself truth has no nature, and the paradox shows it as meaningless. Truth cannot be a predicate. A non-self-evaluating statement can have meaning, but one which uses value in trying to attain a value, in its meaning that is, fails by merely producing a contradiction. The concept of truth-value itself has to be questioned.

Truth, like existence, is an appendage to what is only ever real: in the world's case, physical objects; in sentences' case, their qualitative assertions. Calling the latter 'true' or 'false' makes no difference to the meanings of these statements. Assertions seem to be quite independent of truth-value. They merely say 'how' something is and therefore represent the world qualitatively by representing a qualitative world: in this sense the assertion is 'qualitative'. In short, to be beyond propositional meaningfulness, to be an appendage and not a part of it, in itself, means that truth depends, like membership, on what has a nature, and is by implication natureless, therefore meaningless.

I said that if membership could attain itself there would be no class-specificity; there would be chaos in this department. Determination, identity, for members or classes would matter in no way and classes would break down. Similarly, if truth-value were allowed to secure itself, the nature, the content of any particular statement would be pointless. In the paradoxical 'statement' no statement is made independently of the statement of value: we would not need to compare the statement with the world or with any other propositions to ascertain its value; so meaning, the special content and nature of proposition, would collapse because it would not be taken into account in evaluating the sentence. The statement is a pure act of evaluation but without an object to be evaluated. The qualitative state of the world becomes sententially irrelevant, and even analytic sentences depend on their meanings, not their truth-values, for truth-value. Though it may seem that if a sentence is true then it is true, with truth-value it is not the case that if a sentence is true then that sentence is true, for we depend on the meaning of the sentence, not its value, for whether it is true or not.

We may also notice the positive formulation of the membership or class paradox, in the case where self-membership is needed for self-membership. This appears innocuous, but a reductio is got when we consider the negation, non-self-membership. Similarly, in the truth-paradox, if someone says, 'This statement is true', this may appear acceptable and genuine: if true it is true, if false it is false. But the negative, 'This statement is untrue', produces a contradiction. There is a formal closeness; the analogy is strong. In reality, even the positive renditions of these logical errors are in a concealed way mistaken. We only need to push them into negation to uncover their overall illegitimacy.

The very security of the concepts Truth and Membership is to be doubted. As I rejected existence and membership, I am rejecting truth-values. In the world, things are only how they are, and in language assertions likewise only say how they, things, are. This entails that Truth and Falsity drop out of our vocabulary. But more will be said of the details of this particular paradox later.

Truth, like existence, is ultimately a form of membership, and these equivalences only take a small effort to perceive. Truth, like existence, like membership, is excess conceptual weight, and the paradoxes of class and truth are reductios of membership and existence.

We must be exact in establishing how truth and membership are linked. Truth is the relation set up by the propositions which exactly reproduce the physical universe and thereby belong to it. Truth is the sentential equivalent of pure membership. The situations described belong to the world; they therefore have the more general feature of pure membership at some level. The descriptions have this property too by proxy. What makes for 'membership' of the world is the exact meaningful reproduction of the world. Sheer membership is the residue of that relationship. Sentences reproduce situations, and consequently reproduce their belonging to the world and their simple belonging. Just as the qualitatively physical, by being so, 'belongs' to the universe, when a proposition, through its meaning, reproduces the physical situation, it 'belongs' at one remove to the universe; hence it partakes in the property of general and pure membership as a result; hence it is 'true'. Truth is existence sententially manifested or reproduced.

The sounds or writing in a statement as such belong, and in this inarticulate way and directly, they 'exist'. The 'existence' of the meaningful proposition is secondhand, at one remove, like the proposition is itself secondhand. It 'belongs' by way of its meaning, which in the case of propositions is the nature of the attempt at world-reproduction. Truth is meaningful, secondhand membership: propositional 'existence'.

To be clear and to repeat: 'Truth' is like this: you have the world. Situations and events are physical and therefore are thought to 'belong' to this world. Then you have a statement which exactly replicates an aspect of the world in language. In so doing, it too 'belongs' to the world, but meaningfully, as through or by dint of its meaning, just as the event it replicates does through its physicality. The statement belongs to the world mediately. The pure or sheer membership that can be distilled out of both forms of world membership, is, in the case of physical things, 'existence', and in the case of sentences, 'truth'.

One of the functions of a statement, and this may be a definition in part of what it is for it to be meaningful, is the attempt to reproduce the world. More generally, the meaning of one is the quality, the nature of the attempt to reproduce the world. The success of such an enterprise is equivalent simply to the reproduction of the world, and this will be qualitative in nature. Sentences descriptive of the world have to be 'qualitative' since events are so. In the sense of saying 'how' the world is, assertions are qualitative. Now truth is, as we have indicated, not qualitative. It, like membership, like existence, tells us nothing of the nature of the proposition, its quality, when it is applied to it, no more than membership and existence tell us of the characters of the things credited with them. So 'truth' cannot equal success at world-reproduction in a qualitative manner, since it is not qualitative. Truth is only an implication of reproduction. This state of affairs is similar, then, to physicality not equalling existence or determination not equalling membership.

The meaningful involves description, saying 'how' something is, as in say predication. Therefore truth cannot assert itself for it lacks a qualitative, descriptive, meaningful nature. Truth is always 'outside' meaning, like membership is outside characterization. This being so, it cannot attain a truth-value for itself. Not only in the context of propositions, but in itself, truth is meaningless, for if it is membership it is natureless, and any term denoting what has no character finally is devoid of meaning. Other than as a conceptual misapprehension, it signifies nothing, reproduces emptiness.

Truth, as secondhand membership, is reduced to absurdity by the Liar or Truth paradox. As membership, we know why it cannot attain itself. The Liar and Class paradoxes result from taking membership seriously and when we go further into them we shall see that they are in form the same logico-metaphysical error. Both are class-theory paradoxes.

As before, I shall provide exact reasons for strictly identifying truth, membership and existence.

I can compactly display how membership, truth and existence are equivalent by using the locution 'falls under'. If an object, any object, 'falls under' a concept – and here, as earlier, the actual specificity of a concept is ignored – then, one, a concept is 'instantiated', two, a concept 'is true of' an object (understanding 'F is true of x' to be equivalent to ' 'x is F is true'), and three, an object 'is a member of' the extension of a concept. The quoted formulas have equivalent functions, say the same thing. One may easily be confused when we deal with specific concepts and feel that we are talking about predication, not truth or existence. But I require that the actual nature of the concept and the particularity of the object be disregarded, and we discover by doing this that we escape from predication, and concern ourselves purely with instantiation, membership and truth as such. We see their equivalence.

To say that some object 'instantiates' a concept, or a concept is instantiated (or a predicate is satisfied) by an object, is the same as saying a concept 'is true of' an object. To say that a concept 'is true of' an object is to say that an object 'is a member of' the extension of a concept. Of course, the first statement, of instantiation, is a way of saying that something 'exists'. If a concept is true of some object or other, an object (of that kind) exists. If a concept is not true of some object or other, an object (of that kind) does not exist. So if 'Martian' is true of some object, or better, if 'x is a Martian' is true, Martians exist. If 'x is a Martian' *is not true*, Martians don't exist. Adding to the description of a situation, a mere assertion of a possibility, like 'x is a Martian', a truth-value, turns it into a statement of fact or non-fact, of instantiation or non-instantiation, 'x' means 'some object or other'; x's identity is disregarded.

'x is a member of a given class' is equivalent to ' "x has a given property" is true'. The members of an extension are those things the concept is true of. When we omit concept specificity, the formulas 'is a member of', and 'is true of', or 'is true' have exactly the same function, do the same work. And both express the instantiation of a concept. '"x has a given property" is false', understanding again that the particularity of 'x' is not considered, it merely represents an indefinite object, means 'x is not a member of a given class'. In this pair of equivalences 'is not a member' translates into 'is false' since the only thing that alters between expressions of truth and falsity is negation of membership.

As in equating existence and membership, one of the most important moves one has to make is to disregard concept-specificity and object-particularity, so as to see that we are not talking about predication but that which lies behind it, pure membership, pure existence, and pure truth, the last of which must be distinguished from description or assertion.

Truth is closely associated with fact and existence[17] by many thinkers. The definition of 'fact' by some is that it is what makes a statement true. My theory of truth's origin would explain the relation so: the statement made about the world describes it qualitatively since the world is qualitative. The real, qualitative events are said to exist or belong, hence they become 'facts'. Similarly, the linguistic representation of the events is likewise said to 'belong' linguistically to the world and more generally to 'belong'. That last belonging is truth. A situation that belongs is a 'fact'. A sentence that belongs is a 'truth'.

Truth-values are not predicates. Truth cannot complete an incomplete subject like other predicates. As the paradox shows, it cannot complete – that is, make a valid, genuine statement out of – a subject which is not in itself a complete statement already. So '"The cat sat on the mat" is true' represents a way in which truth-value can be attached, conventionally, to a full statement. But take a subject in itself: 'This statement is true', where the subject is 'this statement', a thing to which truth could apparently be applied if it were predicative , does not form a meaningful sentence despite first appearances, any more than in 'The cat exists' or 'The cat belongs' neither 'exists' or 'belongs' are genuine predicates. If the linguistic assertion is assimilated to the attribution of a class characterization, then introducing a value in one and membership in the other, produce ill-formed sentences and absurdities.

My theory of truth explains the feeling people have had that truth is somehow redundant; if it, like existence, is membership, it is empty, vacuous, superfluous to the only genuine type of statement: the qualitative, contentful assertion. Membership is superfluous to the nature-possessing; existence irrelevant to the qualitative; truth redundant to the assertion. But by a consequential historical accident we have been conceptually saddled with these identical errors. And when some say that

---

[17] The Greeks had a veridical sense of 'is', I believe.

asserting a sentence and asserting the truth of that sentence are the same, what basically is going on is a failure to distinguish 'how' from 'that'. The sentence says how things are; but truth says that the sentence linguistically is.

Truth has no meaningful nature, just as membership has no characterizational nature and existence no qualitative nature. Things 'exist', or so it is thought, without existence being part of their nature; things 'belong' without belonging being part of their character; sentences are 'true' without truth being part of their meaning. Truth is attached to things with meanings, but the paradox shows it cannot duplicate the meaningful function; even when a statement asserts its own truth nothing is really said. It may seem strange that I say that truth has no 'meaningful nature', but I am considering that when it is allowed to secure itself, it renders the special meanings of sentences pointless. Truth is sententially meaningless because self-evaluating propositions are not statements. Value is external to sentential meaning. And truth, like existence and membership, is natureless in the sense that we are told nothing about the meaningful quality of the assertion that is credited with it.[18]

Truth, in the way of membership and existence, is in itself contingent. We surmise that this is because it, like the others, lacks a nature. It is never in the nature of a statement to be 'true'; and even analytic statements, as we shall see, are not necessarily correct, nor are self-contradictions necessarily incorrect, in virtue of their semantical forms, their analyticity or self-contradictoriness. So they won't be necessarily 'true' or 'false'. We shall see why in a later essay.

Like membership, truth cannot establish itself, and when this is attempted we get formally similar paradoxes or meaninglessness. Another manner of expressing the fallacy in the truth-paradox is by saying that in it truth-value is treated as a proper predicate. The same mistake is made in the class-membership paradox. And maybe this formulation is more readily understood than

[18] The natureless – Truth, Existence, Membership – must be the same, for only in virtue of a nature could they be different.

pronouncing that truth and membership 'attain themselves' illegitimately. I believe this implies that the general statement of class, metaphysical and semantic forms of membership not being predicates is not so immediate as I thought in causing the paradoxes, and some of them will bear even closer scrutiny. For instance, the concepts of reference and especially self-reference seem important, the latter appears to make a predicate out of membership, but membership makes self-reference possible.

Not making membership a predicate or 'attain itself' is not all in my solution of the paradoxes for I do not even propose retaining membership at all, as others have. I do not intend to solve the paradoxes within the constraints of membership, but I realize that something is elementally wrong with membership itself as a concept. I reject it totally because it is natureless and void and irrational and meaningless, producing paradoxes when this is not recognized, one of which is the topic of this thesis.

Cantor's Paradox

The culmination of my investigation into the dead heart of membership and solutions of the paradoxes, arrives in considering the next paradox.

Not only are the class and liar paradoxes soluble with the abolition of membership, but other famous and outstanding contradictions are so as well. And, as in the class paradox, the 'nature' of membership and the reasons for its invalidity emerge in these others.

Cantor's paradox can take this form. The power set of any given set is the class of sub-sets of the original set. The power set is numerically greater than the elements in any set by a fixed amount, 2n where n is the number of elements or members in the original set. But in the case of the set of all sets, its power set contains *more* sets than the set of *all* sets does, though of its very nature all sets are in the set of all sets, including those in the power set.

The apparently simple and frivolous solution to this is to reject the concept of membership, thus allowing no set or class to consist of members. But classes would not disappear as a result. What would replace the former members? Sub-classes. So the power set would not be greater than the number of sub-sets and the power set as a separate concept goes. In the case of this paradox what effectively happens is that the sub-sets of the power set become the constituents of the class and no contradictory consequences follow since the essence of the paradox springs from the numerical difference between a set and its power set, coupled of course with the nature of the set of all sets or the class of all classes.

The foregoing may seem baffling, but I can give good reasons why classes or sets should not consist of members. But if they do not how can sub-classes or sub-sets be formed? Plainly what is meant by a 'sub-class' is not what was meant by that term in the context of membership. Firstly, though, why should there be no members?

The reasons I have already given for membership's invalidity are strong ones why there should be no members in classes, why class theory should not be based upon membership. But now I will give new reasons for sub-classes' supersession of members. An individual is a member only if its unit-class[19] is included as a sub-class of any given class. This provides a hint, but maybe no more than that.

Let us look at classes which consist of real, physical objects, like stones, whales, metallic objects. What will any logic text-book insist on as a requirement for membership of the classes of such real things? It will say that something must be a stone, a whale, a metallic object in reality in order to be in the class, in order to constitute it. But classes are logical abstractions, logical objects or perhaps logical conveniences, and how can solid real things be components of what is not itself solid and real? If we consider the class of metallic objects: if the components of this class are and must be really metallic, so too must the 'class'. This however would seem stupid.

How can real, physical things fail to form a real physical object

---

[19] A unit-class is a sub-class containing just one member: each member has a unit-class.

if they are its parts and if the criterion for being a part of the object is to be a real object of a certain kind? If membership commits us to holding that real objects be components of abstractions, this is another reason for conceptually rejecting it. There is no gap, with membership, between the abstract and the non-abstract, as there should be. Any class theory textbook will say that x must be an actual cat in order to qualify for membership of the class of cats.

We preserve the abstractness of the class by insisting that only abstractions be its components. These will be sub-classes. If cats, whales, etc, cannot be components of classes, it must be sub-classes of these creatures and other physical objects that are. This presents us with the problem of having to formulate exactly what a 'sub-class' of such classes must be, consequently what a class must be, if they are not allowed to consist of members.

A characterized class is an Idea, a Concept, a Notion or an Essence of necessity, which does not range over 'things' but over other ideas: sub-ideas, sub-classes. That is what a sub-class is: it is a sub-idea. What else could be the constituent of an abstraction except an idea? What else could ideas be ideas of except things with the appropriate properties; and what else could the abstraction the class is be an abstraction from except the ideas which are its components? Imagine I come from another planet and had never seen a woman before. In seeing one and being acquainted, I could subsequently have an 'idea' of a woman, as in contemplating her, remembering her. To think one needs a collection of a certain kind of thing before having an idea, an abstract idea, of that thing is mistaken. One thing is enough, and the idea we form is 'abstracted' from reality.

Notions are 'ideas of ideas'. Ideas start with only one instance of the thing we bring under a notion, and the 'thing' may itself be ideal. Ideas of the latter kind, sub-ideas, build up into, by increasing variety and generality, and, by association with the null class, achieve, an overall notion which we call the 'class'. This is a process of abstraction. Sub-ideas – ideas of things – are varied and rarefied until we have the overall notion or class. Naturally we do not have before our minds ideas of all the sub-classes, sub-ideas, but the notion is a formal thing and not quite real. Notions, Ideas, Concepts, Essences to repeat are not seen as percolating through 'things' but through subordinate ideas. In this way the class becomes the Idea of say 'Woman', 'Cat', 'Whale', 'Number', 'Month', and so forth.

Sub-ideas are derived from what I call 'originals', which are sometimes solid things, but they can be other ideas. These originals have the place 'members' have in the conventional but mistaken theory of classes; but originals are not parts of classes like members were. Classes are now something we do to A, B and C; they do not consist of A, B and C. Membership makes classes into collections, extensions; the notional explanation makes them into something close to Essences, Intensions.[20] This point is of the last importance. Notions are primarily what they mean, not collections. I do not regard 'membership' as a merely dispensible and in itself harmless façon de parler. Membership is part of the concept of extensionality and I believe concepts do not have extensions. Objects do not 'fall under' concepts.[21] And interpreting classes as collections is responsible for Cantor's paradox.

When we express as 'not predicable of itself' the property of 'non-self-membered' that appears in the class paradox, we seem to be struck with the same difficulties. But, as we shall soon see, whilst the predicate 'not self-predicated' is not itself illicit, when interpreted intentionally, where it means 'included in its complement',[22] its extensional interpretation, the one involving membership, produces a paradox and is illicit.

Resuming: each individual sub-idea is an ideal unit in the class and is equal to any other in terms of being unanalysable into

---

[20] 'Intension' here pertains to 'meaning' as opposed to objects a concept is true of.

[21] The membership fallacy solves the problem of universals: exemplification is membership. With no exemplification we have no universals. Some form of non-realism must be correct.

[22] The 'complement' of a class is the class having the negative meaning to the class. Thus: 'Man' has the complement 'Not-man'.

smaller sub-ideas or to members. For the notion consists of all such sub-ideas and to divide more comprehensive and rarefied sub-classes into less rarefied, less comprehensive ones is to indulge in redundant duplication. Each sub-idea is already part of the class no matter how limited it is. Sub-ideas are not 'collected' but are operated upon mentally by a process of ideal rarefaction or abstraction.

Sub-ideas are at one level and as such are equal. The 'notion' is at a conceptually higher stage: it is the class. Consider say the sub-class of the class of women which is equivalent to the idea of all women, that is, which is derived from a hypothetical acquaintance with all original, individual women or which is simply the idea of all real women. Is this sub-class not equal to the Notion? No. Classes are extensive over, consist of, sub-ideas. They are ideas of ideas, abstractions of abstractions. But sub-ideas are ideas of realities or originals. So the class of women is equal to the idea of the ideas of women, whilst the most comprehensive sub-idea to the idea of all real women.

Ideas of ideas are at a different plane of abstraction from ideas of originals. Therefore the notion of women, or any other notion, is never a 'member of', predicable of, included in, itself, but simply it is itself. Not being collections even of sub-ideas but an abstraction from them, Notions are the achievement of a wide and final idea which always, crucially, includes the null-class. The relation of the original to the Notion is that its idea is 'included in' that notion, whereby I mean that its idea is a sub-idea of that Notion or part of a sub-idea in that Notion.

A notion is an essence, and the notion of Essence corresponds to the class of all classes.

Just as the sub-idea is ideally irreducible, the Notion is ideally unrarefiable, that is, within itself. For the Notion is hierarchical: outside the notion, consisting of ideas and idea of ideas, we have the originals. From these last sub-ideas are abstracted. From the sub-ideas the notion is abstracted. Therefore the essence or notion, within any notional structure and hierarchy, is always at the top of the process of abstraction. But notions cannot be originals for one of their own sub-ideas, though they can be originals for other notional structures. They can be originals for other notions, but not for themselves, so they cannot be included in themselves, only identical to themselves. If one sees it another way one may understand this more easily: can the essence of 'number', for example, contain 'number' within itself? There is only one place for an essence and that is at the top or at the end of the abstractive heap or process. Because membership commits one to thinking of the class as a collection, it is possible to envisage classes which are members of themselves, which is what one needs for the class paradox I have examined. But with membership gone, and classes seen as notions or essences, not as collections, we understand that essences cannot be included in themselves: an essence cannot be the essence of itself. Until in any given notional structure we reach the top, we have not yet got the given notion: self-inclusion is impossible. Within any given notional or essential structure you can only have one abstraction, not a multiplicity of abstractions, for that is what a notional structure is: one abstraction. So an infinite regress cannot be set up as it can with membership.

A notion can be an original, but an original cannot be a sub-idea, so the notion of class will not have the same number of sub-ideas as it has originals. The proportion of originals to sub-ideas conforms to other notions. In 'Notion' (the class of classes), {HORSE} is an original. {{HORSE}} is a sub-idea. {HORSE}, {CAT} are originals, but {{HORSE}, {CAT}} is a sub-idea, not an original, because it is an abstraction of {HORSE}, {CAT}. A sign of this is the double-brackets.

The Notional Class Paradox

Can the notional or intentional interpretation of classes save classes from the class paradox, or can the latter still arise in this context? Let 'not self-predicated' be called, notionally, 'included in its complement'. We see that all classes are not included in themselves, whereas only some have the properties of their opposites. The notion {RAT} is not included in itself, but is included in {NON-RAT}. The notion {NON-RAT} is similarly, by rule, not self-included, but is identical to itself. So {INCLUDED IN ITS COMPLEMENT} is the correct rendition of 'not self-predicated'.

In what class is {INCLUDED IN ITS COMPLEMENT} included? Is it included in its complement or is it not included in its complement?

If it is included in its complement, it is included in its complement. What is its complement? {NOT INCLUDED IN ITS COMPLEMENT}. Therefore it would have the property of not being included in its complement if it were included in its complement.

If it is not included in its complement, then it is not included in its complement. It has that property: it is included in {NOT INCLUDED IN ITS COMPLEMENT}. But the complement of {INCLUDED IN ITS COMPLEMENT} is {NOT INCLUDED IN ITS COMPLEMENT} so it is included in its complement.

The class paradox seems to have revived.

Actually, what does '{NOT INCLUDED IN ITS COMPLEMENT}' mean? {NOT INCLUDED IN ITS COMPLEMENT} is a fictional class, it isn't a notion on its own. Notions have the possibility of being included in their complements, but they don't have the possibility of being included in the complements of their complements, which are themselves. If {NOT INCLUDED IN ITS COMPLEMENT} were a genuine class it would be the class of classes included in themselves, or originals for themselves. Reverting to the concept of membership a class can be a member of itself or of its complement, one or the other; likewise for notions it would seem. But we have the rule that a notion cannot be its own original or self-included. Therefore it can only be itself. This means that {INCLUDED IN ITS COMPLEMENT} is not *included* in either itself or its complement, but that it is equal to, the same as, its own notion. It is beyond inclusion as far as it or its complement goes.

To get the above clear, remember that in membership {NOT A MEMBER OF ITS COMPLEMENT} meant {MEMBER OF

ITSELF}. The equivalent of this does not happen with notional inclusion where the polarity is between the notion itself and inclusion in its complement. So we don't get paradoxical results in trying to judge in what the class we are concerned with is included. This class is not included in itself or its opposite.

Given what '{INCLUDED IN ITS COMPLEMENT}' means, we see why it is beyond inclusion in its complement or itself. For the complement of {INCLUDED IN ITS COMPLEMENT} is '{NOT INCLUDED IN ITS COMPLEMENT}', which is a fictional class, an illicit property, being another formula for self-inclusion. And if it was not included in its complement it would therefore have an illegitimate property: 'not included in its complement'.

The rules for classes establish an asymmetry in inclusion. One may object concerning complements: either a notion is included in its complement or it is not included in its complement. The latter seems quite a legitimate property, for the class {NON-RAT} is not included in its complement, though like all classes it is self-identical. Surely, one urges, more needs to be said to express that {NON-RAT} is not included in its complement than merely saying it is *just* self-identical. Well, concerning complements, what property does {NON-RAT} have? I can't say it is self-included; that means I can't say it is not a rat. (I can say it is self-identical). But if I say some notion {NON-RAT} is not included in its complement I am saying it is not a rat. Therefore the asymmetry is thus illustrated: I can say of the notion {RAT}, it is the notion {RAT}, and it is not a rat, i.e. is included in its complement. But with the notion {NON-RAT} I can say it is the notion {NON-RAT}, though I can't say it is not included in its complement because I can't say it is not a rat, for that would be self-inclusion. Complement inclusion works only one way: this is the asymmetry in inclusion.

The meaning of {INCLUDED IN ITS COMPLEMENT} therefore rules itself out of inclusion either in its complement or non-inclusion in its complement. Otherwise, given its meaning, the class {INCLUDED IN ITS COMPLEMENT} would always end up 'not being included in its complement', or 'self-included'. This class has not *got* a complement. In brief if it was included in its complement, it would be included in itself, and if it was not included in its complement, it would be included in itself.

So let me put this in manageable terms. Since predication is notional inclusion, whilst there can be non-self-predication, or better, since this is misleading, 'having the contradictory predicate' ('inclusion in compliment'), there can be no self-predication, for this last is self-inclusion. Therefore 'having the contradictory predicate' ('non-self-predication') will have no negation or opposite (no complement). And it cannot be self-predicated.

To remind ourselves of why the rule that a notion cannot be self-predicated is not arbitrary, remember that it is because self-inclusion or self-predication infringes the rule of concept or essence formation. A notion, essence, is the end-result of a process of abstraction and for any given notion is only to be found at the completion of the abstractive process. Therefore it itself cannot be one of those things from which it is abstracted. It can't be self-included; it cannot have itself as a property. {NON-GREENNESS} cannot be non-green, it can only be {NON-GREENNESS}. The notion only identifies with itself.23

Grelling's Paradox

Grelling's paradox is a semantic one closely related to the class paradox. The insights we have gained here help to dispel it. We need importantly to stress intensionality, what concepts mean, in solving this and other puzzles.

Some words have the same property as what they mean. 'Awkwardness' is an awkward work; 'short' is a short word;

---

23 This solves the difficulty of whether the metre rod in Paris is or is not a metre long. The metre rod is a concrete concept, a one over many, that which is the standard for other things: it is metrehood. As such it cannot be self-predicated, be a metre long, but can only identify with itself: 'Metre'. As such it is one of those things not a metre long. Therefore it is included in its complement. That though does not prevent it from being the standard metre, the notion of metrehood.

'polysyllabic' is a polysyllabic word; 'English' is an English word. These are stock examples. Such words are called 'autological'. Some words, on the other hand, do not have the same property as what they mean. 'Monosyllabic' is not monosyllabic. 'Anglais' is not an English word. Words of this type are called 'heterological'.

Now what about the word 'heterological'? Is it heterological or autological? If it is heterological, then it doesn't have the property it means; but that is its meaning. If it is autological, then it applies to itself and is heterological. If 'heterological' is heterological it is autological, and if autological, it is heterological.

Obviously, from the way we approached the class paradox notionally, 'autological' is 'self-included or predicated' and 'heterological' is 'included in its complement'. 'Heterological' cannot be either heterological or autological, just as 'included in its complement' can't be included or not included in its complement. 'Autological' is banished from validity as was self-predication, there is no such property, meaning that 'heterological' has no opposite.

The insight into this paradoxical fallacy is got when we understand that concepts are what they *mean*. They are intentional. 'Polysyllabic' is what it means, not how it is spelt. 'Monosyllabic' is what it means, not how it is written. 'Short' is what it *means*, not the word's spelling or length. A meaning can neither be 'short' or 'monosyllabic' or 'polysyllabic' or 'awkward'; not within themselves; meanings aren't those sorts of thing. In themselves, concepts or meanings can't be self-predicated, only identified with themselves. When a concept applies to things other than itself, we have predication; but when it applies to itself we naturally enough have identification. Meanings are not the sorts of things that can be 'fat' or 'short' or 'monosyllabic'. Things can be. A meaning can't be short, but an associate of meaning – the written or spoken letters or sounds, or the contentless sort of *thing* a meaning is: a concept – can be short or whatever may be appropriate. In itself, a word is only its meaning.

Grelling's paradox trades on not distinguishing meaning from the associate of meaning. The accompaniments to meaning, sounds or writing, are wholly accidental; they are in no way essential to those meanings; they could have been otherwise.

Are 'useless' and 'meaningless' heterological? They are what they *mean*. 'Useless' and 'meaningless' cannot mean 'useful' and 'meaningful'. But the words as things – associates – can be *used* meaningfully and usefully. The words are then not treated as *what they mean* but what sort of *things* they *are*.

And a word like 'meaningful' *means* 'meaningful'; as what it means it is itself not meaningful, but rather *identifies* with its meaning: 'meaningful'. It is not self-predicated. What appears to be 'meaningful', in the sense of a predicate, pertains not to its *meaning*, but to the kind of *thing* it is devoid of its special significance. Because autology doesn't genuinely apply to meanings, it cannot function in the intentional treatment of words. The reason why the meaning, a concept, cannot suffer self-predication whilst the word as object can be heterological, is that within itself it is only its meaning, just as within itself the notion is only what it means, within its own notional structure. This, remember, is responsible for predicative asymmetry. Naturally, just as self-predication and complement inclusion signify respectively, the internal and extrinsic as regards notions, autology and heterology signify and apply to the internal and external in respect to words' meanings. And internally, the word is only its meaning. A good illustration of what is essential and non-intrinsic to meanings is the word 'English'. That word is not autological because 'Anglais' and 'Inglese' have the same meaning, but are not English words. Meanings as such cannot be English, French or Italian. Words as the sorts of things they are, but still not as their specific meanings, as being objects, can suffer heterology because heterology doesn't apply to what words mean; when however we get inside a word we are in the domain of specific meaning, which means autology has no foothold.

Therefore the overall comment on Grelling's paradox is that intension should come to the forefront and accidents of meaningful expression should not delude us in spotting the essence of a term: its meaning. In the paradox the wrong notion of the word is used, the one which stresses accompaniments to meaning, which is akin to the wrong identification of classes, not as notions, meanings, but as extensions, sets of objects.

The Liar Again

We can now see that the truth-paradox is even closer to the class paradox than I have suggested, in form.[24] For a meaningful statement to belong to the world it has to represent or correspond to it. But these are not truth: truth is pure membership. A sentence that evaluates itself, says of itself that it is true or false, does not refer to the world (and it is not analytic) but to itself. In self-evaluation the statement is made to belong, not to the world, but to itself. Self-reference itself is a belonging relation, for to refer to the world is to belong to it as a proposition; to refer to oneself is to belong to oneself. I will later argue, not in this essay, that pure reference is itself a form of pure membership, and that truth is the reference that applies to sentences, though reference also applies to parts of sentences, so reference is a more inclusive concept than truth. Anyhow, what you refer to you belong to.

I have already established however that truth is membership, and for the purposes of solving the liar paradox this is all one needs. If evaluation is the attribution of membership or non-membership, self-evaluation is the attribution of self-membership or non-self-membership. But self-membership and non-self-membership are self-predication and non-self-predication or complement inclusion. Self-membership and non-self-membership for sentences mean respectively having and not having the predicates they assert, their own predicates. Therefore the negative self-evaluating sentence will give rise to an obvious paradox: that of the Liar. So the truth paradox has this form: If 'This statement is not a member of itself' is a member of itself, it has its own predicate and is not a member of itself. If it is not a member of itself, it lacks its own predicate, and is not not a

---

[24] Here, I am explaining the form of the paradox.

member of itself, and so it is a member of itself.

We infer that self-evaluation is no longer in and for these formulas ascription of truth-value, because the membership is part of the meaning of these sentences not external to it as a truth-value should be, self-membership isn't membership, and is now self-predication and complement inclusion. The light is on'. If I want to say that statement is true, I assert that it belongs to the world and thus belongs. If I want to say that statement is false, I assert that it doesn't belong to the world and thus doesn't belong.

If I say 'This statement is true', I am asserting that it belongs to itself and thus belongs. It doesn't belong to the world because it doesn't refer to the world, but to itself.

If I say 'This statement is false', I am asserting that it doesn't belong to itself and thus doesn't belong.

But since the truth-values in the above self-evaluations are parts of the meanings I can't infer that they are truth-values, that pure belonging is asserted, for we see that belonging has no nature and can't be in sentences' meanings, can't be predicates. In evaluation, the evaluation is distinct from the sentence evaluated. In self-evaluation, the evaluation is not distinct from the sentence evaluated, and this makes truth-value into a predicate, meaning that self-evaluation is not genuine evaluation.

All I am left with are the statements: 'This statement belongs to itself', and 'This statement doesn't belong to itself'. The self-evaluations aren't real evaluations. The sentences though, like the legitimate one above, 'The light is on', try to set up the conditions for evaluation by asserting membership or non-membership of what they refer to.

So when I say of 'This statement belongs to itself' and 'This statement doesn't belong to itself', that they are 'true' or 'false', I am again asserting that they belong or don't belong to themselves and thus belong or don't belong. And again the 'belongs' and 'doesn't belong' are not truth-values, and are excluded, negated. And all I am left with are statements to they effect that the quoted statements do or don't belong to themselves, from which a paradox can emerge. If the 'is true' or 'is false' in self-evaluations were evaluations then they would not be predicates. Since they are predicates, they are not evaluations. To evaluate a self-evaluation is still to self-evaluate, since the sentence belongs or doesn't belong to itself, and not to the world. Belonging is external to a sentence's meaning when it refers to the world, and internal to its meaning when it refers to itself, in evaluatory contexts. Belonging is thus seen as an internal predicate.

A self-evaluation is by definition a sentence in which truth-value is a predicate. There are two essential expressions of self-evaluation: "This statement is true" and "This statement is false". They have the following forms: "Statement X belongs to itself" (thus it belongs) and "Statement X does not belong to itself" (thus it does not belong). And an evaluation of a self-evaluation is a self-evaluation, for it has the form: "'p' belongs to itself" or "'p' does not belong to itself", where 'p' is a statement. The predicate of self-evaluation is "does/doesn't belong to *itself*".

Whilst belonging to oneself, or not, as the case may be, is nominally allowed as a genuine predicate, simple belonging or not belonging are not. Thus we have: "This statement doesn't belong to itself" doesn't belong to itself, and "This statement doesn't belong to itself" does belong to itself.

Self-evaluation ("This statement is true/false") is impossible, for it is not evaluation, and evaluation is impossible, for it is attributing membership or non-membership.

What is the 'complement' of a sentence? The sentence which asserts the contradictory predicate. The sentence 'The wood is burning' is one of those objects, being a sentence, which is 'not burning'. Thus the sentence is included in the class of 'non-burners', and is therefore included in its complement. The sentence, 'The wood is burning', is *not* burning.

Because self-predication is not possible, the sentence in itself can only be self-identified, that is, be its meaning; mean what it means, it is what it says. The property of being included in its complement has for sentences, as for other things, no complement, no contradictory[25] The liar paradox, which is none other than the class paradox in the domain of sentences, cannot arise. One move solves both paradoxes.

I will examine possible candidates for sentential self-inclusion. Firstly, 'Some thoughts are expressed in writing.' In itself, the sentence is only its meaning and exactly its meaning. Meanings' essences are not written or even expressed. They are specific kinds of thoughts. The sentence doesn't say of itself 'I am being expressed in writing'; a meaning as such can't be written; even this last quoted statement is not really a statement for if a sentence replicates something, i.e. says something about something, it cannot replicate itself. Statements that attempt this have no meaning finally and aren't statements. 'This sentence has five words' is meaningless, firstly, because meanings are essentially non-verbal, they are thoughts. A thought or meaning isn't intrinsically the number of words used to express it; it isn't any number of words. Other languages may have the same meaning expressed in more than five words. And secondly, just because a sentence in trying to pin its predicate on itself has to replicate itself, and because you can only replicate linguistically other things than the actual proposition, a self-replicating proposition is not possible. The general ruling that self-predication is impossible expresses the reason why a sentence may not have its own predicate by means of self-replication. If I say 'This thought is a thought', I am not giving my words meaning, not even uttering a tautology. 'What thought?' I can ask. Nothing is being thought. Nothing is said. '"All nature is akin" is a sentence." This is not itself a sentence, for in itself it is only what it says. And it does not say that it itself is a sentence, but that 'All nature is akin' is a sentence.

So, to resume analysis of the Liar paradox notionally, what is said is, 'This sentence is included in its complement'. That is because we are self-evaluating, not evaluating properly; and to translate this into more recognizably linguistic terms, it is a

---

[25] And we see, as in Grelling's paradox, it applies to the sentence as words, as objects.

statement to the effect that it lacks the predicate it asserts, or that it has the contradictory predicate. But we know it has no contradictory, no complement, given what it means. What it entails is that it is included in its complement's complement, itself, for its complement is 'not included in its complement', 'self-included.' Since it has no complement, it is an illogical statement; wrongly formed; meaningless. *Other* sentences may be included in their complements, but because *this* one has no complement, it is not a sentence, for it violates the laws of predication, the laws of abstraction. It attempts self-predication. As does the notional translation of 'This statement is true', i.e. 'This statement is included in itself.'

Notions

An observation I must make in order to clarify the asymmetry in inclusion spoken of earlier, is that positive notions seem to be included in their complements, whilst their negations (their complements) are just self-identical. Even 'Notion' (the class of classes) is not a notion; and because it isn't a notion it has no complement. If it was deemed a notion, it couldn't be a notion (it can't be self-predicated), and it wouldn't be a notion if it wasn't one. What originals could 'non-notion' come from? From such things as defied abstraction. Notions come from things susceptible to abstraction; a non-notion comes from things not susceptible to abstraction. So 'non-notion' being unabstract can't be included in 'Notion'. 'Membership' is a non-notion. The notional universe-class is derived from all nature-possessing things, and it has no complement, for the originals of the latter would be devoid of nature and unabstractable.

We see that the solution to the class and truth paradoxes is to be found in that of Cantor's paradox, namely, that they are caused by membership which turns classes into collections and allows self-membership. We de-collectivize the class by interpreting it intensionally and rejecting membership.

Going into the nature of the notion more explicitly, I can illustrate notions that are the equivalent of what under membership would be classes of arbitrary individuals, like {A, B, C,}. Now that notions are not collections the class must be the idea of A or B or C, the notion of their disjunction. We have then: {(A), (B), (C), (AB), (AC), (BC), (ABC), Ø}. A v B v C is the characterization, and arbitrary classes become unified notions.

(AC) and (AB) as sub-classes, sub-ideas, are not differentiated by greater comprehensiveness, but by variety. They are not the exact same idea. (ABC) is more ideally comprehensive than either, but it is not ideally reducible or analysable into the others; for the whole sub-class confronts us ideally: each is a thought unit but not a member of a collection. They represent stages in and parts of the process of abstraction that terminates in the notion.

Take even numbers: (2, 10) gives us an idea of even numbers; but (2, 10, 6, 8, 14) gives us a more comprehensive idea of even numbers; whilst (12, 28) merely gives us a different one from (2, 10). All the even sub-classes together with the null-class or idea, give us the final idea: Numerical Evenness. The point, to reiterate, is that notions are not collections, but an abstracted unity of sub-concepts. The idea 'dog' consists of something we do to the ideas of two, ten, two hundred dogs taken together, and not just the ideas of each individual dog. Similarly, the notion 'Flower' is the idea of ideas of flowers; the rarefied, comprehensive idea composed of, derived from, achieved through, less abstract ideas. These last are ideas of individual or groups of real flowers. The abstractions from the originals are not distinguishable into sub-ideal or non-ideal components, like members.

This theory of the 'Essence' or 'Notion' was contrived to evade specific paradoxes. But can one apply the same type of criticism to it that destroyed the member? Could one say that the property of 'sub-class' could get you into any class whatever and therefore be rejected like membership was on the grounds of lacking a nature? The reply is that essences are intensional, their meanings, whilst classes with members are extensional, their groups. Essences are so to speak 'vertical'. One starts with originals: sub-idea A, sub-idea B, sub-idea C, and so on. One gets or abstracts sub-ideas of these: {sub-ideas A,B,C,} .... etc. Then one performs a further act of abstraction and one terminates by extracting the notion: {SUB-IDEA}. Thus one only gets out of the property of 'sub-idea' what one puts in. One never gets from the property 'sub-idea' say {HORSE}, {CAT}. One only gets sub-ideality, the essence. Of course one can get from this what one can get from all essences, namely, {NOTION} (the class of classes).

Unlike essences, classes with members are extensional or *'horizontal'*, and capable, because of membership, of specific catastrophe, as was shown. The sub-ideas of the horse-notion insofar as they are *sub-ideas* can only render 'sub-ideality' as their essence. The sub-ideas of the horse-notion insofar as they are sub-ideas of original *horses*, can only render the notion {HORSE} as their essence. There can be no catastrophic sub-ideal transfer among notions, which are what they mean, and not collections. For a sub-idea to enter, be 'put into', a notion simply means for it to be abstracted, for its essence to be distilled.

I suppose one of the main lessons in my study of and arguments against membership is that extensionality, the result of membership, does not express predication, or that predication cannot be so expressed. Rejecting membership entails rejecting extensionality. So one can say that the paradoxes arise when and because predication is treated extensionally. Saying how things are is asserting membership of a class, which is asserting membership of the class of physical things.

The Null Class

The null class as a sub-class in all classes presents an intuitive problem. The null class must be the idea of nothing. Nothing is unreal. How can it be conceived? From what real original can we derive its idea? We do have the idea of nothing, though it is unreal; only the idea: mathematicians use it, for example. Doubtless it has some conceptual function. But when I contemplate the notion of 'Woman' it does not seem as if I conceive 'Nothing' as an idea it contains. But I believe that the null-class is close to the very heart of the notion. This class is crucial, for nullity expresses abstraction. I believe the null class may well appear in notions to signify the ideality and unrealness of the notion, which is after all a creation of the mind. Nullity signifies abstractness, for in the world things are not abstract. To be seen so, to be so, is to partake in nullity; and the notion is highly and quintessentially abstract, therefore in itself somehow unreal. We note that the abstraction is what it is thought to be – its meaningful content – and what it is thought to be, a concept, an essence, is divorced from particularity, and therefore from reality and solidity. Nullity is not to be seen, I think, as another sub idea, but as a feature of notionality, something that signifies an operation upon sub-ideas that makes them into a class. We think it in thinking notionally. Creatures that can think abstractly make nullity an ideal possibility. I suspect that my illustrations of notions in terms of sub-classes is only an approximation to what a notion really is like, but I have no better idea to work with at this point; it is at least familiar.

Nullity resides at the heart of the abstraction, and disciplines which contain nullity, like mathematics, thereby demonstrate their metaphysical, unreal nature.

Any notion will involve the null-class and this shows the difference and distance between the sub-ideas and the notion. Even a class derived from only one original will contain the null-idea, so the notion will be more abstract than the idea of this single original: the sub-class.

Summary

To summarize: the class or notion of say, days of the week, would be: {(Monday, Friday), (Monday, Saturday, Sunday) ....Ø}. Notions range over ideas; classes are abstractions of ideas, not collections. The class or notional calculus must be based on inclusion rather than membership. The rule for inclusion in a notion is that the sub-idea be an idea of 'real' things or originals (a wider term) with the appropriate determination. Membership, on the other hand, has it that one must be a thing with the requisite determination. To say that something has a predicate is to say that its idea is included in the relevant notion or class.

Apropos of Cantor's paradox, 'Notion' – the class of all classes – will include every sub-idea of notions. 'Notion' will have as originals all other notions. 'Notion' is what it means, and so is not another notion, is not a notion, but the essence of essences. So it means what nothing else means and does not have itself as a property; it is not self-predicated, but self-identified. It means 'Notion'. An essence partakes of essentiality, but Essence (Notion) identifies with it. The class of classes is not a class.

The Paradox of the Greatest Ordinal

The manoeuvre that solves Cantor's paradox is applicable in a special way to Burali-Forti's paradox. A contradiction is obtained when we consider the class of all ordinals, or ordinal numbers. This class, if well-ordered by the 'less than' relation has, as have all well-ordered classes, an ordinal. Now the ordinal of a class of consecutive ordinals – starting from the lowest – will be greater than every ordinal in the class. So the class of all ordinals has an ordinal that is greater than all the ordinals it contains: all ordinals. But that ordinal is itself one so it must be in the class of all ordinals, and at the same time it is not.

This paradox of the greatest ordinal shows better than any so far introduced how interpreting classes as extensions is wrong. The problem arises solely because the ordinal class is taken to be a collection with members. When membership is abandoned, well-ordering is impossible. When membership is supplanted by the sub-idea, one plainly cannot order these last into a series: they do not consist of members and the components which resemble members, the components of notions that is, the unit classes, cannot be ordered, otherwise the membership fallacy would be re-introduced in a veiled way.

Therefore the class of ordinals is not an aggregate, but an idea, the idea of Ordinality. Plainly, that essence pervades all ordinal numbers and does not exclude from the notion any ordinal at all. One could not, I suppose, envision 'ordinal number' defined in a way that is currently accepted, but the concept of ordinal number goes beyond any extensional definition of it. We can still apply them, and employ them, but remember the sub-ideas of ordinal numbers, not original ordinals themselves, are parts of the notion of ordinality.

Membership is to blame for this paradox; not only does it mean collectivizing ordinals, but it allows for belonging and not-belonging.

In the four major paradoxes examined there is the phenomenon of belonging and not-belonging simultaneously. This is plain in the class paradox. We can discern it in the truth paradox when truth is seen as membership. In Grelling's paradox, when we spell it out in extensional terms, 'heterological' means 'not self-membered' and 'autological' means 'self-membered'. In the greatest ordinal paradox we have a number that does and doesn't, or should and doesn't belong to its own class. In Cantor's paradox we have classes that should not and do belong to the class of classes.

There is even a belonging/not-belonging paradox in existence when we say such things as 'The Yeti does not exist'. A reference is made to something, so how can it not exist? In referring to it we assert its existence. This is called a referential contradiction. If we translated the paradox into the form, 'x (The Yeti) belongs and doesn't belong', we can clarify the problem. But to say 'x belongs' is fallacious in the first place; giving membership a place in our conceptual scheme is the faulty move. Reference will be more fully examined in a later chapter.

Solving the Paradoxes

My solutions to the paradoxes can be seen to be strategic and metaphysical. However, I am not doing logic, I am engaging in the metaphysics of logic by asking what a 'class' means, what 'membership' means, and solving difficulties thereby. All the paradoxes are dependent on the membership fallacy and are essentially paradoxes in class theory, even the semantic ones, the liar and Grelling's paradoxes. We need deftness to pick out how exactly the fallacy manifests itself, but the paradoxes are far from trivial: they reveal profound errors in metaphysical, logical, and semantic assumptions, not in the inferences from them. All the paradoxes studied are *reductios ad absurdum* of membership in its various domains: the world, classes, and meaning.

Central to my strategy for problem-solving is to reject membership. There will be no neat solutions within it. Membership is an impossible concept, has no nature, cannot characterize, cannot relate. This fallacious concept makes classes into collections, and allows for belonging and not belonging. In the end the difficulties can be overcome when extensionality as a means of expressing predication is rejected. I make plain what has so far only been implied: notions are only objects externally; internally they are intensions, their meanings. But with membership, classes are both internally and externally objects, and objects are the sorts of things that can be their own property, that can belong to themselves, rather than identifying internally with themselves, that can be for example 'non-green' rather than being 'non-greenness'. 'Non-green' is a property of an object, but 'non-greenness' is a concept. Objects 'fall under' concepts, and you have a collection; and when a class is an object, not a meaning, an intension, both internally and externally, it can fall under its own concept and thus belong to the collection it itself is.[26]

Existence in the Predicate Logic

Existence makes its appearance in logic in the form of the existential quantifier used in the predicate calculus. What I have said must apply to it here. Logicians hold that if someone uses the sentence 'Some animals are nocturnal' or 'Something is an animal and is nocturnal', then it can be formally translated, as can such like sentences, into 'There is something such that it is an animal and is nocturnal'. Because existence is banished from the world, from descriptions of it, and from philosophy, the progression must be wrong. 'Something is' does not mean 'There

---

[26] Therefore with membership there is no way to stop self-predication, but with intensionality one can.

is'. In the first a 'descriptive' statement is offered; in the second an existential assertion is being made. A descriptive statement says 'how' something is, whilst an existential statement says 'that' it is. Put in this way, we observe a disparity which disallows the use in predicate logic of the existential quantifier. We live in a non-existential world which, in language, can only be described. The 'is' of predication is not at all existential: its role is to introduce a physical description. The 'there is' is however existential, thus not descriptive of a qualitative world. One reason for interpreting the word 'some' as an existential quantifier is that existence is the denial of zero, or nothing, which 'some' is also. But to deny nothing need not mean affirming existence: it can be to deny existence too, as I show in the first part of this essay. Likewise, to deny something need not entail denying existence. When I attribute 'nothing' to a concept, as in 'there are no moons of Venus', I am not asserting absolute nothingness, but qualified negation. I assert at the same time that objects are otherwise; hence I assert something.

Here is an example of how we must replace 'there is' or existence in philosophy. We do not say There is a hidden dimension', but 'The universe is partly hidden', or better, 'Something is hidden'. To be 'something' is not to 'exist', and modes of being something are not 'modes of existence'. To be something is to be how something is, to have a nature. 'Nothing' is thought, wrongly of course, to have a nature: things are said of it in maths, metaphysics, indeed, in everyday speech. So supposedly having a nature, it is thought to be something, and being something it can 'belong'. Possessing a nature is surreptitiously allowed as the criterion for being 'something'.

In everyday speech, loosely, and in philosophical discourse, incorrectly, but just as a matter of convention and knowingly so, we can continue to say 'There is ...', but we must not slip into the mistake of thinking it expresses anything significant to things, to inferences, or conceptually. Definite descriptions which do not 'refer' are nevertheless not meaningless in the sentences they form part of. They are not existence claims, and are meaningful because their sentences attempt to describe the world even if they do not succeed. The attempt and its quality is what is needed for sentential meaningfulness.

Because of the likeness between the paradoxes and the concepts used in them, we have been able to arrive at the root of the existential fallacy, the indication of which is so necessary to establishing and discovering causality as a valid concept.

4

The Positive Exposition

Overview

So far I have produced three arguments against the validity of 'existence' which have attacked it through its dimensions. They are: its lack of coherence with a 'world' and necessary connection; the contradictions or paradoxes engendered by existence in a pluralistic world; and the deduction that physical things are 'how' rather than 'that' they are. Of these the last is the most important as far as is relevant to causality since it tells us what the status of physical things is exactly and provides a starting-point for our search for a viable causal theory, though in their own ways both 'world' and existential-sensitivity arguments have done this, only not in so radical and comprehensive a fashion as I propose to do in this essay. But as far as the positive definition of existence itself goes, there is a fourth and the most telling argument against it in the form of exposing the membership fallacy in its various philosophical guises.

I do not seriously doubt that a categorical statement to the effect that things in the world are not matters of fact, do not exist, even though supported by argument, will be seen as strange, if not nonsensical and blatantly counterintuitive, and maybe as self-contradictory, amounting to declaring that things are nothing. I am rather saying that 'existence', in any form, is an invalid concept.

But existence is so fundamental to our thinking both within and without philosophy that it suffers exceedingly from vagueness through having been left unquestioned to a large extent. Circularity abounds and lack of definition is blatant in the works of ontologists concerning this important concept. Philosophers tend to ask such questions as 'What exists?' and 'How does it exist; what are the forms of existence?' instead of whether the notion is at all valid, and what it means. Few define it, indeed many say that it cannot be conceptually grasped, and all assume its validity. Some, failing to find any one 'impression' or experience corresponding to it in the real world, have identified it with objects themselves.

"The idea of existence ... is the very same with the idea of what we conceive to be existent ... Whatever we conceive, we conceive to be existent. Any idea we please to form is the idea of a being; and the idea of a being is any idea we please to form."1

This leaves 'being' still mysterious: it contributes nothing more to anything and is identified with 'object', and this is plainly unsatisfactory. 'Being' fails in a descriptive function so it cannot be equal to things in so far as they are descriptive.

On what grounds though do we say that things exist? It seems a profound cultural, indeed multicultural pre-disposition, so we must engage in a preliminary investigation of its origins or causes before we can excusably launch ourselves upon the vindication of causality.

My list of the origins of existence in our thought is brief and far from comprehensive no doubt, but it should suffice as far as causality goes. The following is not intended as an argument so much as a survey. I don't want to render existence by this history anything profound, so criticism as to lack of profundity is beside the point; indeed part of the mistake is to conceive existence as profound and unquestionable.

Not putting the sources in their order of importance, we can say firstly that we make a comparison and contrast between the notions of nothing and something and deem, as I have read somewhere, that existence is the 'standing out from nothing'. If nothing is nothing, and 'nothing' is an absolute, and the imaginary

---

1 D. Hume, *op.cit.*

is not absolutely null, but a type of thing, namely an imagination, I do not see how it can meaningfully be compared or related to anything. The contrast must be imaginary and not significant to objects, to which existence, if it is genuine, must be meaningful in a physical sense. If we say 'how' a thing is we have given its full nature and have no further qualifications to make about it. We do have the idea of nothing and I doubt whether it can be more than that: ideal. In that case, existence must be purely ideal, artificial and physically insignificant.

Another contrast we make is between what is imaginary and untrue and judge the worldly things that are not so to possess a certain feature or to be of a different order which we call being real or existing. Propositions are true or untrue, so it is held, but situations are supposed to enjoy a parallel status in the world to propositions, such that they can either be or not be in the way the assertions are true or false. What I am saying is that one of the origins of existence is as a parallel to truth, only applying to situations rather than to statements.

A third source of existence as an idea is discovery. When we become aware of something, find something new, we tend to ascribe to it some sort of characterization that made or makes it discoverable. As in the previous existential origin, what has been done here is a transposition of human phenomena onto the world. Things themselves are credited with qualifications that properly speaking are only human and personal. In this case discoverability is detached from discovery to form an attribute of anything we confront or become immediately or indirectly acquainted with: Pluto was discovered; Pluto exists. Everything, though, we are acquainted with is thereby judged to have the capacity for discovery. This capacity is one of the origins of the notion of existence. Also, the re-discovery of things not immediately known is a potent source of the idea, for it strongly suggests persistence, the continuing ability to be discovered.

Furthermore there is the very important area of change, of beginning and cessation; and this is linked to Time as we confront it: past, present and future.[2] We interpret change, beginning, cessation, in an absolute way such that it is not really change at all: smoke that is dissipated, clouds that vanish. Science does not recognise this absolute treatment of change allowing only for transition, not complete cessation. Philosophers often say not that a certain state changes into or becomes another one, but that something ceases, something else begins. We see the world as a series of conjunctions, not as a development; at least empiricist philosophers tend to do so, especially in epistemology: what is not observed, as transition is not, absolutely is not. Time is how we are most commonly faced with change, and both these can be brought under the term 'process', which, as I say, is interpreted in an absolutist fashion. This is superficial and, given a wider experience of the world, counterintuitive, for we hardly think that things begin from no source. With only the evidence of our senses however we are hard put to be anything other than superficial in our judgments concerning process. Trying to be more thoughtful we conjure up 'substance' which has a permanence missing from conjunctions of states, but the permanence is featureless and absolute.

Then, and I would say, fundamentally, we have 'belonging'. Early in our intellectual history, we must have seen this as something we could say of physical things, abstract things, divine things. Not perceiving many concrete, material relations, we ascribed to things immaterial ones, the most basic of which was 'belonging'. We did not see that things 'belonged' because of their physicality, but physicality and belonging were identified, reality and existence. Belonging is not a material relationship: a chair is assigned to the class of chairs in virtue of being a chair, not because it merely 'belongs'.

Belonging became a thing in itself: it was what made things 'belongers'. It was taken as significant; but things do not 'belong' because of belonging. The spuriousness, immateriality

---

[2] This certainly is a prime source of our ideas of existence and non-existence. The latter is suggested by the past and the future, and the former by the present.

of belonging should point to the unreality of existence. The concepts were never formally identified, despite their similarities. Existence was never seen as a relation but as something positive, absolute. The connection between the concepts, the origin of existence in belonging, was tacitly understood but not admitted and only emerged in the systematic theory of classes, where belonging's fallaciousness awaited recognition and exposure.

The relativity of existence, that it operates only at 'levels' and in contexts, should have been plain from our metaphysics. This intellectual error – belonging – raised a host of conceptual problems, even absurdities. Sometimes people say that there is no level on which we can absolutely say that something does not exist. Anything has a context in which it does exist. This applies to 'possible', unactualized objects, I suppose, and perhaps even to 'impossible' ones. Any idea that leads to so many qualifications, that supports impossibilities, must be suspicious; yet it has not been suspected because it is so basic, so accepted.

Things by now seem to perform or do 'existence'; it is like an action, the most simple one. Situations 'correspond' to propositions and acquire the worldly equivalent to truth-value; are discoverable; and because we do not observe the continuity of things, the mechanisms of change, but see beginnings, cessations, and are aware of temporariness; and because we misinterpret belonging, we, from all these sources and doubtless from others, say that things 'exist', and that the concept of existence is valid and self-evident.

As far as is relevant to the study of causality, there are three 'dimensions' of existence, which do not however define the concept positively. They are: contingency – 'Whatever is may not be' – that is to say, things do not necessarily exist; that at least is the consensus among empiricist philosophers. Independence, which is partly a consequence of contingency, partly a result of its definition; the existence of one thing is completely apart and separate from that of another; there is no implication of a logical nature between one thing's existing and another either being or not being; and the lack of qualitativeness. This last does not mean that existence is not a quality, but that it lacks what is common to qualitative things: their 'howness' and describability.

The pristine definition of existence is 'membership' about which something needs to be said. When this is said of a thing, one is given the most basic information. This information is contextual, vanishing and seemingly does not carry any implication for anything else. One is really saying nothing, or one says as little as possible, therefore it sounds basic, about the thing as such. Membership is somehow separate from anything which characterizes the thing. This is of course what one wants to say or convey in asserting existence. One understands the situation when one realizes that 'is' expresses a relation, an unreal, somehow metaphysical and hypothetical one; and in the world nothing can be unreal.

The 'is' becomes fused into the adjectival thing, bringing with it these three qualifications or dimensions, and we call the thing a 'fact.' Where the 'is' is not just fused but completely identified with the thing we get a 'being'.

But we are still left with the inability of the 'is' to cohere with the qualitative nature of the thing which breaks the fact apart and leaves it open to destructive criticism. For instance, in my use of the cube analogy we can point out that the volume in a way 'has' surfaces, a set of boundaries; surface and volume are after all spatial; but shall we say that the qualitative thing is the qualitative aspect of the thing's existence? Existence is not in any way qualitative. Not so much that it does not 'add' to the thing as that it completely fails to be descriptive, and things are descriptive complexes if anything. So it cannot expand or in any way contribute to the physical thing. We beg the question when we look for what cannot be there, when we try to discover existence as something physically significant, but finding no special existential property or archetype, identify the thing with its existence. One option surely would be to say that existence has no grounds in reality.

In addition, fusing belonging and the characteristic thing is the source of the error of identifying existence with reality: and owing to the vacuity of belonging, this is made easy. Reality means physicality, here qualitativity, and existence means immaterial membership, a pseudo-relation.

Qualitative blankness is important in this study of existence in relation to causality, and so is existential contingency. Indeed, because worldly things are judged to be matters of fact they are deemed contingent. But why should existence be thought of as contingent when ascribed to things?

One reason – and I am sure there are others – is that it is said the contradictory of any statement of a matter of fact is conceivable, hence not self-contradictory; so it is possible that things be other than they are. They do not have to be. But maybe a different kind of necessity operates in the world; non-logical natural necessity. This prevents us from properly applying logical criteria, and as the world consists supposedly of facts, facts are deemed alogical. If we are not aware of this non-logical necessity but judge logical necessity as the only kind, then the alogicality means complete lack of necessitation amongst the factual.

A source of existence has been suggested as discovery, and the discovery of things in the world, the world of facts, is not in the end a matter of conceptual demonstration. Therefore discovery is not something that lies wholly within the scope of a priori reasoning, and consequently existence is outside its scope. What lies beyond conceptual deductive reasoning is judged finally to be contingent.

Many philosophers in ancient times and modern, deplored the fleetingness, perishability of the things in the world. For those seeking certainty and 'truth', perishability, inexplicability, change and existential fleetingness, seemed to belong to the natural order of things. So the things in the world were seen as beyond desirable, static certainty, hence necessity. For those who believed in a Creator, existence was his property, even, if you like, his whim. Anyway it was grounded in an ultimate freedom; it was a gift that could be easily withdrawn.

But behind all the reasons I suspect lies a subconscious recognition that existence is flimsy and vapid as a concept. The nature of membership seen detached, as a thing in itself, is that it should be inherently unexplainable, mysterious. What makes for belonging if this last is a self-sufficient concept, if it is divorced from its association with materiality? If membership is the rule for membership, then existence is self-contained, self-regulated. A thing exists just because it exists; nothing external seems to impinge upon it, to force or compel it. On the other hand, as existence sank deeper and deeper into our intellectual scheme, it obtained such 'profundity', perhaps more than any other concept, that it became simply beyond explanation, even beyond analysis.

And as I have said, in the end the very definition of existence with its naturelessness excludes it from attributive and predicative status; this means it is always outside nature, it is never within the nature of a thing, and is thus contingent.

What arguments have we against contingency without disproving existence? For one we can cite the results of the world argument. By this we learn that the nature of one thing or event is linked to or determined by that of another. Therefore things' natures, their behaviours, are not contingent. In showing this we reason that things do not exist. Manners of togetherness are necessary and there is even a physical, non-logical sort of necessity which operates against the supposition of a worldly contingency. Our inability to perceive a natural necessity is one of the strongest reasons we have for existential contingency.

In addition to this, from the paradoxes of existence we derive examples of things' existential responding, mutual significance, lack of independence, and control. Using existence and non-coincidence together, we arrive at the conclusion that some kind of existential change is compelled on objects which are on a collision-course. This is but an instance of relevance among several existing things, such that contingency of being cannot be maintained. These arguments are parts of antinomies though; they go against the orthodoxy and there are perhaps good contrary arguments. These contradictory theses do not have the purpose of establishing themselves one over the other in particular, but of providing good reasons for rejecting existence. One can, depending on cogency, accept any of the paradoxical arguments though.

Accompanying the relevant dimensions and the pure definition of existence are counterarguments to their applicability to things in the world. The existence-relevance and world arguments deal with independence; the first section of the existential fallacy argument handles lack of qualitativity; relevance and world arguments again, apply to contingency. The argument against existence as it is purely defined is recognizing the membership fallacy, which includes studies of logical paradoxes raised by membership. Arguments against membership as such are arguments against the dimensions of existence. In case these 'dimensions' are thought to confer a nature on existence, we only have to notice their negativeness which is generated by membership's own nullity: lack of qualitativity, lack of necessity, independence.

Qualitativity

Existence then is rejected, but it is also replaced by the concept of 'Howness'. We say what things are not and what they are. The reasons for holding things to be universally 'how' they are are principally empirical. This means that they are partly intuitive and self-evident as far as ordinary objects go, and hypothetical as far as scientific objects go. Colours, sounds, tastes, smells, feelings, the categories into which immediate worldly objects fall, as well as shapes, motions and dimensions, are all qualitative. Scientific objects, products of theories, but sometimes things which feature scientifically and which we know directly, are all, even when quantitatively treated, qualitative: chemical structures, particles, fields, life, to name a few of them. Existence hardly features in scientific discourse, except in disciplines like cosmology where the distinctions between philosophy and science are sometimes blurred; certainly not the existence qualified by such concepts as contingency. There are fewer metaphysical puzzles and self-contradictions when we omit existence and substitute howness. The concepts we bring the physical world under are more compact, neater, less conducive to chaos, and not impenetrable. We are all acquainted with the qualitative world, but existence is an inferential leap which only habit promotes to self-evidence: a hypothesis, not an intuition; interpretation at best and far from physical. I do not register a fire as a 'fact' but as a qualitative nature, a sort of thing. If only we had kept to this primitive way of recognition and classification and had not invented existence, philosophy would be healthier and less full of confusing, redundant elements. But now, to recognize again the howness of natural events, though not so very unnatural, is momentous after centuries of error.

The vocabulary used to describe worldly objects or things needs alteration, so it seems, if existence is to depart, and at this point I introduce several new terms to achieve this.

New nouns, 'descriptives' and 'qualitatives' – not 'qualities' – 'situations' and 'matters of quality', 'characters', will be used. And I will continue to employ such words as 'events' and 'objects'. Qualitatives do not coincide exclusively with objects in the world of non-existence: sometimes they are events, sometimes they are forces, attributes and relationships. They are the stuff of the descriptive world, but are not always particulate. It is my most general term. The notion of the 'qualitative' is equivalent to that of the 'how', which I hope is a suggestive word I sometimes will employ. I apply it to a thing the very essence of which is to be a nature, and which is completely so both conceptually and materially. I hope to show that all the important conceptual categories of the world are only howness in various guises. Using adjectives as nouns may be off-putting, but it is, I think, justified, suggestive, and indeed exact.

Qualitatives are not qualities, neither are they 'things' with qualities, but represent rather a coalescing of the levels of thing and quality. Qualitatives are not, as some would have the quality, universals, but as qualitatives they have an unbounded, unlimited aspect, an inseparable dimension of themselves. From this emerges a real ability to operate at a universal level. How they are, their characteristic nature, is replicable in the way that, say, a vowel 'e' may be replicated in words, by itself, in sentences, in texts. The 'universality' of the qualitative resides in this inherent ability to cross instances, to transcend boundaries of particularity, to be repeated. The shape of 'e' can be repeated, the colour of a blade of grass can be re-instanced, a molecular structure can be shared and replicated. This dimension or feature of the qualitative I call its 'non-particularity'. It is natural to qualitatives and comprises most of any qualitative. Hence emerges its universality, not by magic but as an inherent trait of anything that has or is a nature, that is 'how' it is. I do not invent this feature, but I perceive it, and it is the origin of universality. But qualitatives are particular too in a qualitative way. What this means is that the individuality of an object is characteristic and that no two items can ever be exactly alike in terms of their natures. Thus the replicability of qualitatives is mitigated and only ever approximate, though quite close and they do not discernibly differ at certain levels. The difference, however minute, is real though. A shade of sky-blue can be repeated in purely colouristic terms, but its particular manifestation makes for tiny dissimilarities; its particularity is expressed by these differences. An electron flying around a nucleus may be indistinguishable from another one, but the atoms are differently spatially related and participate in systems that are macroscopically quite individual.

Difference and sameness are qualitatively expressed and originated in the qualitative, and the latter has a universality alongside its particularity. The qualitative is never just particular, it is at the same time non-particular. The two aspects are never isolated from each other, in Nature, but only as a convenience for abstract thought can this be done. That this is artificial must never be lost sight of. There are no separate formal dimensions, there are only qualitatives of colour or of sound, and so forth, things that are their characteristic natures and non-particularities. These non-particularities are neither abstract nor manifestations of things in a transcendent realm. The universality of any qualitative is natural. Howness then mitigates the particularity of the 'how'.

To re-iterate, for this is important to my theory: that which can be replicated in a thing we call its non-particular aspect. Examples are: colours, motions, molecular and atomic configurations. This ability to fall into sorts is native to anything that has a nature. Anyone can test these contentions by reflection and it involves nothing fantastic. Observation and reflection therefrom will give any one the recognition that replicability is natural to that which is qualitative, which is 'how' it is. This replicability and lack of confinement to the particular is universality's source. I can offer two less intuitive but more philosophically convincing reasons for this claim. One, the phenomenon of qualitative sameness which operates beyond the limitations of simple particularity shows that the qualitative innately has a non-particular aspect. Two, the thesis that the non-existential, natural thing possesses an anti- particular, unbounded dimension, can be confirmed by recognizing that since the world is not a collection of individual existents, as was maintained by the membership fallacy, objects or natures are not purely particular, not entirely individual. Positively: if the world is a system of internal relations, the nature of anything involves everything in the universe; so each thing's nature possesses a universal aspect. 'Matters of quality' is a suggestive term and shall be specifically contrasted with 'matters of fact'. 'Situations' will also be used to counter the effects of particulate-sounding nouns like 'objects'. A leaf is a qualitative or a descriptive. The collision of two material objects like that of a bat and a ball, is a matter of quality and also a situation. Characters and descriptives do not 'inhere' in anything not characteristic or descriptival, but are fully-fledged objects like a loaf of bread or a mountain.

These nouns apply as well to every scientific event and object and are not just applicable to immediate, evident things. They even apply to the connections between things that are hidden from our senses.

I make these stipulations not out of nothing and nowhere but on the firm basis of my argued position that things are 'how' rather than 'that' they are. And all I am saying is that things are solely their natures, and not an amalgam of existence and nature.

Qualitatives, when fused into a complex of them, can still be called attributes or properties, even qualities, so long as the latter do not suppose a non-attributive 'thing' that they inhere in. Part of the historical reason for this was that membership required that there should be a substance for properties to be embedded in. 'Substance' was a name for the pure being, the membership of an object. Another reason, again springing from membership, was that to be an attribute or property of something was to 'belong' to it, not to be it, or be how it was. So things are in the fullest sense how they are, generally and individually. The account given of such physical things I call 'physical descriptions'.

The 'How' of Change

An historical interpretation cannot represent or describe a physical event because it cannot be a physical description entirely. By 'historical' I mean an account which includes existential elements or which is in its entirety factual. For instance, descriptions which relate the parts of any event as just existentially conjoined, juxtaposed or following after one another, which see events as 'that' they occurred, are historical. The theory of causality, or maybe the lack of one, which results from them cannot be applicable to a physical event or a physical world. This comes out of rejecting existence and asserting the characteristic nature of the physical and it will topple down many of the results of scepticism. The existence, the matter of factness, to which scepticism reduced so much is itself seen as being a misapprehension. As if seemingly checkmated we have added a few more moves to the rules of chess and ourselves mated the opponent's king. Historicity is discarded from our thinking and things are conceived as 'how' they are. When events are so described, the area of worldly happenings to which the concept of causality applies emerges naturally and necessarily.

When considering the notion of causal interaction we cannot express it as a factual, existential conjunction. Because one has to say 'how' physical change or transformation takes place, causality is a necessary feature of our concept of Nature. What one gives is a dynamic and exclusively physical description without tincture of facthood of a change of state or situation. The descriptive replacement of the factual transformation does not say 'it happens' but 'how it happens'. That is, the event is seen as a completely physical process instead of a conjunction of states which begin, last for a while, then cease. Causality emerges then as a conception of Nature in a wholly descriptive and physical manner. It is a province of the concept of descriptivity and philosophy has hitherto failed to provide the foundations for physical descriptions of Nature. The most profound arguments of causal scepticism are answered by regarding Nature as totally physical.

Causality is behavioural howness. The narrative of events cannot consist of mere conjunctions in space and time or in beginning and cessation: that is factual. Physical descriptions must express a wholly physical continuity because to dissever event from event is to render Nature existential. For collections imply members. The descriptive world has to be continuous and without existential disjunctions. Why precisely?

If the world is complex and the parts of it do not necessarily hang together, it would only be a matter of fact that they do. Also, if they do not necessarily hang together in the manners that they do, in their qualitative modes of association, they again would only be factually associated in those ways: it would be a merely contingent matter of brute fact. Indeed, one can say that a world of facts would be one in which no complexity was possible.

Since however the descriptive world is not existential, no existential elements can be in it or in correct accounts of it: events cannot be distinct existences; so the descriptive world is, as is the world of the world argument, necessarily connected and physically continuous. Continuity, necessary connectedness, applies to events both spatially and temporally. But this argument that separability brings fact into a non-factual world is negative. Positively, we can safely say that the idea of immaterial gaps between physical things in a completely physical world goes against a thoroughgoing worldly physicality, since those gaps would be non-physical. There are also relations between physical things, even if we conceive of those things as merely conjoined, and relationships in such a world as we consider must, like everything else, be qualitative; therefore these relations would be physical, real and not immaterial, therefore significant to the things related and involved. So the world is physically continuous, not a mass of distinct elements.

Remembering the discoveries made in examining the membership fallacy in the last essay, we can say that since membership makes for seeing things like classes as collections, because members are apart, isolated, the universe, without membership in the form of existence, should cease to be regarded as a collection, a plurality of individuals, and consequently seen as a genuine unity or system.

If there is no existence, there is no coming into existence, and events cannot just occur without origin or source and relations between them have to be relations of quality. Evolution and transformation are the rule, and transformation is a seamless physical expression of how a situation changes, how events take place or the manner in which they are constructed, which now because lifted out of the stream of historicity, becomes released from contingency. We replace the idea of material implication by the more precise and relevant notion of the loss and gain of properties in a system of qualitatives. We conceive alteration in this way.

Because qualitatives cannot come into 'existence' out of nothing, materialize from nowhere, they must come or be acquired from a source, that is, from something qualitative. This acquisition is a process or mechanism by definition, a qualitative change of properties. In the descriptive world, change does not just 'happen' existentially, but, because situations cannot 'be' then cease to be as in the factual explication of alteration, it must be a development in which properties are originated from a source which neither is nor is not, and are assumed into another given situation, altering it by their qualitative addition. We have to say 'how', in what manner, such is materially succeeded by such, such is acquired from a given source, how the components of a situation are gained or are lost; how change takes place in a manner not inclusive of brute fact or coming into existence, and this can only be in terms of material process.

A causal process can be seen, in one way, as the nature of the acquisition of new properties by a situation, and the origin of such properties is a 'cause'. And because we need to explain – and there are explanations – how transformations operate and are constructed, what the structure of any given physical state of affairs is, its mechanisms, the justification of the practice of the scientist and the beliefs of the layman is found: their 'causality' is part of their attempt to describe the world and is not a superstition. The dynamic physical description is a way of translating the concept of cause and effect.

Description is the term that explanation comes under. To describe, say how an event, a change is dynamically organized is the same as to give a reason for it, to say 'why' it happens as it does. The change, seen as a descriptive thing, renders our instinctive idea of cause: a connected, material, mechanical process, not an accidental succession of states which endure then cease.

Behaviour is a whole, a material whole, in the world of descriptives where factual conjunction is eliminated. The replacement for temporal succession of states with no real connection is a physically joined continuum, a connected flow or unity in which each link in the behavioural series emanates from, comes from, part following part physically, what precedes, for nothing begins anew or absolutely terminates. Such a dynamic whole contains the concept of implication. And since change of state is no longer factual, it is not contingent; and change is mechanistic and material.

The requirement to describe Nature as how it is means that situations of all sorts do not happen in isolation. If we have to describe the Earth's orbiting the Sun we do not simply state it as a fact, that the situation exists, but have to say how it physically does so, in what material manner, the way in which this is done;

and this is to give a reason and explanation. We do not associate
Sun and Earth as a matter of fact, but as a matter of quality,
that is, concretely. In doing this we uncover causal connection,
which is the organization of united, continuous events; events
constructed and unified temporally. Cause is the 'how' of change.
By describing connected events physically and non-contingently,
we say 'why' they happen, we give 'reasons' for them. 'Reasons'
imply mechanisms, explanations. The process of the Earth
orbiting the Sun is qualitative and the process's qualitative
constitution is the cause or reason for it. Orbiting is also dynamic,
a change, so cause will enter the account of it.

The reason for reasons for events is, to summarize, that we do
not say 'that' as a matter of fact something follows, changes into
or is associated with something, but 'how' something follows,
changes into or is associated with something. The very following
or association of situation and situation has a character itself
which is susceptible to description. How something rather than
that something occurs or arises, how change is, not that change
is, are what we recognize. I ask, when I enquire about the coming
about of an event, not how the event is, not about the nature of the
event, but about the nature of the coming about, the arising, of
the event. Saying how the coming about of the event is is saying
that the coming about is physical, a causal process. Expressed in
terms of change, we do not say that A, then B, but how A then B.
Not that B arises, but how B arises. Because the occurrence of an
event – and situations are not permanent, they do 'come about' –
is a matter of quality, has a nature, it is natural and legitimate to
see the world causally.

Succession and following are physical, concrete in a descriptive
world Succession is an aspect of connection, continuity, which
is a type of mechanical, dynamic, material, qualitative linkage.
There can be no ultimate separation. There has to be flow, contact,
and this material flux has been called 'cause and effect'. These
terms are not to be insisted upon in this theory: continuity and
process, not causes and effects, are what we envision, and causes
and effects are simply distorted interpretations of physical flux.

The wider heading succession comes under is 'association'. We have to say as for succession, how things physically organize themselves, how in the broadest sense they come together. In explaining change we are forced to associate things. To say 'how' in the physical sphere, to repeat, is to say 'why', which is to explain. Explanation is description of a situation's organization. Why it gets hotter as the sun gets higher in the sky is the same as describing how this physically happens. Every event is a process, or a part of one, and so is 'causal', for we see that the concept of physical, qualitative process is that of cause.

Descriptive Necessity

Are these associations found in the descriptive world necessary? The answer is yes.

This answer comes from the implications of howness for necessity. In the world of qualitatives, and its metaphysics, everything becomes qualitative. When one speaks of the particular thing one must realize that its identity what it is particularly, equates to nothing beyond or other than and exclusively to its special mode of howness, its particular nature. 'The individual thing' is its individual nature.

And when a thing is nothing other than its nature, as in the world and metaphysics of qualitativity, it is impossible that it be any other way than that which it specifically is. A nature cannot be other than how it specially is any more than the colour green can be other than green, or the shape of the letter L can be other than that shape. Now this is not trivial, and must not be seen as a tautology. For there are conditions under which a nature can be different to what it is, could have been different, namely when that nature exists. This is the situation in which a nature is contingent. If a thing s nature exists we can say: It might not have been that way, it could have been otherwise, i.e. a tree might have had a different shape or had leaves of a different colour. As we have seen in the world of existence, if things do not have to exist, they do not have to exist in the ways they do. If existence is not within the natures of things, not only are their existences contingent, but none of their properties have to exist. Red could have existed instead of green, but in its nature red could not have been green or anything else, on the other hand. When a nature exists, objects are not natures any longer, but existences, and relative to those existences, attributes are accidental. In the existential metaphysic the criterion of necessity is the necessity to exist. By this standard existent natures are contingent. Thus the necessity for natures to be as they are is not tautological but metaphysical.

Since then pure natures untainted by existing cannot be other than how they specifically are, that is enough for us to say that these are necessary, for we now come to the principle of necessity as it is affected by the qualitativity of the world and the things in it. If things do not any longer exist, necessity cannot be the necessity to be, but, in the descriptive world, the necessity to be how one is. Because qualitatives of every sort – situations, descriptives, objects – have to be how they are, they are necessary. And this applies to causal processes and relations.

When I gave the exact example, not an analogy, of the letter L, I must not be construed as saying that it is the concept of its shape which is necessary, but that each individual letter L on this page, being by nature its particular mode of execution, could not but be that mode of execution. Each is necessary; they cannot be otherwise. We should subtract the 'it' and ask, 'Could this howness be other than this howness?' Since the answer is no, this howness is therefore necessary.

To re-emphasise the two foregoing important points: necessity in the qualitative metaphysics is not if a thing has to be, but if a thing has to be how it is. A qualitative, being a nature, must be its nature. Hence it is necessary.

We must avoid the tendency to say that a qualitative is just as a matter of inexplicable fact how it is, because of the necessity associated with it.

Thus we have seen and we have two instances of the way descriptivity envelops the concepts we apply to the world: if one is asked for the reason, explanation, cause of something, one replies: 'This is how it is'. If one asks 'Is that necessary?' one replies: 'Yes, that is how it is.' Causality and Necessity, as are other concepts, are aspects of howness.

For one event to precede another is for that event to physically 'cause' it, for 'precedence' must be seen in a physical, qualitative light. For one event to physically 'follow' another is for the first to be caused by the other, to come from it. Just as in an inference one stage of argument 'leads to' another, in the world a given event 'leads to' another event, but concretely. Understanding the ideas of wholly physical precedence and succession may be difficult without the temporal aspect, which seems to take all potency out of them; all that must be done is to recognize the complete qualitativity of these notions and they become suggestive of implication.

In wider terms, since the cause of any change is to be found in the descriptive organization of it in its surroundings, causality, the reason for reasons for events, is descriptivity as a concept applied to a changing world. We do not need the ideas of 'force', 'power' and 'agency', and we do not say 'because'; we say 'How': 'the manner in which'. Causality is qualitative evolution.

Scientists say that the equations of physics 'merely' describe the universe, but do not say why it should be so. This reinforces my opinion: description is sufficient and natural for the physical world, which is a system of descriptives, a descriptival system. Commonly, the interrogative 'Why?' assumes an existential metaphysics: Why does it exist? But qualitatively the only possible questions to be asked of nature are characteristic ones: How is it like? How did it happen? One cannot ask questions of existence; one 'merely' describes objects, situations, in the same way as one does not ask existential questions of geometrical figures; describing them is enough, saying how they are. And doing the latter is saying how they have to be.

Causality is, in the widest sense, the world conceived as how it is. A cause or causal process is simply how something happens or how things are related. Causality is howness applied to change, to relation or to association of situations.

But since we do not see how things follow each other materially, that is, the precise mechanisms of change, we deduce another, hidden dimension which is science's task to make inferences about. The necessity to say 'how' entails science, but science also needs the basis of natural uniformity, and the results so far obtained will be of use in this case.

Induction

Take the example of a quantity of salt dissolving in water. An historical account of this event will emphasise its lack of necessity: it just happens. The event's singularity as providing no clues as to what will happen in the future will be stressed; it will be seen as essentially particular. The various parts of the process will be distinguished and separated from each other, there will be no necessary physical links between them, and the precise moment of the event will be important to the description. Though it will have no causal implications for it, the moment will be part of the nature of the occurrence historically seen.

All this has to be omitted from a physical description; the event cannot be seen as a fact and divided into independent, contingent, existential bits. These items are associated as descriptives, salt and water that is, and the event therefore contains a non-particular dimension. This is so, to remind you, because the inherent nature of qualitatives is that they should partly transcend limitation to singular individual instances. The descriptive's replicable nature means that it is characteristically unbounded, and what holds for any qualitative is an unlimited necessity. In terms of its non-particularity, the dimension of the qualitative open to replication, which is most of it, we can say 'All A is B': all salt dissolves in water. As a whole the event is necessary, so in its non-particular dimension, it is necessary as well.

The event is necessary and generalizable on account of its non-particularity. But we cannot be certain that we have given a complete description and that the generalization as formulated holds. There may be factors of importance which we will proceed to investigate. Do we know however that whatever the nature of the event it is necessary for all future and past occasions in which the same types of items are involved? Might there not be considerations which mitigate the universality of non-particular natural necessities? What if the special times, locations and occurrences of events were to enter the physical description as qualitative ingredients? This would effectively make each event no guide as to the behaviour of any other, would introduce into the world a predictive chaos in which behaviour, though necessary, was not uniform. Is this possible?

As I have said previously, distinct times, places, events, can only enter the description so long as they are qualitative. Take 'events': the distinctness that pertains to these is of how they are, what sorts of things they are, and if events are distinguished and identified as only being different instances of occurrences, numerically distinct as in a collection of members, not as characters of occurrences, then these occurrences cannot enter the physical description being only blankly and not characteristically distinct.

The same may be said of times and places: time and space are qualitatives of extension and as such may enter a descriptive formula; but when particular instants which are in no qualitative way different, but only blankly identified, are brought into a proposition of quality they are there under false pretences. They do not describe. There are no 'landmarks' in spatio-temporal dimensions. Particular events, times, places, then cannot qualify how behaviours are unless they make descriptive contributions to them. The old problem of the uniformity of Nature arises when instants in time are allowed to bear upon the events which happen in the dimension of which they are arbitrary distinctions. Time does not consist so much in singular instants so distinguished, but in the quality that these instants commonly possess: the kind of extension. The essentially temporal element in time is the quality of extension, the qualitative nature of the extension, not the distinction between one moment and another. That kind of distinction stands outside the qualitativity of time. And it is not time as a qualitative of dimension, but times as separate, blankly distinct occurrences of the same kind of qualitative that is of concern here. Suppose we have two items that are exactly alike in terms of character; what distinguishes them except their non-qualitative, numerical distinctness or identity? Plainly this is the kind of distinction and uniqueness offered by those who would enter temporal, spatial or instantial dissimilarity into the physical description in the hope of confounding natural uniformity. Just because such uniquenesses are not qualitative they are of no account in the physical formula.

A general point that may be gleaned from the membership fallacy is that it is an error to see the world or anything in it as a collection. This happens when times and places are judged real to physical events and descriptions: time and space are not collections of times and places, but are each of them brought under a universalizing principle.

A feature of the qualitative is that it possesses an aspect which is unlimited and transcends particularity. This aspect I call its non-particularity. Particular instances, times, places, used in 'physical' descriptions do not possess this ability and feature, thus are not capable of comprising genuine qualitative descriptions.

Suppose we postulate a law which demands that after a certain quantity of time t, y obtains in the world and during that quantity of time, x holds. Is this a legitimate description that could be made of a physical universe? For several good reasons the answer is no.

If one makes the above move one is really saying 'During this time, x is the case, and during that time, y is the case.' Particular stretches of time are being selected to enter the physical description just as if particular instants, only longer were picked out. Time is not included in the description solely as a quality of extension, but as locations in it, that is, a characterless distinctness is offered; and time is seen as a 'collection' of two distinct times in respect of this law.

But there is a less negative reason why such a 'law' could not validly enter a physical formula.

Physical formulas include time as a qualitative or character, and this is the case even when time is being quantitatively qualified, as in most scientific formulas. What then holds for any duration holds for all of them because the qualitative of time as a kind of extension is what is signified in the description, even if quantitatively. Just as for other qualitatives represented in descriptions, temporal ones must be partly universal, which the supposed 'law' is not. Descriptives, to repeat, must have a universality alongside their particularity: they are not solely particular. All times share in temporality, so temporal laws must be applicable to all times. The 'law' fails to observe this necessary requirement.

'Bent' Predicates

There is a problem relevant to special times raised by the logico-linguistic philosophy; it concerns a fictional predicate called 'grue' which emeralds could have. It means that emeralds are 'grue' if they are 'green before the year 2050 A.D. and blue thereafter'. To avoid sounding too contemporary I call this kind of attribute a 'time-element' or a 'locational' attribute.[3]

Let me say to begin with that there could never be any justification whatsoever for giving such things as emeralds locational attributes, and the possibility of such a nightmare for induction does not arise, for grue is meant to be an equally valid predicate for emeralds as green given the evidence, and our choice of inductive practices would be unlimited, making our present ones almost without any special recommendation.[4]

Locational predicates are supported by no evidence whatever and are empty speculations without any empirical basis. I should think that we can only give things attributes if we have evidence

---

[3] There are five authors I have consulted mainly on this problem: N. Goodman, *Fact, Fiction and Forecast*. S. Blackburn, *Spreading the Word*. R. Sainsbury, *Paradoxes*. N. Swartz, *The Concept of Physical Law*. J. Dancy, *Contemporary Epistemology*.
I have changed the time reference in the definition of 'grue' from 2020 A.D. to 2050 A.D. – i.e. a time later than the time of observation.

[4] The point is that anything can be made to seem lawlike, even predicates which, depending on our imagination in inventing them, appear chaotic.

for them. For grue and other attributes are of their nature such as will never be observed. A predicate with a time-element is effectively never evidenced and remains in the realm of pure speculation for ever. As such, no inductive practice could be based upon something for which there is utterly no reason; and that is what evidence is: empirical reason.

To attribute some predicate for which there can never be empirical reason when that to which the attribute pertains is entirely empirical, is irrational in every sense. And induction is meant to be a form of rational inference.

Why do I say that attributes like grue can never be evidential? The reason is not even epistemological but logical. 'Grue' and others like it irreducibly contain a mention of tense or a time-element. This means that finally grue is not a colour. Also attributes like grue are meant to represent a state, something static and unchanging. An emerald is grue before and after the colour change and the date. It doesn't become grue, it is always grue and does not cease being so. This is emphasized by giving the predicate one name. Both these considerations expose the impossibility of grue as an inductive predicate. As all of grue, that is, 'green before t and blue after t', is an attribute of emeralds now, at one and the same time, and as the past and the future are precisely not happening now, the predicate grue would allow non-present elements to be actually at present attributed to emeralds. I can say at present 'I walked'; I can say at present 'I will walk'; but I cannot say 'At present I was walking' or 'At present I will walk'. Mutually exclusive tenses appear in the predication; one cannot locate the future or the past in the present; or expressed in another way, 'grue' asserts 'earlier it is blue later'.

You see, just because grue is not essentially chromatic it can be treated so. One might think that two exclusive colours could not at the same time be attributed to one object, but grue is not a colour, it is a time-location attribute, and therefore the whole predicate can be attributed en bloc and continuously or at any one time like a genuine colour predicate such as green. One does not approach grue as one would a real colour, saying 'x is green before this time' and 'x is blue after this time', for one does not describe a change since the essential part of the above is the 'this time', not the colour components. The 'this time' does not alter, is constant. What one is doing is like, seeing a door, one time open, another time shut, giving it the predicate 'open-shut'. Of course, one cannot leave these incompatibles as they stand, so one inserts the unifying time-element, thereby transforming the predicate from something about two states to something about one. Only now, whereas the incompatible states required separation, because the new predicate isn't about those states, but about a given time, this time, being a constant, is not divisible, separable, but one. So the predicate is a unit, not a conjunction. If the predicate was about the states of the door, it would be a conjunction; but being a time-element predicate, it essentially is not.

'Grue' then can never be evidenced nor conceptually and physically possible. We must remember that at any point in time the emerald will be 'grue' and that does not solely mean 'green before t', but 'blue after t' as well. In the year 2051 A.D. emeralds would still be green before 2050 A.D., and that attribute is still concretely applied to it even after the change. Grue is static. Part of its present state is not present: a contradiction. We must remember what 'grue' means, not just what part of it means, and that all of grue is predicated of emeralds all the time.

That grue is static may be shown thus: 'Evidence' for an attribute concerns, not so much the emerald or emeralds, but us, our beliefs. What grue or green are concerns exclusively, objectively and absolutely emeralds themselves, not us however. We must finally translate predicates into properties in the real world. Grue and Green are in objective, non-evidential terms mutually exclusive: something cannot be both at the same time. But we, so it is held, can think that a thing may be one or the other and not be mistaken as far as 'evidence' goes. That grue and green are in actuality mutually exclusive can be seen if one allows, as one must, the statement 'all emeralds are grue', or even 'this emerald is grue', to carry the implication that if emerald x is examined after t, it is blue, and if it had been examined before t, it would have been green. Therefore a grue object is *actually* green before t and blue after t. But can something that is grue be satisfactorily characterized by being 'green before t' alone? No, because being green before t carries no implication that it won't be green after t, therefore that it is grue. So green before t is not a sufficient characterization of grue. Now an object that is green is green before t, assuming t to be some time in the future, even if it changes after t. But since green before t is not a sufficient characterization of grue, green and grue are mutually exclusive even before t. They are at no time the same. Grue is the sum of its parts, not part of the whole. A green thing may be green before t, but it will never be blue since the colours are incompatible. Since grueness necessarily requires blueness, and greenness of its nature rejects it, the properties of their natures exclude each other. When something is green before t, or another is blue after t, they are not grue, for both parts are necessary for grueness. Essentially, Grue is compound. Green and Blue are not complex at any time. So grue is never *just* green or *just* blue. The difference is not merely complexity versus simplicity, but the incompatibility of blue and green; but both are necessary for grue. Green , and Blue are homogeneous and uncompound; grue is not homogeneous and compound.

Being just green differs from being grue; being green before t does not differ from being just green; so being grue differs from being green before t. The world is such that anything that is just green is green at a certain time: before t, after t, *at* t. So there is no difference between being 'just green' and being green before t. Similarly for blue.

What is grue? Not only is it what a thing is at a certain time, but also how a thing will be or was, at one and the same time.

Grue is not just green now, but blue later, and because grueness excludes greenness, it excludes it *all* the time, in objective, if not in supposedly evidential terms. Therefore at any given time an object called grue is never just the colour it is then – if it is *just* the colour it was then it would be not be *grue* owing to the uncomplex and homogeneous nature of those colours – but is different from green or blue by that which makes grue different: the reference to time; and this means it differs by referring to the colour it will be or was. Words 'refer'; qualities are how they are. It differs by being how it will be or was. Thus all of grue is predicated at one and the same time and grueness is static. The impossibility of the present and the non-present cohabiting, means the logical exclusion of grue, such that evidence for it is never to be had. It may be 'true' now that I did something earlier, say, went to bed, but it can't be a *property* of me now that I went to bed earlier. Because grue is static it is more than the colour it is at any one time. No inconsistency is made in the earlier paragraphs where I accept the grue predicate as defined by others. From that I derive its non-chromatic nature, its staticness. I do not assume these last. Any property that is more than the colour it is at any given time is not really a colour property.

Another reason for saying that grue and green are mutually exclusive and that the former doesn't change, is that if a grue emerald is green before t in a way quite compatible with being simply green, and someone holds that after t it will be blue, upon what does he base his prediction of a colour change? Is it quite arbitrary? I do not suppose so, for part of the difficulty of the paradox is that it is rational to project a colour change, given the evidence. What the prediction is based on is that before t (and consequently after t) the emerald is grue rather than just simply green (or just simply blue) So grue is a property that does not change and is something over and above the given colour at any one time. And this is illogical. An unfounded prediction would be irrational. Projecting green after t is predicting green before t won't change colour, based on the belief that it is not grue, but green Even before t there is mutual exclusion between green and grue.

Suppose you tried to attack green in the way grue was attacked. Suppose 'grue' and a new predicate 'bleen' ('blue before t, green after t') was invoked to express green such that the latter becomes a time-attribute, being 'grue before t bleen after t'. The time-attributive 'green' is in the same position as the formerly

time-attributive grue, but with the difference that grue and bleen
are primitive in the way that green and blue are usually. 'Green'
excludes grue and bleen, all the time, so it is the 'colour' it will
be or was namely, either grue or bleen. Therefore it is, as grue
was judged, static, and the illogicality entailed by that situation
invalidates it as a property, as grue in conventional terms was.
So the tables it appears have been turned when green is treated
positionally, as grue was.

There is a difference though. In the case where 'green' is taken
as 'grue before t, bleen after t', we observe that this is not the
only way of characterizing 'green'. For there is no phenomenal
difference in an emerald that is grue before t and bleen afterwards.
So there is no need to posit a change, since doing so, making
green a conjuction of other properties results in an illogicality.
Green is neither a change, nor is it a conjunction, and this evades
the difficulty of bringing the non- present into the present, of
violating temporal rules. Green is static, essentially non-temporal.
The same cannot be said of or done for 'grue'. The latter has
a definite phenomenal disjunction and the preceding argument
against grue's logicality stands. There is a non-temporal way
of expressing green; there is no such way of expressing 'grue'.
Needless to say, but I will say it, 'grue' and such predicates could
never be taken as primitive in the first place.

If grue and bleen are taken as primitive we are asserting their
simplicity. If it was the case that either was analysable, they
would lose their fundamentality. However the argument that
'green' can be rendered 'positional' or complex is strange, for it
presumes the non-positionality of grue and bleen. Why should
green be defined by terms of which it is already a fundamental
element? The definition would fail through circularity and infinite
regress. 'Green' is defined as 'green before t, blue after t (grue)/
blue before t, green after t (bleen)'. How would the 'green' that
appears in the defining part of the formula itself be defined? In
terms of grueness and bleenness?

On a different note, someone might hold grue to be akin to
a prediction of a change, and object 'Ah, but it is not a matter

for evidence either that emeralds should stay green after a given date, but a supposition.' This is a problem which does not undermine the metaphysical foundations for induction, but one which concerns the validity of inductions. To some extent we are predicting the future, but in a qualified way. We are saying that unless something physical happens to change it, which might possibly happen, 'emeralds are green'. This is not so much a prediction even as a report and a tautology: it reports the evidence and uses the a priori theory of causality and that of induction to qualify that report in an unassuming, uncontroversial way. If there is no change then of course things remain the same.

In reality, grue is not a prediction of a change because it does not alter, therefore the inclusion of elements which can only be non-present is incoherent. All of grue is happening now. A tensed predicate is grammatically acceptable, but one cannot construct one so that it is tenseless at the same time.

'Green' is a predicate that has no time-element, so that future, present, and past are of no consequence to it. That is why green is not tensed. No viable physical description contains mention of times as if these were real to it. But for grue, future is in the present nature of it, whilst green limits itself pure y to physicality. Tenseless reporting does not rule out physical change; to say 'x is green' is not to say 'x will always be green'. When we report we are deserting and add to that description the triviality that so it is unless materially changed by unforeseen conditions.

Saying that evidence for green is evidence for grue is quite simply wrong The latter is not in essence a colour, whilst green is, so that which is a colour cannot be evidence for it. What evidence does 'green' give for an attribute centred on time t?

Grue's conceptual impossibility, grue's evidential impossibility make it illicit as an inductive practice. This is generalizable: all locational attributes are logically impossible. An illustration of the essential fallacy is the analogy of saying of the French tricolor: 'Here it is red there', when 'here' is the place where it is blue. Likewise, in 2040 A.D. the grue emerald is blue in 2050 A.D. Locational attributes like grue aim to be complex and simple all at once from the same perspective. They are fallacious because they are homogeneous and non-homogeneous at the same time and from the same point of view. We exemplify this with a representative property 'Blite' that applies to swans, insofar as they are black in Australia and white elsewhere. 'Blite' is homogeneous: swans are blite everywhere. But at the same time it is not homogeneous, being different, mutually exclusive colours in different places, yet one has to mention those different colours at once. One cannot avoid mentioning how things are elsewhere in mentioning how things are elsewhere in mentioning how things are here. 'Blite' says: 'here it is white elsewhere' or 'here it is black elsewhere'. The contradictory homogeneity/non-homogeneity causes the locational attribute to differ from the non-locational attribute – non-homogeneity –and to differ from it all the time or everywhere – homogeneity – so that the rules of temporal succession or of spatial location are violated. In blite's case swan is more than just the colour it is at any one place.

But I will bring the issue into the mainstream of my thinking on physicality and argue against grue from that viewpoint.

I can of course disallow grue as a possible physical description since it contains a time distinction, but that will not be satisfactory in indicating why specifically it is wrong in the light of my causal theory.

Grue is not a colour predicate; in its supposedly physical form it is not a colour for it contains an essential time-element. Grue is not a change, but is static: an emerald is grue before, during and after the colour change. Grue is therefore neither a change, but a state, nor a colour, so it is not a colour-change. The time element is irremovable.

But at the level of colour, which grue is not, because of the discontinuity between green and blue, there is a real descriptive change. As are all changes in the qualitative world, this one is a necessary causal process too, and this change process does all the work of the grue attribute and remains disidentical to it, meaning that the 'grue' is redundant. And since that which essentially makes grue different from the colour change is the time element, which paradoxically makes grue a state, not a change, that time element is nullified by having been supplanted by the necessary physical process at the level of colour. Grue is superfluous then. The change is real, so that grue becomes unreal and impossible. Grue cannot equal the qualitative colour change, and both cannot be real since they would exclude the other, render the other unreal.

The colour elements in grue can be analysed out and they represent at that level a real and necessary change. So as far as grue is an addition to this level, the colour level, it is a superfluous addition. Change happens whether or not the time element is added, at the colour plane.

In terms of colour, change is real, but not at the level of grue, and if the change was not materially accounted for, and the attribute grue allowed to remain, that change would be just a matter of fact. 'Green before t and blue after t' is not a description of mechanism, but a conjunction. We need a physical connection, and conjunctions are existential.

'Green' does not mean 'grue before time t' because, apart from being a circular definition, the latter is not a colour. Indeed, no definition that equates 'green' to 'grue' by any manipulation, or which interprets 'green' positionally in time, i.e. 'grue before t, bleen after t', can be correct because green is solely a colour, the quality of light. 'Grue before t' involves a time and as such is not a colour, a type of light.

Some philosophers, whilst rejecting grue in physical laws, countenance it in a weakened form in which the locational element is indefinite or indeterminate: 'green up to some time or other and blue thereafter'.[5] This indeterminacy is not valid in a qualitative world.

We have said that any qualitative must necessarily be the way it particularly is: it could not have been otherwise. The time or date at which the colour does change in reality, for it must change at some specific time even if when precisely is not specified, must be part of the qualitative 'grue'. But indeterminacy vanishes

---

[5]   See N. Swartz: *The Concept of Physical Law*, pp 20-21.

consequently because in a qualitative world all events are necessary. The actual time of the change becomes, through being included in the qualitative attribute, a definite and necessary part of it. The change must occur at that precise time. We finish where we did not want to; with grue in a strong form.

Having a definite location in time is also disallowed for a qualitative description, and if this indeterminacy is insisted upon nevertheless, the qualitative plainly becomes contingent as to its date of change of colour and in that regard is just a matter of fact in a non-factual world and a contingency in a non-contingent world.

In any form 'grue' cannot be an attribute in a physical world. Really it s two states linked by a change which is entirely qualitative, no. one state inclusive of a date. And the new problem of induction collapses into the old one: how can we justify Prediction? 'Bent.' predicates[6] like 'grue' violate the requirement for non-particularity – for they specify a point of disjunction. If two problems like the old and the new problems of induction have the same solution, they are the same problem.

Times, places and instances cannot enter the description of any event, and this can be broadened. The differences between events can only ever be characteristic or physical; and this means that if, for example, on two separate occasions we place the same ball at the top of the same incline and two different results ensue, the differences will be materially caused. We already see that events, when similarly associated to begin with, should resemble each other in what subsequently happens. Salt dissolves in water on all occasions if the surrounding conditions are unchanged.

The issue of physical difference is poised on a knife-edge of misunderstanding. What if we say that on one occasion a certain set of initial conditions led to a given consequence and on another occasion to another consequence? Shall we maintain they are merely 'different' as kinds of events? This judgment entails a contingent and factual vision of events, and we need to say more than that about such a happening. When objects and events are

---

[6]   They are called so in Blackburn.

connected and continuous in every way as descriptives are in the world, the mere difference between them becomes a change

Change is a temporally continuous, connected difference. As we know now a change needs a reason, for it is a process, a causal process and has a mechanism. So conjecture that A, B, C and D are events; A, B and C are closely alike in a non-particular way – say they are the result of placing a ball at the top of an incline – but D is different – the same initial conditions but another result. Since the world is descriptive there is a connection between the events even at the non-particular level. Since A, B and C are repetitions, i.e. connected non-particular similarities, D in the series represents a non-particular change, being connected by the initial conditions but diverging in what happens subsequently. This non-particular alteration from what is effectively a descriptive unit, the repetition, requires and has physical explanation. But there can't be change at this level, for this is the universal level where what holds good for any one instance holds for all times.

The stress between universality and change is resolved by saying that in the case of D the initial conditions, the relevant states of affairs in which it happened, were only superficially similar to the genuinely identical initial conditions of A, B and C. If there is what seems like a 'change in the course of Nature' we for one know that it is not really a change, but on the supposition that it was, it has a necessary physical reason. The reason is that the initial conditions were not the same, and it is up to us to identify the differences. To avoid misunderstanding, I am saying that we should think there is a physical non-particular change, though there can't really be one, and thereby recognize that there should be a reason for it. The 'reason' is there is no change because there was no initial identity of a real nature between the repetitions and the anomalous event.

If unsupported 'objects' started to rise instead of falling, we know that, because of the universality in descriptives' natures, the 'objects' involved could not really have been the same things, or have been in normal circumstances, so that nature has not really changed. Such a supposition of change is really self-contradictory, for objects are their particularly and universally necessary behaviours, and the necessity of the non-particular aspect of an object makes change impossible. The 'same' thing under the 'same' conditions behaving differently is a violation of the thing's we are talking about nature such that it is isn't the 'same' thing. A change in the universal dimension of a thing is effectively the existential creation of a completely new object, an absolute change such as only existence can support. So that possibility is entirely alien to a qualitative world.

The foregoing reasons show that there must be 'cause' for physical difference between events in a series; later I show that there are reasons for physical similarity in a novel way. They are negative and positive facets to justifying and founding causal induction.

The identity of existential metaphysics stresses the individuality of instances in an absolute way, whilst that of descriptivity stresses relative identity and concerns itself, naturally enough, with the natures of things. Emphasising this aspect, qualitativity is amenable to universalization and particularity or individuality are subordinated.

A Digression

Making a short but important digression, we must notice that because the world consists of events, the dimensional, that is, spatio-temporal ordering of these events, inherently involving changes as it does, for the world is not static involves and means causes and mechanisms. A description of a qualitative world will not give, if it is to be at all faithful, simply accounts of conjunctions and juxtapositions, i.e. x is here, now, y is there, then, and so on but reasons, causal processes, mechanisms for the orderings that events have in their dimensions. The very arrangement of the universe's components must be caused and necessary. In brief, the relative ordering of events and objects in the natural dimensions is part of an unaccidental physical causal process or operation, and will imply a system of material influences. Mere location will not satisfy as a description.

Resuming

Qualitative necessity can be stated as a principle in the following manner. In general, things are how they are. But the world consists of things hat are in part particular; they are not just particular though, as the pluralist holds. from the membership fallacy we learn that external relations imply a collection, and when there are no collections, there are no external relations. Pure particularity also entails a collection, and a prohibition on the latter entails prohibition of unqualified particularity. The lack of external relations and the lack of particularity are at bottom the same. It means that things inherently transcend their limitation to themselves. Still, there is a vestige of qualified particularity, and when howness applies to particular things, it must be consistent with it. Things are therefore how they particularly are. Since each thing is by nature how it specially is, it must be as it specially is for a thing must be its nature. Qualitativity means that the selfhood and nature of anything is exactly in the form of its mode of qualitativity, not in a trivial, but materially necessary sense, it has consequently to be as it is, for what it is is how it is. If 'it' were different, 'it' would not be 'it'. By 'it' we mean a special howness.

Not having the possibility of being otherwise, how things are is how they must be. The world too is descriptive and is how it must be, and we cannot ask: Does that event have to be? We can ask: Does that event have to be the way it is? To which the only reply can be 'Yes'.

Physical descriptions cannot include dates, places, instances, because these are as such outside qualitativity, and represent a collectivizing of the world or of its components which is disallowed owing to the membership fallacy. Qualitativity makes for a real universality. Objects cannot start or cease behaving in their non-particular characteristic ways. For example, there cannot be a time when salt started dissolving in water, or a time when it finishes having that typical behaviour. In this respect, things are timeless. There is then a secure ground for induction via universality. It appears that we do not have to achieve qualitative necessity before we secure qualitative induction. The very universality pertaining to the qualitative does that on its own. Mention of instance is inapplicable to the physical description, so that I when fire burns paper at any given time, I know that given a repeat of all the relevant conditions, it will do so in future. That is a matter of fire and paper's non-particular natures.

Things, changes, associations of objects, equate to how they are, and it is self-defeating and senseless to say that 'they', which identify with how they particularly are, could have been otherwise. One might as well say that the colour red could have been blue. This opens up a new realm of definition. Qualitativity has so much replaced the stumbling-block of existence that, not only are worldly things how they are, but in this world Necessity itself is Howness. How implies Must. Rather, 'must' is 'how' seen in a certain light. A thing's necessity consists in how it is and in being how it is. Instead of saying of worldly events: This is necessary, we say: This is how it is. Denying existence and thereby producing necessity is as a strategy negative and not very informative. Positively embracing qualitativity is much more useful and illuminating to this end. In the world of descriptives 'must' is 'how' and 'how' is 'must'.

Every succession of event by event is a completely qualitative, that is, physical matter, and a matter of quality as contrasted to a matter of fact. The succession therefore must be the way it is, both particularly and non-particularly. Necessity is thoroughgoing and affects both dimensions. So suppose we have a situation that is followed by another: this may manifest itself temporally. We know that since the relationship is a descriptive affair, whenever the first situation, in terms of its non-particular aspect, is repeated, the attendant one will physically follow it, in terms of its non-particular aspect. That is, the same types of things go together. That is their nature, how they are, and how they must be.

If we notice that A is followed by B, we know in an abstract, disembodied way, that whenever A-type situations recur – that is, when A recurs non-particularly, B-type situations follow –

again, non-particularly. The nature of A is to be followed by B, particularly and universally. This lies at the basis, in a primitive way, of many of our inductive beliefs and practices. Relationships, just as much as single events, are matters of quality.

When such an association as the above is temporal we can be sure that it is causal because it is a change process. Cause and Change can to a large extent be identified.[7]

Well-known epistemological difficulties mar this neat scheme and we have to rely upon experiment and empirical testing to see whether we have got the relationship between A and B right. That does not alter the conceptual validity of the scheme though. The philosophical problem Is Induction justified' is replaced by the scientific problem 'Is this induction justified?'

Though Induction has been conceptually justified, particular inductions have not been deductively justified: they remain inductive, not deductive and this is my response to those who maintain that any principle which renders induction a priori justifiable destroys its inductive character; such as the uniformity of Nature. The inferential form and its content must, as with causality and causes, be clearly distinguished. As I pointed out in an earlier essay, philosophy justifies the inferential 'form' of induction, not the content of specific inductions. The principle of the uniformity of Nature will not turn our arguments for 'The Sun will rise tomorrow' into deductions. The philosophical justification of Induction tells us, as I have said, why it is proper to reason in inductive fashion, and identifies Induction with those justifications. I hope you will see that the condition for legitimately inducing is the universality pertaining to qualitative objects and events in the world and that the 'form' of Induction is this universality.

Though the world is a system of necessary relations, some elements may be absent and changed in a recurrence of a similar causal relationship. Thus they are incidental to that type of event, though not strictly accidental. Their contributions to it are minor.

---

[7] So in this chapter instead of concentrating on necessary connection I have been concentrating on change. Changes are physical; changes are necessary; changes are lawlike.

We empirically discover the relationship and natures of A and B, and we know a priori that this relationship is a matter of quality and always has the general form it has. The empirical domain is subjected to a priori deduction to produce Induction, which is not a separate principle. But at the actual contentful empirical level we cannot have a priori certainties: at the level of particular inductions. Causal relationships between worldly objects may not be what we think they are physically. This epistemological uncertainty cannot be erased when we get down to actual inductions. At the justificatory level, where this type of reasoning is legitimated, we do have certainty. Applications of inductions are probabilistic and may even be erroneous, firstly, because we don't know if we have correctly identified natural laws, and secondly, because we may wrongly formulate natural laws.

I think it important that I repeat the principle: since it is a matter of quality that A is followed by B, and things have to be the ways they are non-particularly, A, as a kind of event, must be followed by B, as a kind of event. This is the principle we have in mind when we seek to use inductive reasoning in daily life. This is not a psychological, but a logical belief. The relation above is a causal one and is wider than it appears, for it goes beyond macroscopic or even small scale processes, but applies to what may be called 'constitutive' laws. That which causes swans to be white will always cause their whiteness. That which causes other swans to be black will always cause their blackness. In addition, that which causes a swan to be a swan may cause it to have some other property which all swans must have.

As a general diagnosis one can say that the problem of justifying induction largely arose because writers did not recognize that objects and events in the world are not merely particular. They contain universality within them, and one is justified in the general method of arguing from the observed to the unobserved, the 'particular' to the general, via this universality. And there is a contradiction in holding that the course of Nature may alter, for it is to say that a law of nature is not universal, namely that a law of nature is not a law.

5

The Descriptive World

When I say that things do not exist I do not mean that they are nothing, but that they have been wrongly described and classified, and moreover the emphasis is on 'exist' not on 'things'. Existence is invalid in any formulation. In this section I hope to give insights into the nature of the descriptives which replace facts and the sort of world they compose. I give a conceptual vision of the main features of this world, a. least insofar as they are closely relevant to causality. This should give shape to a project which could easily spill over into areas that are not significantly related to the main topic of this thesis.

The world is the realm of the 'how', of that which is how it is, and the nature of the descriptive world can be seen if it is contrasted with that of the existential world, the world existentially conceived. Of the latter it was legitimate to believe that a given event did not have to 'occur' because it was accepted that things' existences were contingent. In the descriptive world this can no longer apply; there is no contingency at all and the difficult mental shift needs to be made in which the 'is' of existence is systematically replaced by the 'is' of predication. 'Is', since it is 'membership', strictly does not express predication at all.

Questions of Necessity

When we ask such questions of the qualitative world, the universe of the 'how', as whether an event has 'to be the case' and being the case, whether an event has to take the exact form it takes, we are really now asking if a descriptive has to be descriptive and if the sort of descriptive it is is necessary The first query is not a simple, self-answering, tautological one, but the question is 'Does it have to be real?' This is only apparently self-answering in the context of the descriptive metaphysics, not the existential one where things have natures too, but those natures also 'exist' where things are not 'natures' but 'existences'. The question can be expressed in this way: Does the descriptive have the possibility of being other than descriptive, like the fact has the possibility of being other than a fact?

We know already that qualitatives have to be their particular modes of qualitativity since they are nothing other than those modes of qualitativity; we know this from the previous essay, and the second of the two questions, does the descriptive have to take its exact form? is answered.

I said that superficially the first question is self-answering. If it were really self-answering it would not matter which metaphysic one chose to answer it in. This means it *would* be tautological. But neither in the existential nor descriptive world is the question as to the necessary reality of the descriptive or the necessity of the fact a tautology. A tautology would not be about the world, but would be asking in form: Is A, A? That one needs a metaphysics to answer the existential and descriptive questions shows that the questions depend not on logic but on choice of 'worlds'. The questions are metaphysical, not logical.

The answers to those questions may be difficult to grasp with the spectre of the lingering but inapplicable existential conception, but examples may be given which are analogically helpful. Consider the number 7. Does it have to be a number, and does it have to equal 7? Or in the case of the colour red: does it have to be a colour, and does it have to be red? A similar analysis is given of the reality of the descriptive, and the necessity of its particular form. The point of the answer to the first question is that when one conceives or speaks in a descriptive mode one has no other possibility than describing; one cannot use existential words or concepts and one can never not describe. Descriptives have to be real, to be descriptives, that is.

A profound area of difference between existential and descriptive worlds can be highlighted by the following consideration. One can ask of the 'world': do there have to be facts? But if one were to ask: Do there have to be descriptives? One would be using factual criteria wrongly in application to the qualitative concept of the world. Descriptives do not exist, so neither can they be utterly asserted or negated, come into nor go out of existence, that is, be nothing. As descriptives, they are continuous. One cannot conceive that the descriptive world was ever anything else but qualitative. Within that world there can only at most be change, and in no part of it, in its history, is there a being or a void, if by this you mean non-existence: not even the 'vacuum' is one such. Thus existential creation is also ruled out for the world. We may use terms like 'there is ...' but that is because custom constrains us linguistically, and all we mean by them strictly is 'something is so'.

The root of the problem is that no existential question can be posed of the non-existential, descriptive world. Of something that is purely characteristic one can only ask characteristic questions. Therefore descriptives cannot be utterly negated, only modified. Their non-existence cannot even be contemplated; they only have their natures which cannot either be or be potentially nothing. They are 'eternal', and the descriptive is not confronted with the equivalent of nothingness as being is. If you can only say how things are, you have no latitude for saying that they are not how they are, for denying their howness.

So to the question: Why is there something rather than nothing, why is there anything at all? We can reply in a seemingly paradoxical way: Because things do not 'exist'. Neither do they 'not exist'. Being something equates, not to existing, but to being how something is. When something is like this its absolute assertion and its absolute negation are both impossible. Consequently things are real because they are qualitative, hence beyond being and non-being, or nothingness.

Anything is its qualitative nature, how it is; and the philosophical question is now 'Need the world be how it is?' not 'Need the world be?' This is a question answerable by philosophy – indeed, it has already been answered affirmatively.

Several points then: the existential metaphysics permits existence and non-existence, and it allows descriptiveness and existence. The existential metaphysics is incoherent and incorrect. The descriptive metaphysics only allows descriptiveness: it neither allows existence and non-existence, with the things that pertain to them, like contingency, nor does it allow non-descriptiveness, for that is patently non- descriptive, so only descriptiveness is permissible, therefore possible. If one can only say 'x is round' or 'x is blue', one cannot say 'x is' or 'x is not', for the latter is not descriptive discourse. Since one cannot utterly negate or assert things, one can only say if they are not one sort of thing then they are another sort of thing. If only descriptiveness is possible, descriptiveness is necessary. Within descriptivity it can in no way be coherent to deny descriptivity, but the existential world can legitimately be denied. A descriptive equivalent to existential nothingness is not available as an option. The descriptive has not the possibility of absolute negation.

This only tells us that a descriptive world is necessary, not whether the content is; though we do have in what I said prior to the last paragraph the affirmation that the content is necessary, I will leave consideration of this until later. Explicit consideration that is, for I wish to add that in the emptiest, least satisfactory sense, we can hold that once things in the world cease to be regarded as factual, they must be as they are and are necessary.

Change

The qualitative is its mode of qualitativity and cannot be different, it cannot 'go out of existence'. How can this assemblage of properties be reconciled with the temporariness of qualitatives in the world? If it, where 'it' means its special nature, stops being itself is there not a contradiction? Can 'L' cease being 'L'? Or do we have to accept that the descriptive is completely annihilated and has effectively gone out of existence, which I said could not even be thought of? Plainly more needs to be said about the descriptive in order to account for this difficulty.

In order to include the transitory quality of descriptives into our account of them we can only posit change, the formula of which I attempt henceforth. Things cannot absolutely cease or begin out of nothing, anew, so it must be the case that new, that is to say, foreign qualitatives are added to or old ones subtracted from, effectively both, the qualitative system said to undergo a change. This process is itself qualitative, therefore mechanical. I distinguish between the definition of change given in the previous essay, temporally continuous or connected difference, and the conceptual mechanism of change which is what I am engaged in describing. The simple description given strongly resembles that of physical causation and change must be seen as a guise of causation. So the study of change is not tangential to the major concern of this thesis.

Things in changing do not cease to be descriptives, only the kinds of descriptives alter. Of course, the momentary qualitative identity something has is destroyed by altering, but in a non-absolute and descriptive manner. A thing, in identifying with a mode of qualitativity, cannot at the same time possess another contrary nature: it cannot both spin and be still; but it does not equate to a qualitative mode in a static way. Descriptives inhabit a world: there are other descriptives which are different from them. They are accessible to and influence each other. This is the essence of modification in the world. Having real, meaningful access to one another, matters of quality can impose themselves in different ways upon each other and thereby they are saved from inertia. They can contribute to other matters of quality and in this way stop them remaining in one state. The contribution they make to one another ensures change, and they inhabit then an animated world in which things can be affected and altered, mingled and distanced.

Things are mutually interpenetrated and cannot be seen as atomic. For example, two objects may not alter 'in themselves' but they are not by themselves and they modify each other, making the nature of the qualitative influences each imposes on the other alter: gravitational pull, as an instance. Because these imposed qualitative influences constitute part of the natures of the things, the things change. This relativity and variety makes for instability, and there is a perpetual mutual accommodation, an endless jostling in the system. One change in the fabric means that everything else alters and a train of alterations follows which is irreversible. But I think that this account of change needs to take time into account; influences between part and part take time to pass, otherwise if modification were immediate one can envisage immediate mutual accommodation which makes for a static universe. If A modifies B, making it into B1, and B1, modifies A, what A becomes, i.e. A1, cannot obtain at the same time as A. So time is involved.

We must expand our comprehension of the qualitative, the event, to include change. The mode of alteration of situations, change of state, must be regarded as an innate facet of worldly things, be it a relation or an event or even the world itself: the qualitative is a changing thing. If the history of the world is the world, then qualitatives cannot be seen other than temporally and we cannot begin with the idea of unchanging qualitatives Regarding things in isolation would be to divorce them from the origins of their changing which is the environment. Change always has a mechanism. This being so, the physical relationships of alteration are themselves native inherent to the thing. The whole account of any descriptive is not given until we include modification; and not only is the qualitative identity that something is inclusive of change, but, since events cannot be divorced from their context, the world, they must involve their material relations to what is beyond them. Physical connections responsible for change make things what they are. Avoid then giving accounts of change which exclude mechanism as these would result in a factual description, not a physical description. Qualitatives are contextual.

Loss and gain of qualitatives result in differences to the variously associated things. A system of qualitatives from which certain ones have been lost, or which has gained some, differs from what it was prior to the loss or gain. But that does not mean destruction of qualitatives or creation of the same in any absolute sense, only a changed relationship prodding changes in the system and in the qualitatives lost or gained as well. When these qualitatives are distanced from the original system, but not completely separated, or are received into a system of qualitatives, but not created anew, the migrating qualitatives and the systems become what each are like in the new kind of 'association'. Not only are systems changed by loss or gain of qualitatives, but these added or subtracted ones themselves change as a result of leaving or entering the system. The distancing of qualitatives from a system is as much an 'association' though, albeit a tenuous one, as is the assumption of qualitatives into a distinct system. Joining or leaving qualitative systems results in the alteration not only of the systems but of the qualitatives that join or leave because the natures of the things involved are results of their relationships with each other and the wider world. But why for instance should a qualitative leave a system? Not only in *leaving* it does it change, but surely *in order* to leave it it must change? The reason is the relativity of the system which is itself as a consequence of this relativity not absolutely stable or static. Change not only comes from without, but goes on within a system because of its complexity.

Change is always a diversity of descriptive relationships over periods of time, a shifting and re-arranging of matters of quality, influencing themselves mutually, but never destroying themselves completely, or creating themselves anew from nothing. Only, new kinds of systems are effected out of a melange of descriptives in the world. The creation of associations is ceaseless and they themselves create others, the world being systematic and interlinked. Generally the descriptive world is unstable because of its interrelatedness, but not, for this very reason, chaotic.

Continuity

Some idea, abstract and simple, has been given of how change is possible in the descriptive world, but the things in this world are, as we say, persistent as qualitatives. How are we to view this perseverance? How, in the light of change, can things endure as qualitatives? The answer lies in the nature of qualitatives, which implies that they are developing. This is an outcome of their contextuality and relatedness which become part of their nature – not something external to it.

A stick is broken, imagine; it changes. But most of the same parts of the first amalgam, the stick, remain in the second 'arrangement', the broken item. They have only been so rearranged by the imposition of an external matter of quality, a force say, that though the parts remain, a new kind of system or association is effected between them. The qualitatives remain as parts, and that is how they only ever were: partial. The descriptive is always a 'blending in' with others and retains this character throughout development, which we see is set up by that very blending. In that way it continues. So in the case of the stick, being qualitatively disunited in a certain way, the parts are altered. The 'new' qualitatives are the old ones in different systems, and they react to the difference in arrangement, they don't stay precisely as they were.

So the qualitative is a mode of alteration and through relativity it persists. The relativistic form of the qualitative's nature lies at the heart of our understanding of persistence.

Qualitatives' natures are in the end relative. A nature is not 'absolute' in the sense that one burrows into its innards and discovers a thing that is not a matter of relativity, but a pure simplicity, a thing in itself. This relativity opens them up to the ability to change. Do not suppose then that if 'A' becomes 'B' something of a complete disjunction is happening. A and B are at heart characteristically relational, and the transition is nothing other than a change of relations, and endurance is possible. Picture it: put the relativistic nature of any one qualitative suggestively as Δ (A). B is Δ. A and B are simply associations, systems of relations. All that is needed for one to become the other is a relational shift, as I figuratively instance it above. The non-relational, simple, absolute nature, on the other hand, can only statically persist or else be completely annihilated; it can't develop. And a point that must be recognised is that the complexity of things does not imply fundamental simplicity, but a fundamental relatedness.

'Persistence' sounds existential and static. Here it is envisioned as a feature of things' howness and is not something separate from change in terms of source. 'Persistence' is better expressed as 'continuity', continuity as an unbroken development.

From the start, a qualitative is never pure and simple, if one means by that 'apart' or isolated. Partiality is its characteristic as far as change goes. Always it is blended with others, always a part of a given association. No particular stage of the development should be taken as the pure state which others are corruptions of. Qualitatives should be seen as stages of development, at least as we encounter them, and transition is of their nature whenever one captures them. The mode of development is the whole thing and the stages of it must never be seen as fundamental. The stage is part of a continuity and itself persists by appearing in different guises, different associations which are brought about by dint of interacting with other stages in the environment. It never disappears and always interplays with systems. But to require the continuity of the qualitative in a pure state is to mistake what is always a stage of development for something static, pure and simple, and above all complete. The clue and key to the problem is the contextuality of the thing. Always 'environmental', it participates to its very core in relativity, of which change is an outcome and through which continuity is possible.

At the individual level we need to escape the conception of things with unaltering identities. Since change is the rule for the qualitative event, just because of the latter's relativity, persistence has to be developmental, thus a matter of unbroken development: nothing absolutely new is created, nothing absolutely terminates. Only existence allows that. New relativities form, old ones end. The qualitative is a relativity, internally and externally. Since the origin of both change and continuity is relativity, one can say that what finally persists is relativity: there is enduring relativity. That though is figuratively speaking. We must not reify continuity by supposing a continuer, a something that persists. We must merely regard continuity as a feature of development: the latter's seamlessness.

On the ground bass of a relative world we have change and persistence, only, relativity must not be comprehended simply as an abstract concept but as the relativity, in addition, that the world physically is.

Though we are aware of apparently static 'things' when we consider a part of the world's development, flux is natural to the descriptive world. So we don't see the world atomically now, we see it as temporal blendings and inter-mixtures which appear to organise into 'things'.

What has been learnt about change so far has implications for identity and induction, to which I shall soon proceed. Consider two events that appear to involve the same objects at different times, events which are descriptively indistinguishable. One may say that the same characteristic event has taken place. Perhaps it is the repetition of a mechanical process. Since though, they bear distinct temporal relations to each other, are stages in a development, that of the world through time, they must be subtly but effectively different in a descriptive fashion. They represent a change. This means that over a length of time in a various world, an object does not remain 'itself, as understood in the sense of the same developmental stage. Because the context alters, so does the thing. Therefore objects are contextual not only in space but in time as well, and there is no absolute, static selfhood for a thing over periods of time. The 'outside' world for the thing includes 'itself in the past. Things have no isolated identity in time; even the supposedly 'same' object varies physically from itself in time. This is what change implies. The thing is a mode of variation. Selfhood can only be grasped if it includes change. So static individuality applied to descriptives can only produce conceptual errors. And obviously, when we come to induction, what is crucial is how much a thing is different from its earlier 'self'.

Identity

Identity must be examined and defined within the constraints imposed by all-pervading relativity, change and continuity operating in the world. But the prime requisite is not so much these three elements; it is the need for descriptivity.

Before engaging in these determinations, and in order to avoid confusion and attain precision, I want first to distinguish two uses of the term 'Identity'. One appears in sentences such as: 'The countries of Europe must retain their national identity', and, 'His identity has been lost'. Another use appears in 'A is identical to B'.

The second sense takes the concept of identity to be a relation, and it is sometimes signified by 'equals' or 'is the same as'. Plainly this sense cannot be given to the term 'identity' in the first set of sentences. The first sense treats identity as 'uniqueness'. Identity in the second sense is a relation between uniqueness and uniqueness, but is not the same as 'uniqueness'. I find this distinction confusingly blurred in many writings on the subject, and in this section when I speak of identity, unless I specifically say otherwise, I mean it in the first sense as 'uniqueness'.

Going further, what is the link between uniqueness and 'is identical to'? An intimate one obviously. Suppose an object has the defining attributes A, B and C. We will say that these constitute its uniqueness, its identity. If one of these attributes goes, the object 'loses its identity'. Uniqueness and relative identity seem to meet, for the object is no longer 'the same as' it was. In a changing world momentary uniqueness cannot help but alter. The relationship between uniquenesses before and after change itself changes. But we are not required to call relative identity 'uniqueness', rather it is implied by this last. The relationship between identity as uniqueness and identity as relation is that the relative identity depends on the uniqueness identity. Change and difference in uniqueness causes change in identity as relation; the relationship is asymmetrical with the uniqueness being the condition for relative identity. Uniquenesses are the terms in equality relationships. A 'loss of identity' is a change in distinct characteristics, uniqueness, such that the relation between the uniquenesses is not oneness any more.

Identity as relation is still mysterious. I call it an inter-uniqueness relation and can offer two hypotheses as to what is meant by it. Firstly, and least interestingly, the 'is' of equality denotes repetition of the term, nothing but repetition, and this can be admitted to be artificial and verbal. Secondly we have the more intriguing proposal that relational identity is a predication of the whole uniqueness of itself. With the conventional view of predication, as membership of a class, this can be expressed by saying that when a uniqueness belongs to itself, it is identical to itself. But I won't pursue this further until more has been said about uniqueness.

In descriptive terms, the uniqueness or identity of something is a 'location', a descriptively particular one, including a mode of alteration, past, present and future, within the system of the universe. This characterisation of uniqueness hardly differs, it will be noticed, from that of the qualitative thing. By a 'location' I mean a singular physical relationship in respect to the environment.

As howness includes necessity and change, so it includes identity. In case my description seems circular I will expand it later in a way that is easier to grasp and devoid of metaphor.

In the world, identity is a qualitative singularity, but as each thing is contextual, that contextuality works its way into the singularity. The thing's uniqueness is an amalgam, a sum and system of its contextual uniquenesses I   and locations, just as the sun in the contexts of earthly vision, in the hidden dimension, in all the other relationships it bears to the universe's inhabitants, has all these as its contextual uniqueness, its identity. And these contexts do not exclude but complement each other.

Change however is of the first importance in understanding the concept, and since nothing begins or ceases utterly, continuity is written into the qualitative as well. So in practical terms identity involves the closest continuity a thing has at any one moment or stage with the nature of the thing at a previous and succeeding moment: that is to say, the closest developmental connection in the world. If I am pressed, this continuity has to be expressed in spatio-temporal terms. Since qualitatives have continuity, the uniqueness of a qualitative will be the uniqueness of a continuity, and what individuates a qualitative individuates a continuity.

As a result of these stipulations, relativity, change and qualitativity, the identity of the descriptive world is distinct from the one we are used to in a basic way; we might as well say that the common idea of identity has no place in it. 'Identity' was an outcome of the existential interpretation given to the world. Existence implied the isolation of facts, of existing things. This was a fruit of the independence credited to existents from each other. Isolation goes intimately with identity, and under existence was absolute. When existence is invalidated though, so is independence and isolation along with it; and if isolation disappears, absolute identity is overthrown. This sort of identity is an aspect of existence and has the existential naturelessness and blankness, and is a reason why we cannot apply it in physical descriptions in the form of distinct instances, locations in space and time. Shortly, the identity of the past was a form and consequence of existence, which saw existents as independent, therefore isolated and distinct.

If identity is to be retained it must be transformed in a manner agreeable to the qualitative world, and cannot be a characterless uniqueness. Identity must be seen as a descriptive, not a factual singularity. But the idea of singularity is dubious for in the descriptive world there is essentially no isolation. There is no utter individuality which it is the tendency of existence to confer on objects. Descriptivity injects relativity into our idea of identity. Of the descriptive one can only speak descriptively, and this is relevant here. No two things ever have the exact same relationship to the rest of the world, and since these relations make them what they are, different relations mean different descriptive natures. So no two things are ever descriptively exactly alike. This qualititive uniqueness is sufficient. I am here giving the real cause of identity in the descriptive world, not trying to say how we go about distinguishing things, and this is in case anyone asks how we distinguish 'two' things empirically to start with. The relations a thing has to other parts of the causal network make that thing. Since a thing is a mitigated particularity – its particularity mitigated by its non- particularity – it follows that the relations a thing has to other parts of the causal network are the sources of its particularity and its inseparable non-particularity. The inevitably diverse relations are the origins of the uniqueness in both particular and non-particular aspects of the thing. For a thing's non-particularity likewise has its uniqueness.

In reality, the universe of descriptives, the identity of a thing is precisely 'how' it is. But there is inextricable overlap, no real individuality, no total schism or disjunction between thing and thing. More subtly, transformation is part of identity, and this too is an example of something never being completely separate from another: there is no existential total persistence. Does this mean that identity changes, uniqueness changes, and isn't that a contradiction? Only if identity were seen statically and simply. But in our world, identity involves a kind of development; it cannot be still, for descriptives, therefore their identities, are in an important way developmental; they are processes and events. The 'it' is not static and unchanging.

Perhaps there can be no genuine identity and it is only imagined by us onto the world, on its items. There is however difference, pervasive difference and variety, and this is all that is required. A 'genuine' identity cannot be what it says it is if it is based on a misconceived premiss. Also it seems that while identity as a relation is dependent on uniqueness, uniqueness is itself dependent on difference. In a descriptive system one should expect uniqueness to have a basis in relativity, and difference is real.

The relational identity of repetition I mentioned is artificial, unworldly, but the developmental sense, where there are stages of an uniqueness, seems real and acceptable. The stages of a development can be said to constitute the 'same' object, to have relational identity. Here stage is related to stage, and though descriptively dissimilar, nevertheless comprise a developing continuity and singularity. One cannot say of a stage that it is identical to itself. Sameness applies, paradoxically, between different stages of one unique development and the wrong characterisation of self-identity is like this: . The conceptually correct one is this way: $| X | \leftrightarrow | Y |$.

This last conception takes account of development and continuity, features of the qualitative. The other one fails in this respect. Continuity is distinguished from relational identity in that continuity involves the arrow of time, whereas relational identity is independent of time's directionality. And a reason why the identity of a thing with itself expressed as an absolute, static numerical relation is unacceptable, is that it is not physical, not a physical relation. The only kind of relations possible in our world are qualititive, real ones: they are effectively, these relations, *things*. That status cannot be claimed for the absolute self-identity that we are used to with the existential metaphysics. I can scratch myself, for example; but to be myself would be for that 'being', if seen as numerical and absolute, to be a physical object, a thing that other things could affect and interact with. But that cannot be so with the non-descriptive identity as relation, which is a relation nothing can affect or alter, being a logical relation.[1] Developmental identity is a physical relationship, with the relation being the thing itself as it 'moves' from one term to the other. For me to be self-identical is for me to be how I am.

The real opposite to qualitative sameness is the difference responsible for uniqueness, which can be momentary, the uniqueness of a stage of evolution where the contrast is with other stages of other unique developments; or which can be overall, the uniqueness of a whole development, though here it is arbitrary to a large extent when a development is complete. This, I guess, is up to us and maybe this may lead some to say that if the world is

---

[1] Identity as a relation is part of the predicate logic and modal logic, where it is conventionally seen as, at least in the case of self-identity, logically necessary. But this kind of identity is very strange, is it not? Does one ever physically or phenomenally encounter it?

temporally finite, development lasts as long as the world lasts. I said the descriptive world is 'eternal', but this is compatible with temporal finitude since there is likely to be no time 'outside' the universe.

In the end identity is simply 'how a thing is', for we have the guarantee that no two things will ever be descriptively exactly the same. No two descriptives will be indiscernible. How they are will, we are sure, be the mark of descriptive individuality.

Just as identity as uniqueness is the nature of a thing, how a thing is, so identity as relation – the qualitative continuum – is also how a thing is. For the relation between terms, stages, is the thing itself as it develops in a real sense, and it involves those terms physically, those stages. So howness will render relational identity as well as uniqueness. What we do is stress various aspects of the qualitative to concentrate on and reveal these concepts, like change and necessity. The descriptive uniqueness and relational identity vary from object to object: one object's uniqueness and relational identity are different from another's. This is quite unlike non-descriptive uniqueness and relational identity, which, being devoid of character, are devoid of characteristic difference.

There is very little difference between persistence, continuous development, sketched in the last section, and identity as relation as here expounded, except to mention that in the latter we mean continuous, uninterrupted development of a uniqueness, and that we focus on stages of this development.

One good reason to maintain that the old concept of identity was featureless is that the existential vision of the world demands that no property of anything is had of necessity and any of them can be lost without loss of identity.[2] This is at least the opinion of some. Therefore it seems the identity of things cannot, on this interpretation, be located in what is qualitative about them. Identity does not reside then in the descriptive make-up of things

---

[2] A J Ayer (see *The Central Question of Philosophy*. 1973. Penguin pp. 196-198). But others hold that physical things necessarily have properties that make them what they are (S.Kripke: *Naming and Necessity*, 1972).

and is not qualitative: therefore it is blank and characterless.

Further reflection results in the paradox that in a factual world there can be no identity. With the understanding of the existentially conceived world, which I reject, we note that attributes or properties are not the home of identity because, relative to that which makes something an object and fact, existence, that is, all properties are contingent – none have to exist. So it seems that in a world of facts there will be no identity, and it can only have a place in a descriptive world, one of events and relativity where there is strangely enough no 'real' and absolute individuality.

So there is a seeming incoherence we arrive at: the existence concept renders things independent, isolated, hence possessed of 'identity', but it also renders only contingent their properties so that the 'itness' of anything will not include properties. No given existent needs to possess any given attribute in order to have identity.

What can be the nature of identity in the light of this in a world where things are thought to exist? It seems that the identity of things in such a framework is the uniqueness of their non-attributive facthood: their beings without any qualities and the individuality of such beings. The pure being of the fact is the indispensable element in facts and in the distinctness thereof resides their identity. The indispensibity is relative to facthood, not absolute in the sense of a non-contingent existence. This escapes the difficulty of how a thing is to be identified if it has no properties by using the isolation of the existent as a form and source of identity. This also evades the difficulty of having properties that are not indispensible simply by not having any properties at all which carry the identity. For the attributes we can substitute the non-attributive element in the fact, its existence, as bearer of identity. We don't take that element to be separable from a thing, in the existential way of looking at things, but say that its identity resides in it being a certain existence, not in its nature.

The identity here described is a numerical uniqueness. By 'numerical' I merely mean 'non-qualitative'. A qualitative identity will be like that described earlier, with individuation involving relationships with, distinctions from other things. Since the existential metaphysics permits both existence and descriptiveness, both numerical and qualitative identities are possible. However, the coherence of the two dimensions of the existential metaphysics is finally impossible. The identity here described is that which pertains specifically to the existential world, to existence.

The good reason for saying that existence is at the heart of the old-style identity is that these things, objects, would not be things or objects, would not be real, without existence; and if identity resides in what is indispensible to the object, thing or fact, essential to it, then that is its existence. Curiously, existence and essence seem to converge here and when people talk about 'its very being' they are using 'being' in the sense that it is indispensible for objecthood (essential) and the seat of a thing's identity (again, essential).

Returning to descriptive identity, change with identity means difference without complete disjunction, continuity without staticness, continuity as seamless alteration, and unity without sameness. Transition is essential. We need to get away from the idea of an underlying invariant which supports change. Change penetrates to every level of the physical, even the non-particular level, where however it is law-like and consistent with universality. When people disputed about identity they assumed there was something simple, static there, most of the time. The notion of the 'thing' invites singularity as a consequence it appears. But there is thoroughgoing relativity down to the very centre of 'things'.

In the revised identity we use with descriptivity we note that every qualitative aspect and relation a thing has is needed to identify it. None may be absent, none contingent, though expedience forces us to partially identify objects.

I should stress that the relational identity which absolutely equates a thing to itself is artificial and devoid of character. This kind of absolute, numerical identity – as a relation – misconceived and unreal as it is, springs, I believe, at bottom from the absolute and uncharacterized uniqueness that the existential concept endows identity as uniqueness with. This would be natural for a relation holding between characterless terms and absolute terms. So the qualitative identity as relation which holds between stages of a development that are not absolutely the same, is the one we adopt. With the existence concept there can be no gradations of relational identity: a thing is absolutely itself or it is something other completely. Intuitively that is not how the world appears; we qualify and make gradations of sameness and difference.

Quite possibly – I offer this as a hypothesis – the absolute existential identity as relation is a belonging relation. The uniqueness belongs to itself.[3] This is in respect to numerically relational identity; but the identity in equations is often merely a sign of analysis. The absolute artificial identity seems more at home in the artificial world of concepts, but to repeat, it cannot be applied to the real world. Identity as a relation between concepts is absolute because concepts do not change; they are essentially timeless. Identity as a belonging relation is suggested by relational identity seeming to be a predication of a thing of itself. In the class theory with membership, to say something has a certain predicate is to say it belongs to a certain class. In the light of the foregoing it would be natural to say that identity as relation is a belonging to oneself: the belonging of a uniqueness to itself, where the uniqueness is seen as if it was a set. With the reformed notional theory, what was self-membership in extensional class theory is self-identity. Identity as a relation in membership is imperfectly rendered as self-membership, I believe, for if that theory had understood what was going on in some of the paradoxes I examined it would have recognised that they showed self-membership to be impossible and that the latter was only a misunderstood way of expressing identity as relation.

---

[3] The uniqueness here is a 'member'. Being completely unrelated to anything it is like a universe, a set. Such a thing can only belong to itself; there is nothing else. Formally, this notion of relational identity is to be expressed thus: $\{\varepsilon\} \ \varepsilon \ \{\varepsilon\}$.

Again, relationally, when a thing just 'is' itself, no qualitative property is given. This is so when 'is' is unqualified and absolute, as in the ordinary notion of identity, when 'is' is not physically various, as objects are. But when 'is' has no nature like this it can only be a form of membership, as we have seen.

The membership fallacy has tentacles reaching into every part of this philosophy, and it would be fair to observe that membership in the areas of classes, language, and the world is modified somewhat by the contexts it appears in. How can the extensional metaphysics say that the world or realm of physical things exist? Things belong to the world by being physical. The world is physical too, not abstract, and is to be seen as a concrete class or extension. So the world belongs to itself. But to belong to oneself is really to be identical to oneself, and so the world 'belongs' in a pure way; it exists. Now take the concept the things in the world fall under: physicality. If the extension, the world, *belongs* to itself, doesn't the concept physicality have itself as a property, i.e. isn't *it* physical? That would be silly. The concept physicality (worldness) has the property not of physicality but of self-identity. Self-membership is not, we have learnt, to be called in the end self-predication, but is a confused way of expressing self-identity; and the concept physicality *is* self-identical.

Identity, Change and Induction

Considerations on identity and change have important results for induction. We have discovered the lack of absolute sameness of things from one moment to the next, though in an innovative way one can say that stages of one developing uniqueness are the 'same' descriptive object. The argument that the same initial situations are followed by the same events holds good theoretically, but since nothing is exactly the same as another thing, through time especially, that is, the same as 'itself in time in the more strict sense, we must emphasise that what individual moments share with other moments is what cannot be excluded from a physical formula inclusive of Time. A time cannot be simply singled out without reference understood to its qualitative resemblance to other periods. What is necessary for one moment holds for them all generally, and natural laws are universal. Only if moments vary physically among themselves could momentary uniqueness take its place in a law of Nature. Even then the uniqueness will inescapably have a non-particular aspect, and have universal implications. And because of non-particularity, even changing will be universal and law-like and theoretically predictable. Though the edge of our metaphysical certainties is somewhat blunted by change when we are concerned with induction, necessities of times are necessities about Time. The non-particular dimension is a fundamental reality of the universe and is more potent than particularity as we can witness. It allows systematic science to arise and the success of the latter is evidence of its pre-eminence.[4]

Necessity

Howness, qualitativity, demands the re-interpretation of change

---

[4] These passages concerning change, continuity and identity, lead me to see that they can be put under one heading: the concept of substance. Here, as elsewhere, the membership fallacy is relevant, for the old existential idea of substance can plainly be seen to be explicable as features of membership.

Substance was thought to have the following functions: its purpose was to exist, that is, to be the ultimate existent; to persist through change unvaried; to be the focus or seat of the qualities a thing had, though not be itself qualitative; to be independent of other things; and to be the home of a thing's identity. All these functions can without too much difficulty be seen to be accomplished by membership. Members are substances. They exist quintessentially; they are not qualitative, but are the fundament of qualities; they are independent in an absolute way of other members; they persist unvaried, for that which has no nature cannot vary; and individual members are, as we have surmised, uniquenesses. With existence gone however, the sections on change, continuity and identity show how substance's functions are replaced in the qualitative world. Ontological thinkers have used the notion of 'stuff' to express vaguely the feeling for what ultimately exists and holds the forms things take together. A 'transcendental glue' and a 'basic material' are expressions used in the attempt to grasp what is felt is needed in any final metaphysical theory of the world and its items. My opening section on necessity shows that the qualitative of its nature needs no support to be real, to be a thing.

and identity, but also, as I intimated in the last essay, necessity has to be re-evaluated in its terms. The descriptive world contains its own necessity, which is a situation that may be derived merely by noting the absence of existence. But just to say, 'No existence therefore no contingency', is not enough: it is not sufficiently detailed and positive, and what necessity means in the light of descriptivity is probably of greater importance than what change and identity mean.

The necessity in the descriptive world is a natural necessity, not one that is verbal, prepositional and tautological. Though not a logical one, it is discoverable and its outline is made clear by *a priori* necessity. As one may expect, worldly necessity is physical and qualitative. One equates an event to how it is particularly and asserts that it must be that way, could not be otherwise.

I used the analogy and example of the letter L to help convey the peculiar requirements for necessity in a descriptive metaphysics. We are not considering here the tautology of whether L is L, as if 'L' is some kind of symbol, some kind of variable, but the qualitative question of whether it has to be shaped as it is shaped. Given that L is how it is shaped, the answer is plain, but one needs the underpinning of a special metaphysic to make this situation come about. Or suppose it is raining. Existentially one could derive no relevant necessity about this; but tautologies that do not speak about the world would be available and forthcoming. Tautologies which say that if it is raining then it is raining, for instance. We could not determine whether it had to rain as a matter of physical necessity. The consensus was that it was a matter of fact to which any sort of necessity was simply not applicable.

In the descriptive world 'being the case' is replaced by 'being how it is', and in the latter case there is a necessity. Not a necessity of fact, but a new kind.

The criterion for necessity alters when the world is seen qualitatively. Because the world is how it is, necessity becomes the need for something to be how it is, not the need for something to be. This new requirement for worldly necessity is met by all descriptives. The state of the weather does not have to be now, it has to be as it is if it is to be necessary. If it is raining, that is how it is; since that is how it is, that is how it must be: it must rain. We cannot, to repeat, set up standards for necessity external to the descriptive context in our kind of Nature, which means that we can no longer contemplate the necessity to exist, but the necessity to be how a thing is, which qualitatives fulfil.

'Must' blends into, is an aspect of 'How', and really is to be regarded as redundant and probably harmful and not conducive to clear understanding if it is seen as something separate from 'how'. The necessity in the natural world is not imposed on it from outside like rules, but is co-significant with descriptivity. This is not an artificial necessity, but living, unabstract, spontaneous, though not of course accidental. The term 'necessity' should be contained as a natural, almost unconscious part of the meaning of howness. When one says, 'This is how it is', one understands that it must be so at the same time.

Necessity must, in the world, take a form, for a worldly necessity cannot be abstract. Indeed, in the world, necessity is the form it takes because, things being necessarily how they are, necessity can only take one form. But the form and content of worldly necessity is precisely how things are. So descriptivity and necessity identify in the world. Therefore the definition of, as well as the criterion for, necessity In the descriptive world is 'how things are'. Necessity disappears into howness, and 'how things are' expresses necessity. Any event such as the flowing of a river, or the wind blowing, is necessity itself.

In a different way, we reason that if how things are is how things must be, being how things are is being how things must be, which is the qualification for necessity. (Being *that* you must be is the qualification for existential necessity.) Being how things are is being necessary. The key consideration though is that natural, worldly necessity is unabstract, so it is 'what is necessary', not 'necessity' regarded as an idea or concept, necessity's manifestation rather than its conceptualisation. 'What is necessary' directly equates to 'how things are', and what necessity is, is how things are.

The new standard for necessity applies to the descriptive world as a whole. The world must be the way it is, and one can only consider it qualitatively as one might a geometrical form: it does not exist, it is just its nature. Since the world must be how it is, and being the descriptive world, since this is the criterion for necessity, the world is necessary. Not necessarily 'existent' but descriptively necessary.[5] Necessary, but not 'created'. This is reinforced if we recall that nothing begins or terminates in an absolute sense. A thing only begins or ends absolutely *in* time, and one must distinguish the beginning or ending of time from beginning or ending *in* time. The former does not take place in time so is not absolute termination or commencement, not existential beginning or ending. Qualitative ends and starts are more like boundaries, limits, not creations or extinctions. I only say this in case the world is temporally finite.

In addition, since each individual qualitative is necessary, the whole world is necessary. Indeed, the world is Necessity. The necessity of the world further answers the question, 'Why is there anything at all?'

Why is the circle as it is? Because that is what it means to be a circle. Why is the universe as it is? Because that is what it means to be a universe. If the circle had corners it would not be a circle, and if the universe wasn't as it is it wouldn't be a universe. The actual way the universe is, is what the term 'universe' means. Both circle and universe are 'hownesses', not things that could be otherwise; they are necessary. The universe would fail to be the universe if it wasn't as it is; a universe would be impossible.

To encapsulate the foregoing: what a thing is, is how it is, and if it was not how it is, it would not be what it is.

Description is explanation. In describing the universe one defines the term 'universe'. When one achieves the final physical description in the form of the ultimate laws, one knows that these principles explain everything else within the world, and that they are the definition of the term 'universe' in an abstract way. One is then left with the conceptual problem: Must it be so? The answers to this are supplied herein.

---

[5]   The way things are is necessary.

Since there is no other rule ultimately for necessity for descriptives than their need to be themselves qualitatively, such requests as: 'Tell me, does that have to be the case?' become: 'Must that be as it is?' The only answer can be Yes.

One will notice that the equivalences: 'How' is 'Must' and 'what is natural' is 'necessity', conceived as the definition of natural necessity in the world argument, are themselves equivalent. The same thing is asserted in both formulas. This is another point of contact between the world argument and the descriptive interpretation of the world and of objects. By two strategies we have demonstrated natural necessity and given its barest outline. Why can we not probe as philosophers or even as sentient creatures further into its mysteries? Why can we proceed no further than saying that given a recurrence of initial conditions the same consequences must hold? The reason is, I think, that just as the natural world is hidden in a large part relevant to the dimensions where the workings and mechanisms of cause and change operate, so necessity, which largely identifies with this non-evident world, in the world is not, and never perhaps will be, wholly apparent. Hidden Nature entails hidden necessity. It would be a great day for philosophy if our ability to judge the content of the natural world's necessity could be made as certain as that ability to judge the conceptual, abstract, *a priori* necessity. But this does not, from the very nature of the necessity seem possible, though I would not like to rule it out completely.

But are we so sure that natural necessity is beyond our scrutiny? As I said, we are in a way sensitive to it and it forces us to behave in various ways. Senses deceive and logical errors can be made – many of the pronouncements of philosophical reasoning are erroneous – but natural necessity never fails: it compels us, and is not our invention. We are and must be 'aware' of it, only not logically, or so it seems. We are part of it. Nature is the content of natural necessity which is the dominant kind of necessity in our universe. This necessity is probed by science when it attempts to describe the world.

The position is even less benighted than this. We ascertain if something is necessary by seeing if it is real. Conventionally, experience is maintained to give one no notion or example of necessity; but upon the latter's reconception, 'how' is 'must', experience of a thing's reality is experience of its necessity, both that it is necessary and how it is necessary. The child who puts his hand in a flame and gets a painful burn thinks, 'That's how it is'. He means by this, 'That is necessary'.

Another way to express the formula 'How is Must' is in the more recognisable way that Reality is Necessity. The world is necessity itself.[6]

Linguistic Considerations

Plainly, rejecting any existential interpretation of the world and replacing it by a descriptive one must entail our ceasing to look upon accounts of the world as contingent, and certain linguistic implications follow which are important.

Since universal necessity obtains what was a correct factual statement becomes a necessarily correct one. Any erstwhile factually incorrect statement becomes a necessarily incorrect one. In the case of the latter one has done something similar to declaring of a circle that it has four sides: whether one knows it or not there is an absurdity.

For the world there are no 'possibilities' other than what constitutes its reality. Possibilities that are unactualized are not possible because there is no existence in the first place and there is total necessity in the second.

What immediately follows is provisional until we study the concepts of reference and meaning-acquisition. Once reference is made to an object, all the object's properties are understood to be part of the meaning of the referring expression or of the word. To verbally attribute an incorrect predicate or say something mistaken about the objects referred to is to deny the meaning of

---

[6] Kant: *Critique of Pure Reason* (Macmillan) p.125, p.139. The Logical Positivists held that experience gave no idea of necessity, since experience was needed to verify a statement of fact, and this made such statements synthetic.

the word or referring expression after having tacitly asserted it. So if 'Voltaire wrote *Candide*' states a real property of the man, the sentence is analytic. If 'Rousseau wrote *Candide*' is incorrect, then it is self-contradictory. In accounts of the descriptive world analyticity and self-contradiction replace truth-values.

The principle which lies behind the analyticity and self-contradiction of empirical statements is that the natural meaning of a word transcends our whim. Once we refer to something worldly the nature of that something endows the referring expression with its meaning. The meanings of such words as 'Sun', 'Earth', 'the river Thames', 'the corner shop', 'grass', 'lightning', are given by the worldly state independently of ourselves. This meaning is objective for such expressions, even if they need discovery. For example, the temperature at a given time of the Sun's core is part of the meaning of the word 'Sun' even if we do not know it. Thus also one can see that objective meanings involve change since the world of qualitatives changes. Objective meanings include relations because these help to individuate or identify the areas of the world that are signified by referring expressions. They individuate both in descriptive and in existential metaphysics. What a thing is will include how it is distinct from and relates to other things, and how it behaves as well.

To affirm or deny the objective meanings of words or referring expressions is analyticity or self-contradiction. These are definitions of analyticity and self-contradiction: the affirmation or denial of the objective meanings of expressions. Therefore they are defined in terms of semantic, sentential form, not in terms of modality or justification or truth-value. This formula is equivalent to describing analyticity and self-contradiction as saying or failing to say how things are.

We count a proposition analytic or self-contradictory whether we know it or not. Discovery that the object named does not mean what we thought it to mean or quite what we thought it to mean, does not affect our using the expression, for its meaning is independent of ourselves. We still say 'the sun' even when we believe it to turn round the Earth, or the Earth to turn round it. From the context of terrestrial vision the sun moves round the Earth; from other contexts this is reversed. We tend to call the behaviour of the sun in the hidden, scientific dimension its 'real' behaviour; but all contexts are valid and do not exclude each other and are parts of the objective meaning of a term: only, the role of contextuality must be recognised and explicit.

The chemists who compiled the periodic table of elements were not engaged in conventional definition, that is, were not concerned to make the elements' names mean what they made them mean in compiling the components of that table. They discovered certain things about the elements, placed them in that table, but were fully aware that they did not know all there was to know about the elements they named. Those meanings are objective and not alterable by fiat. If meanings can be extended by discovery of the natures of things, then the meanings were at one time only partly known, and partly unknown.

If the meanings of the referring expressions in sentences had no objectivity we would have a completely elastic and unconstrained language, and activities like science would be games. The theory of objective meaning brings reality into language, and reality is most specially conceived of as a constraint upon us.

But how can a word have a meaning we don't any of us wholly know? Consider the word 'atom'. There was a time when most of the nature of atoms was unknown. Therefore the word's meaning was mostly unknown. The concepts had not been grasped of 'neutron', and so forth. But there was a referring word with its mostly unknown, unconferred meaning. It wasn't as if the meaning hung there unattached to a word though. Meanings, verbal and sentential, only occur when we talk, so propositions that no-one has made are impossible. But the nature was always there.

Reference

What are the mechanics of meaning-acquisition? Certainly one such is stipulative definition; that doesn't apply here. What is the nature of reference? This is a more fruitful area of study.

In my treatment of truth in a previous essay, when I was diagnosing the causes of the Liar paradox, I maintained that what a sentence referred to was what it belonged to. A normal sentence like 'The lawn has been mown' attempts a truth-value by referring to the world. It replicates or attempts to replicate a part of the world, belongs or fails to belong to it, second-hand, and belongs, again second-hand, or fails to belong purely. A paradoxical or illogical statement like 'This statement is true' or 'This statement is false', refers to itself, consequently belongs to itself, and hence belongs. From this we can get a paradox. Referring and belonging mirror each other.

When an expression refers to an object and does so successfully, the existence of that object is asserted. When reference fails, an object fails to exist. In the cases of the referential tautology and referential contradiction, where existence and non-existence are respectively asserted these sentences are tautological or contradictory because we hold that when a singular term refers it asserts existence.

Problems like that of 'the present king of France', display that when a reference fails, existence is deemed to fail, and the attribution of any predicates to a singular term that does not refer becomes a source of logical perplexity, because what does not exist cannot have properties.

So referring mirrors belonging in sentences, where one belongs to what one refers to, and conversely. And reference mirrors existence in the case of singular terms in that to assert reference is to assert existence, and to say that one fails to refer is to assert non-existence. But to assert existence is to assert membership; to assert reference must consequently be to assert membership. Reference is therefore a form of membership in the linguistic sphere. It is not a speaking about but a belonging to.

Now membership is an invalid concept and wherever it appears, not only does it lead to paradox in the end, it is redundant, and its function can be taken over by other concepts, by other operations. The sentence attains meaning by reproduction or replication of that part of the world it focuses on. This replication, of a qualitative world, involves no reference because it involves no membership. All we really needed, we now know, for physicality, was qualitativity. Similarly all we need for meaning-acquisition is the replication of qualitativity; saying how things are.

This applies to both the sentence and the singular term or subject. If the sentence gets meaning by replication, so too does the singular term. In the case of the latter, *not* by referring. Reference is eliminated and replication is adopted in its place.[7]

As with all forms of membership, you gain membership through descriptiveness, not conversely. In this case, you replicate in order to refer; you do not refer in order to replicate. Using a singular term is like taking a picture with a camera; one points it and takes an image, and this image is automatic and objective. Only, in the case of the descriptive world, the image will be a moving one.

If the method of meaning-acquisition is replication, the thesis of objective meaning is vindicated. If the function of a name is to replicate and identify, the process entails objectivity.

Reference is like Being: with Being – the generic concept – existence is the positive and non-existence the negative. With reference truth is the positive and falsity the negative. How should reference and truth be connected? If they are both membership in language, they are identical, though this might not be obvious if it is usually thought that they apply to different parts of the sentence. A singular term replicates part of the world, hence gets a meaning. Consequently, by replicating, it belongs to the world indirectly, and in a simple way it indirectly belongs. This sheer belonging is pure reference for a singular term. The belonging of the replicated object is taken over and is the referent of the referring expression. The object as member, belonger, is the referent of the singular term. Now when the rest of the sentence goes on to say something about the replicated object, in the attempt to spell it

---

[7] The idea of 'referring' results from the second-hand nature of language. Because of the gap between language and the world, the sentence or word appears to point to, to indicate, the world. Hence 'reference' as it is commonly envisaged. Really, what is going on is mediate belonging.

out, it can either describe successfully or unsuccessfully. When description is successful, the sentence shares in the belonging of the singular term, shares in its belonging to the world and its sheer belonging, and that makes the sentence 'True'. When description is unsuccessful on the part of the rest of the sentence, when it fails to spell out the nature of the replicated object, then the sentence fails to share in the belonging to the world and sheer belonging of the singular term, and is 'False'.

The sentence aims to unpack, to spell out, the singular term which always replicates something. Sentence and subject have the same referent, at least the sentence attempts to have this referent, but the sentence may fail to belong, unlike the subject which cannot fail to belong. The sentence may fail to belong because the subject may be mis-referred by the predicate to the wrong class. The mis-description happens whensoever a subject is made a member of the wrong class. Successful membership of the subject of the right class is successful predication.

But reference is membership, so it is rejected as illegitimate, and we are left with the subject that replicates and the predicate that attempts to describe successfully. Thus we have a validation of the theory of objective meaning, since replication in the case of the subject cannot but be accurate, exact and objective; whilst predicative description may fail or succeed. Therefore analyticity and self-contradiction enter upon the scene and apply to the sentence.[8]

I must add some comments which are of interest to the scheme outlined above. The equation of reference to membership may seem as an argument distressingly simple, but this whole metaphysics is intended to be as simple as possible. Since the discovery of the membership fallacy so many things have fallen neatly into place in a manner that is not to the detriment of this philosophy, but rather to its recommendation. A principle as basic as membership simplifies the philosophy, which cannot go

---

[8] Leibniz famously held an analytic theory of truth. He nevertheless did not dispense with truth as I do. The well-known problems that arise in such a theory, problems in modality, need a radical solution which will be provided.

into excessive detail when the concern is something other than is closely related to causality.

Successful reference is got, in the case of sentences, by a situation existing; and in the case of singular terms, by an object existing. This justifies my inclusion of objects existing as 'facts'. A fact is what makes a reference successful.

If reference is belonging, self-reference is self-belonging, which is self-predication. The paradoxes which are self-referential or the results of self-reference, must be illicit formulas consequently because self-predication is erroneous, illogical. Reference is rejected in favour of reproduction, and even here a sentence may reproduce other things, but a sentence cannot reproduce itself. A sentence that reproduces itself engages in self predication, saying something about itself. Saying how things are is the same as replication.

If a sentence replicates the world in order to gain meaning, does a sentence which replicates itself have no meaning? And is this the case with and solution to all those semantical self-'referential', or now, self-replicating paradoxes: that they are meaningless? Saying that replication captures acquisition of meaning has to be qualified. The singular term is a pure replication because it doesn't attempt description; the predicates do and this makes sentential meaningfulness not so much reproduction, as I said earlier, as the attempt to reproduce and the quality of that attempt.

Though we are responsible for setting up the institution of meaning because we are responsible for language, when the words we use replicate and are not defined stipulatively or conventionally, we must recognise that we are not responsible for those words' objective meanings.

Modalities

We avoid mention of any truth-value synonyms like 'correct' and 'incorrect' in defining analyticity and self-contradiction. Analytic statements are not 'correct', they are analytic, and self-contradictory statements are not 'incorrect', they are self-contradictory. But we must not fail to recognise that the designations 'analytic' and 'self-contradictory', as they are here defined, are modally neutral. World-replicating words in a subject-predicate or relational sentence, have objective meanings. Therefore to say something consonant with those meanings is to be analytic. But if the object replicated is part of a contingent world, if the world is contingent, then a statement that reports it correctly is itself contingent, even if correct and analytic. (Correctness results from analyticity but is not part of it.) A contingent world would be an existential world, one in which the membership fallacy is not recognised and admitted, where membership is not existence, where existence is not a relation. In such a world reference is valid, not membership, and objective meanings remain nevertheless in the way I noted at the beginning of this section. Meaning-endowment would probably be, for referring words, replication by dint of reference. But analyticity and self-contradiction would still remain as they have been initially defined: sentential semantic forms.

Therefore though analyticity will always make a statement correct, it will not make it, in terms of its semantic content, necessarily so. So an analytic statement can be contingent. Likewise, if the world is necessary, as it is in the descriptive metaphysics, a correct analytic statement is necessary. But not because of analyticity, not because of meanings, but because of natural necessity. The same holds for self-contradiction. If the world was contingent, the contradiction would be contingent; and if the contradiction took place in a necessary world it would be necessarily incorrect.

The point is that the objective meaning would not *have* to mean what it does in a contingent world, or *would* have to mean what it does in a necessary world. Thus a semantic tautology, or analytic statement, could be converted into a semantic contradiction without involving any element of necessity or impossibility.

Analyticity was defined in its earliest appearances not so much in terms of meaning, but in terms of 'the concept of the subject'.[9] This kind of definition naturally allied necessity and impossibility to the analytic and self-contradictory. When later philosophers tried to improve upon the original definitions they were obliged to include mention of modality and were duped into taking meaning as the source of necessity and contingency and impossibility in statements.[10]

But as we have inferred above in examining objective meanings, it is not sentences that confer necessity and otherwise on themselves but the extra-linguistic world. If the world is necessary, the sentence is necessary or impossible. If the world is contingent, the sentence is too.

What effect does natural necessity have on objective meaning? It makes the meaning of the replicating expression necessary. What effect does natural contingency have on objective meaning? It makes objective meanings contingent. The origin of the necessary statement is the necessary meaning of the replicating expressions or terms. The origin of contingent statements' contingency is the contingency of the objective meaning of the sentences' subjects or terms.

The concept we therefore introduce to explain the conventional attribution of necessity to the analytic statement is that of 'necessary meaning'. To affirm a necessary objective meaning is to be necessarily analytic. To deny the necessary objective meaning is to be necessarily self-contradictory. The reason why the original definition of analyticity involved necessity was because a concept-word is, interpreted just as a meaning, a necessary meaning, a definition, to affirm or deny which is to be necessarily correct or incorrect. But the analyticity of these statements, or their self-contradictoriness, are irrelevant to this modality.

Saying that an analytic statement could be contingent sounds odd, and saying that a contradiction may be so as well sounds unacceptably paradoxical. So I turn to the contradiction expressly. One might say that it is impossible for a contradiction ever to be

---

[9] Kant: *Critique of Pure Reason.* Introduction IV (Macmillan 1929).
[10] Myself included, I must admit, to begin with.

other than necessarily wrong, on any theory of meaning, even objective meaning. Consider this puzzle: take the sentence: 'This object is red and this object is not red', where 'this object' is the same thing. According to my ideas, and supposing the object really to be red, my sentence now becomes: 'This object (which is red) is red and this object (which is red) is not red': I still have a contradiction and there seems no way in which even the theory of objective meaning can escape the inference that any contradiction is necessarily wrong.

I don't deny that necessarily all contradictions are wrong, for that is merely saying all incorrect statements are incorrect. What I deny is that the contradiction, by being one, is necessarily wrong. To explain my point I introduce a distinction of the contradiction into two kinds: the formal and the semantic.

In terms of form the contradiction is always wrong: P & -P is always wrong.

In terms of meaningful content, which is what language, ordinary and philosophical, is concerned with, a contradiction can be contingent if the objective meanings involved are contingent.

The quoted formulas are formal contradictions, thus always mistaken. But the semantic, contentful contradiction would be this way: 'This object (which is red) is not red.'

If 'this object' could have been different, i.e. if the world was different because of contingency, the meaning of the sentence becomes a semantic tautology, a tacit repetition:

'This object (which is not red) is not red.'

In terms of content, therefore, a contradiction is not thereby necessarily incorrect. In form necessarily it is incorrect. The formal and contentful contradictions are quite distinct and the semantical cannot be reduced to the formal one. What makes a sentence a semantic contradiction are actual meanings. What makes a formal contradiction is not meaning at all but structure, in a logical sense.

This can best be understood in the analytic domain. Some people call such a form as 'p v -p' analytic. They call all logical formulas analytic. But 'p v -p' and logical forms in the predicate calculus tell us nothing about the actual meanings of the sentences. They are about the meaningful, they are not sentences as such. 'p v -p' appears, like its kin, in formal 'languages' and has no meaning outside formal languages, unlike 'square' and 'orange' which connect with 'objects'. They are sentences in a metalanguage of some kind, outside language proper. Logical 'sentences' express only the form not the content of ordinary sentences, anyway, and that is my point.

Formal 'sentences' are not what philosophy uses; it uses semantical ones. When someone holds that an idea cannot be predicated of an unthinking subject, as a matter of analyticity,[11] one can be sure that this will be found in no logical textbook. Assimilating logical and semantical sentences in the sphere of analyticity is invalid, because in the latter meaning is irremovable and essential. Sentences may have the same logical form but have different meanings, obviously. In logical sentences, meaning is dispensed with. If analyticity is a matter of meaning, logical statements are not analytic. Asserting a meaning depends not on logical form of sentences, but on the content, the meaning. The logical form of a sentence cannot be what a sentence asserts; it cannot assert its own form. A sentence is an assertion. Analyticity, being a property of meaning, is the property of the contentful assertion, thus not of the contentless non-assertion – the logical structure or form. An assertion asserts its content, not its form, and meaning is irreducible to form.

If self-contradiction is a matter of meaning as well, formal statements are not self-contradictions. An error is made then in trying to reduce the semantically analytic, or contradictory, to the formally, logically 'analytic' or 'contradictory'. They are different species.

Seemingly, I have divided statements into two kinds: the analytic and the self-contradictory, and have excluded the synthetic. The self-contradictory is more nearly the opposite

---

[11] 'Now for an idea to exist in an unperceiving thing, is a manifest contradiction.' Berkeley: *Principles of Human Knowledge*, Part I. 7.

of the analytic than the synthetic is. All analytic statements are 'correct' and all self-contradictions 'incorrect'. That is a natural opposition, and the earliest definitions of analytic statements explicitly state that their denials are self-contradictions.

One may allow for the synthetic, in the original way, these being sentences which say more than analysis of the concept of the subject or of their terms reveals. Therefore all empirical statements will be augmentative of the concepts of their subjects or terms, be synthetic, but not in a pejorative way: they would be perhaps a sub-species of analytic or self-contradictory statements: those that attempt to reproduce the world. To be extra-conceptual is not to be beyond necessity, because the synthetic statement, like the analytic and the self-contradictory, is modally neutral. A concept is a necessary meaning, but not all necessary meanings have to be conceptual. To ascertain necessity or contingency is a matter of the metaphysics one is convinced by: the descriptive or the existential.

'Apples in the market cost 50p per lb' may sound contingent because 'Apple', the concept, doesn't involve a price. But 'apple', the concept, is not what the sentence is about, not the meaning of the subject of the sentence, which is 'apples in the market'. Costing 50p may be a necessary meaning, albeit non-conceptual, of 'apples in the market'. It would be if that was how it was in the descriptive world.

Modality is not captured by syntheticity, for the real meanings of world-replicating expressions may or may not be necessary, but they certainly will not be conceptual. Synthetic statements may be necessarily incorrect or necessarily correct. Syntheticity will not guarantee either. Syntheticity will not entail contingency either; only the type of world we live in ensures that.

If one were to accept natural necessity but reject objective meaning, sentential necessity would go beyond the conceptual. And if one rejected natural necessity and accepted objective meanings, analyticity would apply not only to the conceptual but the empirical statement. In the first case, the correct sentence would be synthetic and necessarily correct; in the second case the correct statement would be analytic but contingent. This is in the case of sentences which are about the world.[12]

Given though that 'meaning' is broader than 'conceptual meaning', and that 'augmentative of the concept', as the meaning of the synthetic, is not a useful category to put contingent statements into, as well as the arguments in favour of objective meanings, all statements are either analytic or self-contradictory, that is, all subject-predicate statements.

Related Issues

Illustrations: if I say, in the context of the descriptive world, That paper is white', because the paper must be white then I am giving a necessary description of 'that paper'. 'White' is part of the objective meaning of 'that paper', a meaning that could not be otherwise. Again, if two objects have a certain relation to each other, it is a necessary relationship, a matter of quality, then the statement that describes that necessary relation is one giving the necessary relationship between the objects in respect of their necessary meanings.

How are such questions as 'Is Man is an animal' an analytic or self-contradictory statement?' to be resolved? According to one body of opinion the quoted statement is a self-contradiction; according to another the sentence is correct. Now there is objectively a definite response, but it is one that is beyond *a priori* speculation. Either man is endowed unlike animals with souls by a divinity or we evolved from ancestors which definitely were animals. We have to discover, but we cannot define our answer into our terms; we do not decide the meanings of the words 'Man' and 'animal', which, though conceptual terms, are always reducible to real particulars and are not forever or ultimately on the conceptual plane where everything is a matter of opinion.

One allows for the possibility that the object which endows a

---

[12] A posteriori statements could be necessary or contingent. But *a priori* statements could only be necessary or impossible, for they would involve necessary meanings, concepts, that is. I am not convinced by arguments for the *a priori* contingent. (S. Kripke: *Naming and Necessity*: Part 1).

word or term with its meaning may only be an imagination, like 'Phlogiston'. They are not 'non-existent', not 'false', they are misconcepts or deliberate inventions, but they are not nothing.

They can still have analytic or self-contradictory statements made about them. 'Phlogiston was thought to have negative weight', is analytic given the objective, though fantastical character of the subject. 'Phlogiston has negative weight', in suggesting that phlogiston is externally real, is self-contradictory. World-replicating expressions always replicate, and cannot fail to replicate, only, for the sake of analyticity, we must be sure of *what* they replicate.

The problem of attribution of a predicate to an imagination like in 'The King of France is bald' can be handled in the following manner. 'Bald' and 'not bald' differ in this instance. An idea can't be 'bald', but its negation 'not bald' is ambiguous. In a world of positive events our predications must be faithful to it, and we cannot really give negative predicates as qualities. We have to understand that a negative predicate means that something else positive other than that which is denied is attributed to the subject. So 'not bald' can mean 'is hairy' – ridiculous when applied to an idea – or 'is an idea' – analytic when applied to 'The King of France'.

A negative predicate leaves so much leeway open as to what I am tacitly saying positively that I cannot judge from it alone whether the statement is or is not analytic where the subject is not an external reality.

I do not deny that most world-replicating words or expressions have subjective meanings, that is, have meanings we *think* them to have, right or wrong. But it is the objective meaning alone which concerns analyticity and self-contradiction. That we can be right and wrong in our various statements about the world, and can ascertain our rightness and wrongness, proves that words can have subjective meanings, and defuses the possible objection that since all contexts contribute to the objective meaning of a term, the context of how something seems to us, the context of appearance, may be included in the objective meaning of a term and thereby identify objective and subjective meanings. In so far as we can check appearances at the level of other appearances and confirm or correct our statements, we know that the meanings of our terms can be what we think them to mean. Of course we can discover and confirm objective meanings in the contexts of evidence: they are not in principle hidden, they are only independent. I believe that in normal circumstances we can know completely whether our statements are correct or incorrect; and this means, when we are correct, that we have got a meaning right, discovered part of the objective meaning of an expression. 'Correctness' and 'incorrectness' pertain to subjective meanings; 'analyticity' and 'self-contradiction' to objective meanings. In order not to talk nonsense we have to understand a meaning for all our words. This is where subjective meaning enters: we must always have at least a subjective meaning for terms that attempt to reproduce the world. But subjective meaning is not all there is to meaning. A subjective meaning is not known, only believed. An objective meaning is only known, but not believed. We do not have to know the objective meaning of a word for that word to have that objective meaning, however.

Just because meanings are objective, and in the world of descriptives, necessary, it does not follow that they are static, like conceptual meanings. Empirical replicating expressions have meanings that are from a human point of view, dynamic, expanding, developing as we discover them and as the world changes. The paradigm of conceptual definitions should not be applied to meanings of words that replicate objects in the world; the former are inadequate in their abstractness, their inability to change, their partial nature.

The sentence 'Some bachelors are fat' may appear synthetic in the sense of factual, since fatness is not defined into the concept of 'bachelor'. But in a descriptive world, the attribute does indeed define some bachelors. Usually, the word 'bachelor' does not fully replicate, does not conventionally and completely mean any object it is applied to. It has a fixed definition in abstraction, but the object replicated by the term 'unmarried man' is not so limited. There is a wider range of properties that the object has and the word only means part of the object. This object has as many defining properties, we know, as it has properties. If the word meant as much as the object, if they equated to each other, as it should do since the qualitative is never just abstract, every correct statement about it would be analytic. Thus 'some bachelors' means everything we can discover about them as men, and every faithful statement concerning them is included in this discovered meaning, and is of the nature of a partial definition.

The word 'bachelor' when used to signify objects, should mean all about those men: all bachelors are men too. Only when we conventionally try to determine the necessity of any statement about them does the 'concept' enter our calculations. We may use only the conceptual meaning to discover the validity of statements about bachelors, or we may discover non-abstractly the correctness of any statement about some of them. But whatever the method we employ to evaluate it, the statement is still either analytic or self-contradictory. Conceptual analyticity only figures as a matter of the methodology of ascertaining the status of a proposition. All statements are on the same level; but their characteristics can be discovered not only by conceptual but by empirical means.

Meaning has to be broader than conceptual meaning if we are to make physical descriptions in a qualitative world in which the objects' universality and particularity are not to be separated. Full meaning is not static and truncated like that of concepts; full meaning is expanding and animated and needs empirical discovery.

In this thesis I establish the necessity of sentences by establishing natural necessity and we realise thereby that meaning is not the home of necessity. Necessity is its own cause even for conceptual sentences.

Is the Liar Possible?

I have to say a little more about truth-values in this section. Analyticity and self-contradiction effectively replace them. The latter do not involve truth-values. Truth-values are essentially external to sentential meaning whereas analyticity and self-contradiction are essentially internal to sentence meaning. The externality of truth-values allows the paradox of the Liar to arise when they are included in the meaning of a sentence. Evaluation is internalized. Truth-values are reduced to absurdity by the paradox. This cannot happen with analyticity and self-contradiction. One cannot say: 'This statement is self-contradictory', in the hope of undermining analyticity and self-contradiction, for all analytic and self-contradictory statements have these features as internal to the sentence such that they disappear into the meanings of them. Thus, the statements cannot assert their own analyticity or contradictoriness. They have to be reduced to statements which determine their own semantic status without mentioning this status. Truth-values cannot be so absorbed. Analyticity and self-contradiction are not values, they are the semantic form of sentences, for the affirming or denial of objective meaning is formally identical to the sentence.[13]

Merely to assert the form of a sentence as in 'This statement is self-contradictory', would be to omit the content that bears that form. As a result, nothing is said semantically, and a sentence is not offered. The semantic content is what one asserts, what assertion consists of; but the semantic form is the contentless, therefore non-assertible, abstraction and skeleton of the assertion. A form appears only in the context of and dependently upon, a content; so that the omission of the content of a sentence takes with it the meaningful form, the semantic form. At the ordinary linguistic level of assertion a content is absolutely requisite; so mere formal 'sentences' are not really sentences at all: a sentence cannot assert its own form.

---

[13] 'Analyticity' and 'self-contradiction' are uncomfortable mouthfuls. Perhaps we can do what I suggested happens earlier when I say that meanings could change depending on our increasing knowledge. Maybe 'truth' and 'falsehood' might reappear with new meanings, as happens all the time in living languages. 'Bat' for instance has at least two objective meanings: the implement and the animal.

Scientific Laws

Because there are no facts, empiricism's essence must be seen for what it always was: the discovery by non-abstract means of that which must be as it is. Discovery, not fact, is central to empiricism. The necessity of what is descriptival means that what does not happen cannot happen. This affects our judgment as to the status of scientific pronouncements on the world. Scientific laws, if conceived as being in a conditional form, cannot be equivalent to natural laws, or to descriptions of these, more exactly, for it is always possible that the 'law' be unrealized. Laws of the form 'All As are Bs', or 'For anything, if it is A then it is B', may never be instanced; aluminium may never reach its melting point, for example, in the world's history, and the conditional, If Aluminium reaches temperature x it melts, always contains the possibility that the antecedent never happens. Therefore in the world it would be literally impossible for aluminium to melt, for the law to be exemplified.

Negative laws cannot be natural laws either. They concern themselves with the unreal, the immaterial, so cannot be what is natural. They report the impossible; so natural laws will be positive. Physical descriptions report events. Something negative is precisely not an event and therefore physical descriptions are unconcerned with negation.

Positive and unconditional forms for natural laws mean that these laws are categorical. And because abstractions as such are not found in nature as they appear in scientific formulas, natural laws must have a particular component and must concern what is particularly real, but with the qualification that there may be general occurrences like the expansion of the universe, overall physical necessities (if the theories are right) which make scientific formulas posed abstractly nearly faithful descriptions of reality.

'Natural laws' are 'what happens in reality'. They identify with the content of natural necessity and must be materially, concretely happening. Otherwise that which describes them linguistically is not a physical description. I say this because the scientific enterprise is to describe nature as exactly as can be. But 'copper conducts electricity' and 'gold melts at temperature t', are not events that are happening; they are abstract. Qualitatives have both particular and universal sides which in nature cannot be separate.

Scientific laws treat of abstractions; and being partly abstract are partly unreal. They treat of possibilities, hypotheticals, conditionals and may be negatively put. They must therefore be distinguished from Natural Laws, or exact descriptions thereof. Scientific laws are to an extent artificial, but each event in Nature is so to speak a natural law, natural necessity, what is natural. But though this is impractical, the description of every event in Nature, that is to say, the distinction must nevertheless be made and borne in mind between scientific formulas and natural necessities or laws. Though scientific laws are generally and rightly taken from the non-particular dimension of the physical, we need to remember that this is not its only facet, and repetition is only ever approximate if it happens.

The Natural and the Conceptual

In relation to the world we know of two kinds of necessity, the conceptual and the natural, the former being used to discover the latter. What can I say about the connections between these necessities?

Natural necessity, how things are or what is natural, is a totally physical and non-verbal, non-formal kind of necessity, which is not dependent upon concepts. These last are used by us to understand the world since we do not perceive natural relations, necessary connections and change mechanisms in their physical guises. Natural necessity itself needs no foundation, it only needs discovery by the means available to our minds: concepts.

The universe does not really cohere for the conceptual reasons I have given. In itself, only the physical nature of and forces in the universe hold it together, and this nature is revealed scientifically. Salt does not have to dissolve in water for any other than physical reasons; and it is not compelled by any other than physical reasons to remain doing so. The general, abstract reasons which underlie our inductive reasonings are not the ones which keep the relations between real things as they are.

When I say that the world is held together out of the very meaning of the notion 'world', that does not in a physical sense unify it. The forces that keep it whole and makes the parts mutually accessible are physical, concrete and mechanical. But it is still valid that the 'world' is a relativity: the *concept* of the world, that is. Only as long as the concept of the world is a faithful translation into intellectual terms of the real world is the argument valid. Causality applies to this concept of the world, the conceptual world, and not directly to the physical world in which things are brought about for necessary, but purely physical reasons. Only insofar as Causality tallies with the concept of the world is it acceptable. Causes apply to the material world. But if we reproduce the real world correctly we can be sure that what we say holds of the conceptual world fits in some way, is expressed in some way in, the real world.

As philosophers, our concern is the coherence of the conceptual world and what we say of it. We are physically in the natural world though, and even our thought is a component of it. For this reason we are confident that our second order necessity is only a feature of and not separate from the real world.

Duality is bridged because we can use realities in the evident world to function in conceptual arguments – as in the reasoning for an occult dimension. In the role of understanding the real world, which perception alone cannot do, conceptual necessity has its justification.

'Causes are reasons for events whilst causality is the reason for reasons for events.' Does this mean that causality, the concept, is the foundation for causes? No: we need causality because we are not acquainted with causes. If we were we would need no causality, for causes would contain their own perceivable natural necessity and further investigation would not be needed. Our having to posit Causality indicates our incomplete knowledge of the physical world.

If the world is physical, how does it connect with the conceptual mode of perceiving it? The separation between conceptual and physical is not unbridgable: there is a level at which the conceptual mode is valid as a means of scrutinising and reaching conclusions about the world. I cannot say that the world 'contains' a metaphysical dimension,[14] only that we can perceive or interpret the world through concepts in default of a complete awareness of the material world through perception. Conceptual reasoning is only a manner of knowing the world, but it is partial and it misses out a whole swathe of the universe, the particular and particularly various. As philosophers, conceptual necessity opens what is closed to us by our inability to use natural necessity.

Conceptual vision of the world is a stratagem which has finally to be reduced to, to collapse back into, physical descriptions. It is incomplete and needs embodying and conceptually reached judgments about the universe use a necessity that reduces to natural necessity; and not conversely. The 'objects' that feature in conceptual reasoning are ghosts, ruses, ways of seeing flesh and blood realities, which cannot live in their own right; temporary translations of worldly things.

Though the difficulty is to render the conceptual results back into solid results and statements, we, as philosophers, are only concerned with the conceptually seen world; but we must not think it founds or precedes the physical world. Philosophers leave us in suspense and do not perform a translation, but give us disembodied notions, partial glimpses. Calling up the reflected-upon world to supply us with what we cannot see – like not seeing necessary connections so thinking *a priori* of necessary connection – is certainly a feature of pre- or early-scientific enquiry.

The point of having reasons for reasons for events is not that the events themselves need conceptual support, but that we need support for our belief in reasons for events.

---

[14] It does contain a non-particular dimension though.

But why should we look for natural connections if we do not perceive them? Why not accept only what is evident? Though self-evidence does not offer it to us, it implies it and so does practice: it is inescapably practical to believe in necessary connection and use it. Reflection is then called into play. The abstract method of perceiving the world is valid as a method just like using eyesight is valid. The form thinking about the world takes is conceptual, and the capacity to think is as natural an ability as eyesight is, and the sense-items caused in our brains by the world are duplicated by concepts which are 'caused' in our intellects by the data we receive from the physical world. Concepts are the sense-items of our intellectual faculty.

How does the conceptual vision we have of the world connect with and 'collapse back into' what is natural or into physical descriptions? One idea is that it is, I think, by forming the background assumptions of natural science. Science attempts to describe the natural world, to describe natural necessity, and concepts are the broad assumptions we bring to the enterprise; concepts which do not have to be exactly formulated, like the metaphysical principles of induction, but which cannot be absent. Such concepts are the vision of a unified cosmos; the principle of non-coincidence which may lead to us seeing things as composed of particles.

Producing a quasi-systematic theoretical abstraction like a metaphysics is easier than making systematic, precise, and workable scientific theories. History as well as practice shows this. This is one reason to assign to philosophy, conceptual thought of a wholly abstract nature, a temporally prior and not an equal place among the sciences. A person does not overtly have to be a philosopher to have general broad assumptions useful in undertaking scientific investigation. What we discover about the world has its place within the framework given by concepts. But there is interchange between assumption and discovery which allows not only assumptions to determine the treatment of discovery, but discovery to modify assumption. Therefore, it is interpretationally that concepts affect the natural world, affecting our behaviour in it and descriptions of it.

A vision of the world may be judged correct or superior to another if it works. Causal and inductive scepticism do not work because we cannot behave as if they were valid visions. Scepticism of these types would render us helpless if really embraced, though it may give us a great open-mindedness. Scepticisms of these kinds are not practical but remain purely academic and thus fail ultimately to connect with natural necessity (which of course it doubts).

A more satisfactory account may perhaps be given of the connection between natural and conceptual necessities. Conceptualizing is based on the firm bedrock of natural necessity's regularity over space and time. This we perceive in daily life. What this regularity allows us to do is to generalize. We make generalizations about food, about water, grass, the seasons, night and day. From this level we proceed to more and more comprehensive generalizations until some are of the nature of pure, abstract concepts, such as 'world', object, causation. The progression is of degree rather than kind, from generalization to concepts. I make no stipulation here about how the process of generalization is carried out. Rigorous conceptual systems like mathematics, but some other more homely, less 'pure' generalizations, form the backdrop to systematic science.

So we can draw up a historical formula: natural necessity manifests regularity, which allows us to generalize, make predictions; this is pushed through transitional stages of ever-increasing comprehensiveness until we arrive at pure concepts; some of these form the background to systematic science, and the latter attempts to describe natural necessity: thus the circle is closed.

An example of generalization is how my experience of the world is permeated by awareness of relations, so that the concept 'world' ensures 'relativity'.

Our mentality is an essential element in the above formula, which is somewhat strengthened as a hypothesis by considering that an irregular, chaotic nature could not support reasoning. Reasoning needs regularity and we could not reason in a chaos, in which anything is possible, which we could not describe or comprehend. Concepts are used in metaphysical reasoning, so concepts spring ultimately and logically from regularity or coherence.

Because the practice of conceptualizing comes from the nature of the world, we may be confident that some of our concepts and chains of inference may be 'correct' generalizations since their natures emerge from and point back to the nature of the world's consistency or regularity. Concepts at bottom spring from the world's character and thus may say things metaphysically applicable to it. There is no yawning gulf between the physical and conceptual. Concepts are metaphysical descriptions or interpretations of the world as the laws of science are scientific descriptions or interpretations. Neither are quite faithful though, but less or more distorted visions. One may argue from this that such distortion impairs the quality of the necessity pertaining to conceptual inferences, which, to remind you, are distorted because concepts are pure abstractions, which nothing natural is. Note though that the purpose of using conceptual thought is to go beyond the merely evidential, so we should not be surprised if sometimes the results of this conceptual reflection are counterintuitive, that the world the concepts point back to is not precisely the same world we perceive. There would be no point in conceptual thought if we ended up just where we started, with the phenomenal world. So do not be surprised if you are surprised. Counter-intuitiveness does not invalidate the outcomes of conceptual reasoning, however, nor does it impair the necessity. One can say that the importance given conceptual thought about the world marks out the difference between the rationalist and empirical metaphysician. The latter is content finally with what he sees; the former accepts that conceptual thinking may lead to strange outcomes. He is sensitive at least to the purpose of concepts, which even the empiricist uses.

A conceptual reason for the regularity, the uniformity of the world is the communal nature of the things in it. A thing's nature is not had in isolation, but is imposed upon it by all other things, by the world. So we must not see the world as a collection of individuals. Characteristics are not thing-centred but world-centred, 'environmental', and the nature of the world is not generated upwards from the individual, rather the nature of the individual is generated downwards from the world. Things confront us as a community, and behaviour is communal, universal, not anarchic. This applies historically as well as spatially. Broad similarities, overall patterns, which we call in the common way 'Laws of Nature', are the rule, and individuality is suppressed, though not obliterated.

This is supported by results of considering the membership fallacy where we learn that the world really must be a systematic unity. This provides perhaps an insight into what I called the 'innate' feature of things with a nature to transcend their particularity. It may express the communality of things. And we derive from this that the world orders itself naturally.

I propose conceptual necessity's dependence on and evolution out of natural necessity mainly for the reason that our very ability to reason at all displays the natural regularity of the world. Reasoning depends on a coherent world. The quality of that coherence underpins the nature of our reasoning and the concepts used therein. Metaphysical reasoning is justified by its emergence out of and its pointing back to a uniform world. It is consistent with that world. Concisely, the sorts of concepts we have emerge from the sorts of coherence and regularity in the natural world. Natural necessity though, not being inferential, cannot be gainsaid. I believe in natural necessity for conceptual reasons, but natural necessity generates conceptual arguments and thinking.

The validation of reasoning on the presumption of a coherent, consistent, regular, non-chaotic world, is quite interesting. The possibility of reasoning depends on it. Since deductive reasoning is thought valid, that is, conceptual *a priori* reasoning, on that basis, it will be valid in future as well as now. If deductive principles are invalid, they are invalid now, not 1000 years from now. This means that the regularity and coherence which vindicates deductive reasoning, underpins it, can validate inductive reasoning. For inductive reasoning likewise requires the same principle of worldly regularity and coherence, i.e. the uniformity of Nature. Induction and Deduction share the same principle, and the denial of the validity of one is the denial of the validity of the other. Induction is justified if deduction is justified, and justified timelessly.

The principles of deduction and deductions have a universal validity of their nature, a timeless validity. That from which they spring, worldly consistency and coherence, has to have this feature of being constant. Coherence cannot be temporary or it is not coherence, but a facet of chaos.[15] Thus the principle which gives timeless support to deduction, gives it to induction. Coherence is exemplified as lawfulness and chaos as lawlessness. And simply to establish the reality of natural laws is to establish induction, that given the recurrence of initial conditions similar events ensue. If coherence is accidental the validity of conceptual deductive reasoning is accidental; but the latter is not, so the former is not.

The nature of the world and rationality are indeed linked, because if the world was actually chaotic, why should our thought be coherent? Someone says: '*A priori* reasoning has nothing to do with the world'. I say: 'Everything has to do with the world. Could you prosecute your reasoning if the world ontradicted it?' The world is a very important place. Language, and by extension, thought, have as subject matter the world, and insofar as propositions are concerned, replicate the world. Now if the world were fundamentally chaotic and incoherent, language and thought would ultimately replicate that incoherence and chaos. Logic would not be possible, neither would conceptual reasoning. And a chaotic world would not look like this one: you couldn't even have an idea of coherence. A chaotic world could not be described, and a language could not emerge of which the logic could be elicited. The very arguments which demonstrate that induction cannot be justified presume what they deny: that the world is law-governed.

---

[15] It would be an accident of what was a fundamental lawlessness.

Chaos is where anything whatsoever could and does happen. Coherence, seen temporally is regularity, and is universality.

I believe that conceptual necessity is an abstraction from natural necessity, as I have said, and this has implications for various puzzles concerning the foundations of logical thought. Justifying rules of inference, conceptual ones, is problematic because people think that these justifications have to be in terms of other abstractions, and we get an infinite regress since we have to ask what the bases of abstract laws are based on themselves. Some adopt the 'brute fact' approach and say that explanation just gives out. It stops and no further justification is possible even if it is needed.

However another possibility raises its head. The natural world is the basis and justification of our laws of thought. Take the law of non-contradiction. Given what we have called 'contradictory', I can assert that the rule says 'failing to say how things are is wrong.' Doing so is denying objective meanings. The law of sufficient reason (that there is always a reason why something is so rather than otherwise) could be validated by saying that in a descriptive Nature saying how things are, describing them, naturally involves explaining them, cause being a form of descriptiveness. If we fail to say how things are or fail to explain things, we fail to describe the world.

Perception Theory

To the benefit of our knowledge of the world I have avoided excursions into perception theory so far. We know that there is an unobserved realm that is physical. This is the hidden dimension of the mechanisms and natural relations of causes and changes, which is connected to the evident world. I cannot add much at present about this part of the world: in what way the hidden is connected to the evident it is not strictly philosophical to ask. We do not know how intimately the dimensions are connected and cannot go into detail when we consider their relationship. However at this stage I think we can attempt to establish the status of worldly objects in respect to some theory of perception.

We naturally must distinguish between what we can philosophically say of the world, what can enter philosophy, and what scientifically and practically we admit. I hold that the theory of sense perception, and of sense-items as well, cannot be maintained as a philosophical position and should not be allowed into philosophy. I must emphasise that one does not have to deny the theory scientifically, only that it should remain scientific and not philosophical.

Where 'knows' means, not 'perceives', but 'allows', 'permits', 'tolerates', philosophy knows objects, events, and so on. It does not know the specific natures of objects, events, and so on. Philosophy does not know how objects are except conceptually. They are allowed to be matters of quality, but that does not say what sort of qualitatives they are. Like 'object', 'matter of quality' is a blanket term which does not commit one to any kind of scientific interpretation of things. Philosophy only goes that far.

But 'sense-item', 'percept', and such like, presume a science of sense perception which is not philosophical. They are products of a group of scientific theories which may, as far as we can conceptually know, be mistaken and which are inherently uncertain. We cannot logically know sense-items as part of our philosophical furniture because the whole theory of sense-perception, namely, that I connect with the world through various physical faculties, the senses of sight, touch, hearing, taste, and smell, is patently scientific and not an assured conceptual premiss, not watertight and indeed at a level where it can never be strictly philosophically admitted. This has only escaped us because it is so 'immediate' and not seemed to merit a challenge to its assumptions, its validity, even by empirical sceptics, who of course based many of their views on the premiss of sense perception.

Philosophers say without any awareness of difficulty that 'seeing and hearing require eyes and ears' is a conceptual necessity, and even that it goes without dispute that they need 'the possession of optic and auditory nerves'. In an uncomprehensive manner, I could object that it is my little finger that is required for seeing, for all we know. But the radical, general point is that not only are the details of sense-perception scientific, inductive and at best probabilistic and extra-philosophal, but the whole theory is itself physical and scientific, and because of the attacks of the causal and inductive sceptics, certainly not *a priori* and conceptually analytic.

Of course one can maintain 'I wouldn't call anything 'seeing' and 'hearing' unless they involved eyes and ears'. That simply gives notice of a convention to give words certain meanings. But on what is it based? Is it purely intellectual or is it not discovered in daily life starting from infancy that there is a correlation of a physical kind between eyes and seeing, ears and hearing? And isn't that an induction?

All that can be allowed for the items of so-called 'consciousness' is to call them events, qualitatives, situations, matters of quality. As such they are not mental objects, may not be idealized; they are not sensations in the scientific sense. They are not 'in our minds' as far as philosophy can allow: they share the same status as ourselves and every other thing in the world: they are worldly, physical objects.

Because we conceptually excluded scientific sense-theories, 'experience' is to be downgraded and mentioned as little as possible. At most we can speak of taste-events, sound-events, which do not bear the sensual and experiential stamp and connotation. Everything previously deemed an experience becomes a matter of quality, for experience is a non-philosophical hypothesis when it means 'sense-experience'.

Qualitatives are however discovered and is not discovery a form of experience? A form of knowledge, maybe, but not logically in the manner of sense perception, which is supposed, scientific and possibly incorrect. Only by scientific judgement do we classify objects as 'seen' and 'heard' and as sensations. Much perception – theory is not really philosophy, which concerns pure concepts, and we here can only speak of the world philosophically. We can't make physical hypotheses.

We must be careful to make clear what exactly is philosophically rejected, namely that we connect with the world through senses, or, that things are sensed. The manner in which we are related to the world is plainly the subject of an inductive speculation however obvious it seems, and is included in the domain of natural necessity. Though I have attempted to justify induction, among other things, I rightly do not justify inductions in these essays. Sense-theory is neither *a priori* nor self-evident, but a series of inductions based on supposed causal correlations. Not that it is wrong, but that it is not philosophical.

Of course, we are connected with the world; it and ourselves are not separate. So in some way we can say we are 'sensitive', metaphorically, to it. But 'sensitive' does not necessarily mean 'senses'.

The world, as far as it is known abstractly, does not consist of things which are objects in consciousness, just 'objects'. Causal connection of object and object does not objectively render either of them simply items of sense. No object is isolated and privileged; none is subordinate to the other, for if an object is in my field of sensitivity, I am in its; so no object is merely another's sense item, logically. A thing's habitat is not anything else's 'consciousness', just being related to it, but the world.

For me objectivity does not consist in total independence of myself: everything is involved with every other thing. There is *parity* of object with object, mutuality in the relations between objects, and above all, objects are not merely features of my consciousness. If I hold things not to be independent of my mind or myself, I must not be interpreted as saying that they are subordinate to me. That is a misconceived antithesis. To deny independence, in an absolute sense, is not to embrace idealism, but to adopt, in this case, a more coherent form of realism.

Sensitivity between things is not an admission of the theory of senses because sensitivity is a form of a connection that is universal. Even non-conscious things have it but are not judged to have sense-items or perceptions. I do not think that connection, which is the term sensitivity comes under, can be called sense-perception by philosophers, for it would give perception too wide and unnatural a connotation. Things that do not appear to sense, such as those in the hidden dimension, would nevertheless be connected and 'perceived' if the foregoing was allowed: 'sensitivity' equals 'sense-perception', that is. Things would be both known and not known sensually. So we admit the former and leave the latter as a hypothesis of science that may possibly be a form of connection. What that 'connection' is like is outside philosophy's scope.

We are linked, we know, to what is evident in the world. But this does not mean that logically the linkage is of a different nature to the linkage to what is not evident. Linkage to the evident is not special or favoured from a philosophical point of view. What makes it special, gives it its character, is the scientific interpretation given it, the physical theory of sense. And moreover, what it is to be 'evident' is a scientific matter as well like say, what it is to be 'metallic'. The division of the world into evident and non-evident is not a conceptual, logical one, but a natural one.

As for epistemological difficulties about knowing whether one is dreaming, one can say that 'dreams', like sense-items, are inductive hypotheses based upon our notion of the way the world works. I may never, for all I know, be dreaming, even when I believe I am or have been dreaming. Asking how one is to know is akin to asking 'Is the Earth flat?' This is a matter for practical not philosophical investigation. Satisfaction will be attained at the practical level and the question is out of place at the level of philosophy. All I can do from a philosophical viewpoint is to allow the inhabitants of my 'dreams' the same status as the objects that are evident when I am 'awake': they are 'events' like all the others.

Denying sense perception raises problems, like that of the apparent privacy of evident things to each person, which may mean that a theory of sense and sense-items has to be contemplated.

What if one person points to a bucket of paint and says,

'That paint is white', and another, wearing tinted spectacles, unequivocally indicating the same bucket says 'That paint is blue'. Does this show that my theory is inadequate as it stands, and that I must allow private consciousness?

What it shows, firstly, is that an object cannot bear the same relation to two different objects simultaneously. And secondly, that the object is, as we have seen all through this thesis, not a thing in itself, but a contextual, relative object. A given thing is modified by one thing, and the same thing is modified by yet another thing. When I say 'Object x', I mean 'x as it is related to me'. It, being relative me, does not thereby become my 'property'. I am its 'property' too.

So the 'real' colour of the paint is not the paint 'in itself', but the paint in its various contexts. Thus it is quite natural that the paint may be white and blue simultaneously. The paint is white' is a report of the paint in a context; similarly for 'The paint is blue'. It is the context, not the thing 'in-itself which is being described. But this does not make any description acceptable, for one may make mistaken or deliberately incorrect statements about a context as about a thing in itself. Though genuine contextual statements do not exclude one another, contradictions can still arise within a given context.

Another illustration of the difficulties which face a non-sensory theory of physical events is how to explain the disappearance and appearance of certain 'evident' things. If I travel from room to room, place to place, my world changes. If I shut my eyes and reopen them, the visual world disappears and reappears. The evident ceases to be so, newly evident things appear. Does this mean that philosophically we have to take seriously a theory of sense and one of sense-items?

The important idea to grasp in the above format is that of 'change'. The world changes, undeniably. Evident things change into other evident things or into non-evident things, since the two realms are connected. How this is accomplished I say again is not philosophically relevant. No annihilation takes place, only change which involves evident and non-evident dimensions of the world. And we do not need to invoke a physical sense-hypothesis.

I arrive at my position by using scepticism against itself: the conceptual uncertainty of sense theory is used to subvert the uncertainties that that sense theory is responsible for in philosophy. All we know is that we are thrust into a world of solid, bona fide 'objects', and that we ourselves are among their number. I would like to exclude 'consciousness', in sensory terms, from philosophical debate and allow only for the 'evident' and 'non-evident', which do not presume sense-faculties or 'perception' in its conventional usage.

If asking the above is rather too much, and in respect to the traditional problem of the mind/physical interaction, I note that since the common currency of the descriptive world is qualitativity, this is so broad as to cross the mental/physical divide and join what was separate. If qualitativity is reality, then mind and body concur in this. They are in the same category. There is doubtless a species difference between these two, but they nevertheless are mutually accessible. One does not have to be reduced to the other; they cohabit. If you attempt a reduction, you simply indicate that you presume dualism since you show that you believe that both cannot retain their character and cohere.

Conclusion

Two concepts predominate in these essays: relativity and descriptivity. I began with the former and introduced the latter subsequently, bringing them together in this last essay, in many respects. Can one be reduced to the other? Casting my eye over certain features of my synthesis, I believe that descriptivity is reducible to, or maybe synonymous with, relativity. Relativity features in cause and change among the qualitative quite essentially. Relativity cannot be separated from identity and persistence. I located the universality of the qualitative in its contextual, environmental, communal, situation; as well as the particularity or uniqueness in the inability of any one thing to share the same relations to other things in the universe. The world argument identifies necessity with what is natural – the world indeed – and establishes natural necessity in the world. But what is natural is, we learn in that argument, relativity: it is innate. Therefore what is necessary or necessity is relativity. What is natural is, of course, qualitativity as well.

These are facets of 'nature' or qualitativity. And in the last example, the last equivalence, if what is natural is qualitativity, qualitativity is relativity. Relativity causes or perhaps translates into nature or qualitativity because it gives, to use a metaphor, structure to the parts of the world. It endows form and is the source of variousness. Through the superficiality of our senses we often fail to perceive genuine relations and fix upon external, apparent relations. The genuine relations or relativity is the origin of qualitativity, and the chief source of the external, seeming-relations is existence. Speaking of the latter, relativity might explain why the qualitative ultimately cannot suffer absolutes of assertion or negation. Absoluteness pertains to existence. Relativity to the qualitative in all its departments: change, identity, persistence, etc. Descriptivity and Relativity seem on a level: in proving that a descriptive world is necessary we prove that the world is descriptive, quite unempirically. And relativity seems at the heart of any conception of a world. A descriptive world is a relative world, and a relative world a descriptive one.

Concerning causality I said at the beginning that it was a notion obtained by applying various concepts to the world we encounter. The thesis has shown that this is not a complete enough characterisation of its origins. Causality emerges out of the world, not in the incorrect and inadequate Humean manner which would have such concepts as after-images of impressions, but in the form of howness. The archetype for 'howness' is simply 'how things are': the physically various qualitative world. I call causality a form of howness applied to change and association.

Thus there is an 'impression' causality derives from, but it is hampered and blocked by the dud concept 'existence' – a fantastic concept.

Similarly in the definition of causality as necessary connection,

I have strong, overwhelming, empirical evidence for it in that my experience of the world is experience of relations, such that the world could not be conceived to be without them. Using the language of empirical epistemology, I have impressions for my ideas: descriptive things and related things. Both are the basis for Causality.

This is in answer to die-hard empiricists who, in answer to every attempt to demonstrate causality will say: But we do not perceive it; there is no evidence for it. But the whole of the evident world provides the material for our derivation of causality, through both relativity and descriptivity. Philosophical misconceptions along the way hinder this however.

This metaphysics I call a 'hypothesis'. Many of its general theses could in principle be discovered by non-philosophers, so that it could be of conceptual use in more than a limited field.

How convenient is the monism of descriptivity! So many concepts have a place within it and are facets of it, like here, I am sure.

Postscript

The membership fallacy is the logical core of this thesis. It establishes the world argument, disproves external relations, establishes the non-particularity of non-members, consequently providing the basis for justifying Induction. It defines what identity, both as relation and as uniqueness, is existentially. It defines reference and Truth, and solves the logical, semantical, and some of the metaphysical paradoxes I concern myself with here. But it supports these arguments in conjunction with the independent arguments I use in their favour. The world argument, for instance, supports itself; but the membership fallacy confirms it.

Abandoning such concepts as membership, truth and existence is somewhat hard to do all at once, so I can say that they, especially truth, which has an important role in logic, may be regarded as hypotheses which work well within limits, but which are strictly wrong. The paradoxes show us what these limits are. There are examples in physical science where a theory is in some ways mistaken, but where it is usable in a limited domain.

I have a hesitancy about existence though: I feel it should go categorically. But it does have a linguistic usefulness in locating and establishing things which is difficult to replace immediately. Metaphysically though it is out. And though it may seem incredible to propose its abandonment, that the world does not exist, one should remember that existence is a metaphysical concept in the end, and not all metaphysical concepts are valid. I cannot at this stage re-invent the language: all I can do is set the re-invention in motion.

Bibliography

Aristotle, (1956), Categories, Oxford Classical Texts, Oxford.

Ayer, A. J. (1971), Language, Truth and Logic, Pelican, London.

Ayer, A. J. (1956), The Problem of Knowledge, Pelican, London.

Ayer, A. J. (1973), The Central Questions of Philosophy, Weidenfeld & Nicolson, London.

Ayer, A. J. (1982), Philosophy in the Twentieth Century, Weidenfeld & Nicolson, London.

Blackburn, S. (1984), Spreading the Word, Oxford University Press, Oxford.

Cottingham, J. (1984), Rationalism, Paladin Books, London.

Dancy, J. (1985), Contemporary Epistemology, Basil Blackwell, Oxford.

Davies, P. (1980), Other Worlds, J.M. Dent & Sons, London.

Descartes, R. (1968), Meditations, Penguin Books, London.

Frege, G. (1980), The Foundations of Arithmetic, Basil Blackwell, Oxford.

Goodman, N. (1983), Fact, Fiction and Forecast, Harvard University Press, Cambridge, Mass.

Hamlyn, D.W. (1984), Metaphysics, Cambridge University Press, Cambridge.

Harré, R. (1985), The Philosophies of Science, Oxford University Press, Oxford.

Hume, D. (1969), A Treatise of Human Nature, Penguin Books, London.

Kant, I. (1929), Critique of Pure Reason, Smith, N.K. (Trans), Macmillan, London.

Kripke, S. (1980), Naming and Necessity, Basil Blackwell, Oxford.

Leibniz, G. (1973), Philosophical Writings, J.M. Dent & Sons, London.

Locke, J. (1961), An Essay Concerning Human Understanding, J.M. Dent & Sons, London.

Nozick, R. (1981), Philosophical Explanations, Oxford University Press, Oxford.

Owens, J. (1968), An Interpretation of Existence, Bruce Publishing Company, Houston, Texas.

Russell, B. (1959), My Philosophical Development, George Alien & Unwin, London.

Russell, B. (1967), The Problems of Philosophy, Oxford University Press, Oxford.

Sainsbury, R.M. (1988), Paradoxes, Cambridge University Press, Cambridge.

Swartz, N. (1985), The Concept of Physical Law, Cambridge University Press, Cambridge.

Wittgenstein, L. (1961), Tractatus Logico-Philosophicus, Routledge & Kegan Paul, London.

Index